Informal learning in the workplace

Informal learning has become an extremely important issue as post-industrial workplaces seek to harness its productive potential. Managers and human resource development practitioners have attempted to deploy informal learning in the design of corporate cultures. However, most discussions of the subject have tended to be uncritical expositions which do not challenge the underlying economic, philosophical and organisational rationale. *Informal Learning in the Workplace* critically examines definitions of informal learning, focusing on its application in a variety of workplace contexts. The book features:

- theories of informal learning
- the unmasking of contemporary corporate language
- the implications for accounts of workplace learning of post-structuralist and postmodern perspectives
- case studies based on interviews with practising managers and HRM practitioners
- a detailed glossary of key concepts and issues.

John Garrick is a senior researcher and policy analyst at the Research Centre for Vocational Education and Training at the University of Technology, Sydney, Australia. He is co-editor of *Understanding Learning at Work* and *Flexible Learning and Human Resource Development: Putting Theory into Practice*, Routledge (forthcoming).

Informal Learning in the Workplace

Unmasking human resource development

John Garrick

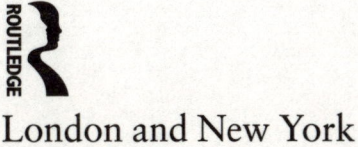

London and New York

First published 1998
by Routledge
11 New Fetter Lane, London EC4P 4EE

Simultaneously published in the USA and Canada
by Routledge
29 West 35th Street, New York, NY 10001

Typeset in Sabon by Routledge
Printed and bound in Great Britain by Clays Ltd, St Ives PLC

British Library Cataloguing in Publication Data
A catalogue record for this book is available from the British Library

Library of Congress Cataloging in Publication Data
Garrick, John
Informal learning in the workplace : unmasking human resource
development / John Garrick.
 Includes bibliographical references and index.
1. Employees–Training of. 2. Occupational training. 3. Experiential
learning. I. Title.
HF5549.5.T7G344 1998
331.25'92–dc21   98–18519

ISBN 0–415–18527–0 (hbk)
ISBN 0–415–18528–9 (pbk)

Contents

Preface
Learning in the workplace

Informal learning has become 'useful' in our post-industrial workplaces. Many workplaces now seek to harness its productive potentials. Industry managers and human resource development (HRD) practitioners are attempting to deploy it in the 'design' of corporate cultures. In the language of contemporary organisational development, this design is to make enterprises more innovative and competitive. This book critically examines definitions of informal learning, focusing on the term's application in various workplace contexts.

Contemporary talk about how informal learning can be 'utilised' to promote 'learning organisations' is challenged as this study shows how so-called democratic and participative workplaces are being 'framed' by an economistic human capital theory and a 'mercantilisation' of knowledge. HRD managers and practitioners from several multinational corporations and public organisations tell 'stories' that challenge assumptions about corporate uses of informal learning and its alignment with competency-based training. *Being* at work entails far more than simply performing the tasks one is required to *do*, and in turn, affects the links between informal learning and formal education.

The analysis is directed towards retheorising 'informal learning' – away from the narrow and instrumental definitions that currently characterise the term. Respect for the dignity of others, equity, and an appreciation of situated ethics have a place in 'workplace learning', especially in the postmodern context. It does not follow that the measurable tasks that one can be observed doing at work – the 'visible' – represent one's informal learning.

Acknowledgements

Many people have helped make writing this book a worthwhile experience. It is, in part, based on two years of field work which took me into the everyday work lives and corporate environments of several Human Resource Development managers and practitioners. They and their corporations must remain anonymous, but they have given generously of their time. Each knows their identity within the text and I wish first to thank them. Their reflections on their own stories, and then on my analyses of those stories, enabled me to generate the theoretical hypotheses and the resulting insights into informal workplace learning.

I would like to thank especially Robin Usher and Nicky Solomon who have read developing chapters and contributed valuable comments throughout the process. I am deeply indebted to them both. Chapters 4 and 5 build on work conducted jointly with Nicky. I also wish to acknowledge and thank Eleanor Olding who was always encouraging and provided critical feedback at the inception of the project (like 'why don't you make it a scathing critique?').

My own informal learning in relation to writing this text was influenced in positive ways by David Boud, Bernard Cohen, Richard Edwards, Andrew Gonczi, Paul Hager, Denise Kirkpatrick, Alison Lee, Victoria Marsick, Kate Sumner, Mark Tennant and Philip Wexler. I wish to offer them my warm thanks for providing me with both a rich store of ideas and suggestions about how I might approach such an elusive subject, and key and timely references.

Introduction

The notion of informal learning has captured a great deal of attention in recent years. There is an increasing volume of published works representing, amongst others, postmodern, critical, interpretive and positivist perspectives. Informal learning is such a powerful and elusive phenomenon, however, that no one perspective can capture its range of meanings. It has to be considered allusively. To adopt a single, exclusive approach renders any findings vulnerable to attack from other approaches. This is symptomatic of a more general crisis of knowledge associated with the 'postmodern condition'.

Debates over informal learning within the fields of practice of management and human resource development (HRD) have tended to focus on *how it can be enhanced*, or *what can be done* to enable individuals to learn more 'efficiently and effectively' in their day-to-day work. The debates have not substantially challenged existing definitions, conceptions and uses of the term. There has been little critique about the uses of informal learning, or of its construction within the master discourse of economic rationalism. A principal challenge of this text is to animate critique of the convenient exploitation of the rhetoric of 'learning organisations'. This rhetoric seeks fully to utilise workers' informal learning for productivity and efficiency gains.

In the United Kingdom, the USA, and throughout the OECD nations, HRD literature has contributed to a highly instrumental notion of 'informal learning'. It is being used by state authorities in reforms of national training and accreditation systems and processes. National training reforms are seeking more 'competitive' industries by promoting more highly-skilled, more highly-trained, workers. Informal learning thus becomes part of the discourse of 'competence'. In this discourse, the purpose of 'skills acquisition', including skills learned informally, is to enhance competitiveness. Indeed, the aim of developing a 'competent' workforce – to compete internationally against emerging 'tiger economies' – underlies the powerful drive to incorporate informal learning into economic discourse.

The connection between economics, workplace learning and education has been referred to variously by Barnett (1997), Burbules (1995), Casey (1995), Marginson (1997) and Usher and Edwards (1994). They note that in the alignment of education with market economics it is education that plays a critical, but secondary, role. With education in a secondary – albeit vital – position to economics at national policy levels, workplace learning and training are both constructed as secondary to industrial relations. This is particularly so within production-oriented industries. This text does not attempt to argue why this may or may not be economically justified. Rather, a counter-argument emerges through the stories of workers themselves. A close examination of the industrial contexts of the stories, and the emergence of clearer understandings of the parameters of informal learning reveal *masks of disguise* worn by contemporary 'learning organisations'. Unmasking underlying 'truths' about much of the language of contemporary education and training reform thus seems to be a worthwhile project.

Informal learning happens in everyday contexts as part of day-to-day life, but it is also a key element of a discourse which has this everyday process as its 'subject'. As such, informal learning is constructed in certain ways. For example, it can be viewed as a component of 'experiential learning', or as an aspect of performing one's work tasks 'competently'. The discursive construction (of a subject) can be problematic in several ways:

> I don't think it is coincidental or 'natural' that we focus on certain things rather than others. Once we start analysing something, once we start making something the object of our investigations, we do so within and through a discourse. It gives us a vocabulary, a set of concepts and pre-understandings, a motivating focus and direction of our investigations – above all a disciplined and systematic way of 'talking about'.
>
> (Usher 1993: 169)

By 'talking about' informal learning in this text, I too am discursively constructing what is sayable about it and, by implication, leaving something unsaid. The unsaid relates to what falls outside the discourses that enable analyses of informal learning. This represents a problem for the development of richer notions of informal learning. Many more questions are raised than are answered. And the stories in this text demonstrate the complexities inherent in informal learning. As an educational concept, informal learning appears less suitable for competency-based assessment than many strategic planners in industry, and in education communities, may have hoped. Indeed, an aim of this book is to expand debate both about the uses of informal learning in workplaces and attempts to 'recognise' it through competency-based standards.

A significant part of this project is to interpret the reflexive moments, the 'internal dialogues' of workers engaged in their daily operations. Clearly, informal learning involves engagement among persons and between persons. But, as Burbules (1995: 13) warns us, 'for this engagement to avoid dependency, there must also be a critical distance'. It is precisely the lack of 'critical distance' which remains a concern in relation to the new bridges being formed between education and learning-at-work, bridges which, to a significant degree, centre on 'assessing' the informal learning of individuals.

The subtle power of the informal suggests that there are more radical ways of viewing informal learning and work as learning environments. Contemporary views which increasingly seek to link 'the person' to work-productivity fail miserably to play with the tropes of irony, tragedy and parody – elements so important to learning. This in turn leads to the failure to hear the voices of difference and other influences not always directly observable at any given site. And yet they are ever present.

It is my hope that enhanced understandings of informal learning may lead in the longer term towards paths of qualitatively better work lives and, in the shorter term, analyses that help make sense of the turbulent postmodern and post-industrial conditions. Such hopes directly relate to how people learn from dealing with their daily experiences and dilemmas at work and the implications of this for their formal education and training. The development of new views about informal learning most certainly has implications for the links between formal education and workplace learning, extending to the ways individuals adapt to and resist work purposes and industrial practices. There are important ethical directions and purposes in this, but they will not please everyone.

1 What is informal learning in the workplace?

'The postmodern perspective' to which this study refers means above all the tearing off of the mask of illusions; the recognition of certain pretences as false and certain objectives as neither attainable nor, for that matter, desirable.

(Zygmunt Bauman 1993: 3)

Introduction

This book examines informal learning in various industrial contexts. It focuses primarily on everyday experience at work, exploring the effects of workplace practices on one's learning. I make two main assumptions about informal learning: that there are indeed rich sources of learning in day-to-day practice situations and that what is learned from experience is dynamic and open to multiple configurations. In particular I draw on examples of human resource (HR) managers and practitioners' negotiations, dilemmas, conflicts, successes and 'failures' in organisational and training developments, and also their personal and professional desires to illustrate the dialectical nature of informal learning.

The term dialectic is not used in the Hegelian sense of a synthesis of opposing tendencies in the thesis and antithesis. Here the term 'dialectical' needs to be distinguished from the conventional Hegelian and Marxian usages of dialectic which would relate learning to a privileged 'system' of needs and societal class divisions. I have drawn on Foucault's post-structuralist theory of power, which represents a major departure from both Marxist and Freudian understandings of power. Critical theory (before Foucault) tended to conceive of societal construction as a composite of economic, cultural and psychological activities.

Post-structuralism, however, abandons the idea of universals, holisms and composites, in favour of fragmentation and discontinuity.

Foucault viewed the individual as constituted by power, and the relations of power cannot be 'established, consolidated nor implemented without the production ... and functioning of a discourse' (Foucault 1980; in Casey 1995: 13). The discursive practices of contemporary work are examined in this study through the stories of HRD practitioners who are caught in discourses which 'frame' their learning in very particular ways, for instance as 'competence'. At the same time they experience informal learning in the everyday so that their stories represent an intersection between discourses and lived realities: they *speak the tensions*. Their stories are discursively constructed at one level and they live them at another.

Post-industrial corporations now use communication practices based on 'team work', self-direction, empowered workers and non-hierarchical work arrangements to design organisational 'culture'. These practices are, in this study, viewed as shapers of the informal learning of employees. They are discursive practices, and their effects on working selves are described systematically. I am more interested in the construction of meanings than with the materiality of construction, although these are interrelated. For instance, material production today is characterised in many workplaces by e-mail networks, various computer and information technologies and automation. New forms of production have resulted in restructuring of work tasks, occupations and organisational practices. But as Casey (1995: 5) points out, the relationships between the institutional processes of the new work – particularly in 'post-industrial corporate culture' – and self-formation, have not yet been adequately described.

'Self-formation' is an astonishingly complex notion. It is deeply problematised by some writers such as Derrida (1982) and Lyotard (1984). Rorty (1989) and Aronowitz (1992) say 'the self' is a convenient 'modern' fiction contingent upon innumerable forces and identity processes. Some philosophers, including Marx, Durkheim and Freud, variously point to the social and historical conditions that pattern the self, whilst Sartre espoused the existential project of self-creation. Foucault, however, contends that the self is 'an abstract construction, continually being redesigned in an on-going discourse generated by the imperatives of the policing process' (Hutton 1988: 135). For Foucault, theories of the self are a kind of currency through which power over the mind is defined and extended. Whereas Freud sought to explain how knowledge gives us power over the self, Foucault seeks to demonstrate how power shapes our knowledge of the self.

For this text I am particularly interested in subjective experience. However, the capacity to act and the authenticity of subjective experience will be viewed with postmodern doubt. Such doubt treats modern identity significantly as a social outcome of contemporary discourses and the language of industrialism. A view of self that encompasses both identity-making processes (including cultural, psychological, biological and multilinear) and outcomes (self-strategies), remains useful in understanding a person's informal learning.

Tensions between individuals and their workplaces raise many questions about the intersubjective nature of human discourse.[1] The dialectical relationship between the self and society, inherent in social action, is described by Lee (1992: 7) as 'a complex process of negotiating a pathway through the circulating discourses which produce the possibility of meaning . . . for the world as well as for the "self"'. To address the dialectical relationship between the self and society and its inherent multiple meanings, I examine various theories about how we learn in the world of work and how workplaces are being organised to 'facilitate' learning organisations.

The various perspectives on work-based learning raise questions about the inextricable connection between learning at work and society. These are questions which should have been central to the massive growth in writing and research on work-based learning in the past ten years. Yet they have not. This 'massive growth' is what constitutes the new 'workplace-based learning' discourse, and its effects are significant within managerial practices, workplace reforms, organisational theory, the sociology of organisations, systems theory, adult education and training. Notwithstanding such powerful effects, this new discourse can either bypass or obscure what actually happens to individuals at work.

In the field of practice of HRD, it appears that many researchers are either satisfied with the literature's concentration upon technical aspects of training and learning at work, or are lured (directly or indirectly) by their institutions or outside funding bodies to write about 'exemplary practices'. Examples of 'successful' practices which empower or make one's organisation, enterprise, workforce – indeed one's country – 'more clever', are prevalent. Perhaps such themes attract a greater likelihood of funding from both government and private sources.

Many contemporary texts on learning at work focus on the range of 'enhancing' procedures and techniques such as coaching, mentoring, job rotations, trial and error, and so on. These 'educative' processes are convenient to assess and amenable to the instrumental requirements of 'flexible specialisation', 'transferable skills', 'performance appraisals' and 'enterprise objectives'. This cluster of terms constitutes a language in which desired human resource products are highly-trained, flexible and competent. It is *the* dominant language of 'human resource development', and has the backing of industry, governments and unions. The language of experiential or 'experience-based learning' is being promoted as a valid form of knowledge acquisition. 'Talk' about work-based learning is thus in the terms of a discourse about human experience that is inseparable from power relations.

I argue in Chapter 2 that influential notions of informal learning have been located under the theoretical umbrella of 'experiential learning'. The distinguishing feature of experiential learning according to Andresen, Boud and Cohen (1995), is that the experience of the learner occupies the central place in all considerations of teaching and learning. They add, 'the ultimate goal of experiential learning involves the learner's own appropriation of something that is to them personally significant and meaningful (sometimes spoken in terms of the learning being "true to the lived experience of learners")' (1995: 208). These standpoints serve as the 'ultimate' (and most 'truthful') justifications of experience-based learning. But this study argues that these standpoints are problematic at several levels, especially at the assumed levels of learner autonomy and intentionality (see Glossary).

Powerful shaping influences, such as local organisational or site power relations, and more broadly industry discourses, cast doubt on the degree to which one should accept the notion of 'the learner's *own appropriation* of something which is to them personally significant or meaningful'. Not only is the subject's sense of meaning mediated, it is socially as well as personally constructed. Andresen, Boud and Cohen (1995) to an extent acknowledge this by arguing that learning is a 'holistic process', but the extent and effects on the person of the discontinuity of contemporary society, the strategies of flexible accumulation and the pragmatic world of labour markets should not be underestimated.

The philosophy of experiential learning somewhat rests upon Kierkegaard, who wrote in his *Journals*:

> in order to help another effectively I must understand what he [sic] understands. If I do not know that, my greater understanding will be of no use to him. . . . Instruction begins when you put yourself in his place so that you may understand what he understands and the way he understands it.

> (Kierkegaard 1959, cited in Kegan 1995: 278)

It is not enough to know what a person knows, or the *way* they may understand because the person is being continuously (and discursively) shaped. Their 'own' ways of knowing are immersed in discourses, power relations and local networks. The comfortable cohabitation of the valuing of experience in learning with a period of deeply conservative Western governments in which market economics rules is worth noting. Indeed, a dramatic blind-spot would exist if the direct and indirect influences of market economics on informal workplace learning and its growing links with formal education were not acknowledged.

With the powerful influence of market economics on workplace learning and its purposes in mind, my examination of everyday experience at work features several contextual questions. For instance, do HRD practitioners actually 'help' workers with their learning? Or are they managers of subtle technologies that help meet economically based objectives of the organisation? Why is it that informal learning is, at this particular moment, a focus of industry's gaze? Indeed, how is this text and its field research constructed through discourses of informal learning? Of course, such questions need not be mutually exclusive. But they highlight the problematic, at times binary, nature of worker and manager perceptions about the purposes of learning, and the discursive construction of its meanings. The complexity of learning at work is such that there are multiple answers to each of the above questions – there is no overriding 'truth'. Here, however, it is the question of what shapes informal learning that is of particular interest rather than narrow questions that seek to quantify, assess or measure it.

The discourses that shape informal learning

Contemporary HRD knowledge frameworks are unashamedly linked to market economics. It is the master discourse of market economics which gives the cues to the sub-discourses of HRD practices: consultancies, re-engineering, downsizing, outsourcing negotiations and image making on one hand, and discourses of quality performance on the other – capability, competence, total quality management (TQM), empowerment, self-direction, learning organisations, and so on. Economic and instrumental rationality are at the heart of the knowledge frameworks associated with each of these discourses as they are applied in Western societies. Knowledge is prized in so far as it can generate a market advantage (or service an operational area that has the capabilities to bring the organisation a market advantage). It is the generation of efficiencies, profit and institutional or organisational prestige that is primarily valued. This, of course, is not a bad thing per se, but in such a regime knowledge becomes characterised by what people actually do – and are seen to be doing. 'Performativity' requirements (Lyotard 1984) including financial and numerical performance indicators, become valorised. If something cannot be *shown* to be effective, it becomes dubious. Dubious corporate overheads are not carried for long in the postmodern world.

A contemporary epistemology of HRD practice is highly performance-based. Yet HRD practices are set against a backdrop of postmodern conditions – globalisation, discourses of 'market penetration', deregulation, privatisation, marketisation, dispersal of authorities (and of knowledge formation) and the feverish search for new 'self' definition. Bauman (1997: 14) describes these characteristics of the world we live in as 'a polyphony of value-messages and the ensuing fragmentariness of life'. Power structures are changing, decision-making centres are shifting and traditional notions of knowledge construction, such as through universities (and their research) are being radically challenged. Postmodern ideas bring a set of epistemological challenges – a questioning of anything that suggests absolute principles of reasoning. Yet, ironically, even with postmodern doubt, faith in market economics at political and national policy-making levels appears to have reached a virtually unchallenged position in framing thought and action. What is constituting 'valid' knowledge is the direct and measurable link between thought and action; the idea and the market power of the product. Such a link, by definition, permeates the processes of self-identity formation, including the attempt to locate where one 'belongs' in the work maze.

What tends to be required of HRD practices is not a promotion of doubt or any problematising of cultural projects or of ethical or social justice issues. It is assumed in a market forces ideology that via 'the market' such issues will be resolved 'naturally', by the 'natural order'. In other words market economists make the ontological assumption that 'free market' economics is close to or even reflects 'human nature'. The outcomes of the 'market place' are thus reflections of nature and not manifestations of culture, history, power and language. Considering the assumption that the market economy reflects 'human nature', any trust in the so-called market place to determine 'valid' knowledge would appear to any sceptic to be naive at best.

Following Foucault's propositions about the intimate connections between power and knowledge and considering scientific discourse as linked to the tightening of surveillance and control, the possible outcomes of market forces determining 'valid' knowledge become disturbing. For example, HRD knowledge and practices can be read as technologies of compliance and control – a techno-science that refines self-regulation and dependency in the guise of worker 'empowerment' and 'self-direction'. Chapters 5 and 6 illustrate how these technologies can work. HRD practices are placed in a paradox by their intimate ties with the determining criteria of market economics. The paradox rejects the principles of absolute reason and yet they are subject to the governing rules of market economics – rules which apply, at this historic moment, almost absolutely.

Most advanced economies are encouraging their industries to make changes that will enhance worker productivity. The changes include:

- the introduction of competency-based standards for workers in most industries
- a greater emphasis on training, work-based learning; experiential learning; and recognition of prior learning
- demands from government, business and trade unions for 'greater relevance' of formal tertiary education courses to industry requirements.

Alone, each of these points carries enormous implications for HRD practices, including the reform of training methods to align with strategic organisational change processes, innovative curriculum development and assessment methods. Associated with the training reforms is a 'master discourse' about economic imperatives (Marginson 1997) including the need to seek greater productivity and competitiveness in the workplace. In the US, Britain, Canada, South Africa and Australia, large-scale foreign debt and poor competitive performance in a range of industries are perceived by the various national governments, unions and industry leaders as significant concerns for standards of living for future generations.

It is precisely this language which is prevalent in current industrial and workplace reforms. However, assumptions underlying economic imperatives should always be questioned. For instance, the widely accepted assertion that industry and workplace reforms are required to compete successfully in international markets links market economics and the skill-formation requirements of the workforce. These links are meant to enable companies to become more flexible, innovative and competitive. Marginson (1993) expresses strong scepticism of such links, wondering how sensible it is to allow market economics to determine educational goals. His concerns centre on 'the production of competencies' or of people as simply 'human capital' (1993: 239). The alignment of educational goals with market economics is seen by governments and major industry bodies as the solution to problems of modernisation and the future and, as Marginson points out, 'in these cases the object is the already existing economic subject. . . . The implication is for a deeply conservative education' (1993: 239).

Teasing out the educational implications of linking market economics with educational goals is an important subtext of this book. At the level of individual experience, this subtext relates to *how* workers actually become (or are made) more flexible. Rainbird for one, notes that in many instances:

> the process of learning the skills required for a new job occurs informally, through one person training another . . . and that new skills are being acquired without the legitimation of a formal training period. . . . Although the scope of a job is being extended . . . this is not always rewarded in the wages structure.
>
> (Rainbird 1988: 177)

In other words, becoming 'more flexible' can be coded language for workers having to accept additional responsibilities, perhaps having to work different (more extensive) hours, but being paid no more.

This linking of skill formation and workplace reform to work-based learning has major industrial relations implications for the roles, purposes and practices of workplace trainers. It is thus pertinent to ask whether informal learning is being structured, recognised and remunerated in the context of reformed workplaces and, if so, how? Failure to recognise new skills adequately has often occurred in the past, not only where training is based on informal arrangements but, according to Rainbird, 'where training is narrow, and competence is acquired largely through experience'.

With often repeated government aims to become more competitive, structural changes are occurring throughout private and public sector enterprises in most OECD nations. Such changes are in part to make the workplace function more productively. They also involve an examination of formal day-to-day work practices, and the informal interactions that result from work organisation and structures. Marsick and Watkins (1990a) hypothesised that informal and incidental learning may become much more prominent in the workplace. And this is true – it has. Yet we know only fragments of what such terms actually encompass. It is with this fragmentary and discursively constructed knowledge base in mind that some of the prevalent definitions of informal and incidental learning are examined.

Some prevalent definitions of informal learning

There is a silence about the power of discourse to delineate the sayable about informal learning. In writing about 'it' I highlight those features of the subject that are constructed by the circulating discourses as being more or less important. Once informal learning is objectified, classified and measured it is also being, in some ways, reduced. Definitions of a term such as informal learning thus become a site of tension for the study; one of its problematics. Concerns about the power of discourse in 'defining' informal learning are therefore reflected in the following discussion and examined in depth in Chapter 2. The question posed by Usher (1993: 169) helps clarify this concern, asking 'is there a difference between learning from experience and experiential learning?' He claims that learning from experience happens in everyday contexts and is rarely recognised, whereas 'experiential learning' is a key element of a discourse which has this everyday process as its 'subject'. This discourse constructs the learning in a certain way, although it appears to be merely a term that describes the process. The point is that there is a difference. Accounts are, of necessity, discursive, 'they are cast in and communicated through language and are understood by us by our discursive frameworks' (Usher 1993: 169).

This study is itself an example of a disciplined and systematic way of exploring informal learning. It discursively represents what informal learning might encompass and thus what it might exclude. In considering the recognised and respected definitions of informal learning that follow, it is worth keeping Usher's question in mind as the discursive constitution of informal learning has tended to fall out of view.

Definitional complexities about informal learning are exemplified in the wide range of writings that have over the years related to this phenomena:

- learning from experience (Dewey 1938; Pfeiffer and Jones 1983; Cell 1984; Kolb 1984)
- learning from the context (Zuboff 1988; Lave and Wenger 1991)
- action science (Lewin 1947; Argyris and Schön 1974)
- non-routine versus routine conditions for learning (Schön 1983; Jarvis 1987)
- the tacit dimension of knowledge (Polanyi 1967; Inkster 1987)
- reflection and critical reflection (Mezirow 1990; Boud and Walker 1992 – see Glossary)
- enhancing informal and incidental learning (Freire 1972; Brookfield 1986; Marsick and Watkins 1990a).

The way one talks about informal learning begins to construct what it becomes. The way Bagnall talks about it suggests informal learning is 'obtained unconsciously, existentially; through the mere experience of living in a particular environment or context' (1990: 1). Informal learning is often distinguished from other kinds of learning by the fact that 'it is non-intentional' (Wain 1987: 48) as against formal learning, which refers to intentionally constructed learning activities.

La Belle (1982) and Mocker and Spear (1982) define it by distinguishing it from 'formal learning' which they characterise as being university or college studies; short professional training courses; or externally planned programmes of instruction. Mocker and Spear also distinguish between informal and formal learning through the concept of 'locus of control' over the content and conduct (ends and means) of these types of learning. For instance, with formal learning, control is usually institutionally mediated and thus less 'self-directed'. Such definitions can have the effect of positing 'informal' as something left over from the formal. Indeed, a standard objection to the inclusion of informal learning within formal education is that informal learning has the potential to render the term 'education' meaningless, if experience is perceived as valid learning.

Influential North American authors such as Knowles (1975) and Brookfield (1981, 1982) link informal learning to the 'autonomous', 'independent' and 'self-directed learner'. For Candy (1988: 160) a key element in self-direction is that informal learning 'occurs without participation in externally planned programs of instruction in the subject area concerned'. Marsick and Watkins reiterate this theme, suggesting informal (and incidental) learning happens: 'outside formally structured, institutionally sponsored classroom-based activities, taking place under non-routine conditions or in routine conditions where reflection and critical reflection are used to clarify the situation' (1990a: 7).

In this definition the processes of reflection and critical reflection are central. Critical reflection, argues Mezirow (1990), enables people to 're-frame' problems they may be experiencing, to realise that a particular situation can be defined and solved in many different ways.

Informal learning, in contrast to formal education, is predominantly experiential, non-institutional and, according to Marsick and Watkins (1990a), distinct from incidental learning. Marsick and Watkins' (1990a) distinctions between informal and incidental learning include:

Informal learning

- self-directed learning

- networking
- coaching, mentoring
- performance planning.

Incidental learning

- learning from involvement
- learning from mistakes/trial and error
- assumptions
- beliefs
- values
- hidden agendas
- the actions of others.

Informal and incidental learning, although interconnected, are not necessarily the same according to Marsick and Watkins, who define 'incidental learning' as: 'a by-product of some other activity such as sensing the organisational culture, or trial and error experimentation' (1990a: 8).

As such, incidental learning is not planned or intentional as it may be with self-directed learning, or where help is consciously sought from advisers, coaches or mentors. A key distinguishing feature in Marsick and Watkins' definition is therefore that informal learning is intentional, incidental learning is not. Such a distinction may, however, be dubious. It seems unwarranted to separate 'self-directed' learning from the beliefs and values that influence 'incidental' learning. Separating informal and incidental learning seems to represent a false dichotomy, however. And existing definitions do not problematise the phenomena adequately. Wain's technical definitions, derived from 'lifelong learning' literature, exemplify this shortcoming:

> Formal education: the hierarchically structured, chronologically graded 'education system', running from primary schools through the university and including, in addition to general academic studies, a variety of specialised programs and institutions for full-time technical and professional training.

> Informal learning: the truly lifelong process whereby every individual acquires attitudes, values, skills and knowledge from daily experience and the educative influences and resources in his or her environment – from family and neighbours, from work and play, from the market place, the library and the mass media.

> Non-formal education: any organisational activity outside the established formal system, whether operating separately or as an important

feature of some broader activity, that is intended to serve identifiable learning clienteles and learning objectives.

(Wain 1987: 51)

Here the formal and non-formal focus is on institutional structures, whilst the focus of the informal is on the learner. Wain's separation of informal from 'formal' and 'non-formal' is problematic. 'Informal' learning may occur in each of these contexts and they are not mutually exclusive. Such technical definitions thus deny a 'boundarylessness' that can accompany informal learning. Marsick and Watkins also stress the distinction between informal learning and non-formal education, pointing out 'non-formal is where education is difficult to access and frequently tied to social class; non-formal education is often introduced as a "second chance" for credentials, credibility, or knowledge and skill development' (1990b: 32).

Marsick and Watkins' contributions have influenced recent managerial and HRD discourses on informal learning in the workplace because their main focus is on ways to *enhance* informal and incidental learning. Their approach is based on a 'human capital' theory of learning and posits 'action-reflection-action' as central to informal workplace learning. This perspective differs from the Freirean notion of action-reflection-action – which is a core method in non-formal education – as it is without much of the political intent implicit in Freire's (1985) critical theory of pedagogy.

Marsick and Watkins' work on informal learning does not address postmodern theoretical insights that problematise the very notion of workplace learning and the *ways* people do learn unintentionally in particular environments or contexts. One of the emerging problems that accompanies talk about 'informal learning', often neglected in the literature, is that it is linked with situated ethics, yet often there are no clear cut ways to resolve these. It is 'incredulity' that characterises our 'postmodern condition' (Lyotard 1984). In this condition, virtues such as liberty, individuality, difference and tolerance contain deep paradoxes – celebrated on one hand, threatening and potentially subversive on the other. The problems of defining informal learning may thus be not so much about its relationship to formal learning, or about how it can be enhanced in the workplace, but connected to the political, social, cultural and ethical or moral issues which underpin questions such as 'what ought one to do' in the maze of workplace activities and dilemmas. This is in part why Wain distinguishes informal learning from formal and non-formal learning on the basis that it is unintended by the learner, asserting that:

it is easily demonstrable that people pick up attitudes, values, skills, and knowledge by simply interacting with other people or being present in a particular social context, and, as Aristotle pointed out, [this is] how we are educated into 'virtue' or moral behaviour.

(Wain 1993: 63)

For this text, particular interest is in the ways informal learning in the workplace is constituted through and by embedded and discursive influences. The range of definitions related to informal learning indicates alternative discourses and understandings of the terms. Although there is no definitive meaning, these definitions are discursively significant – they represent the language of the discursive practice of informal learning.

Conclusion

Many 'stories' are being told about informal learning, and what is clear is that there are many stories to tell and many ways to tell them. There is a performativity and power of language that implies we should look at the way stories are told and at the words of signification. In the everyday corporate and site contexts described in the following research, informal learning has very different significations for each of the participants. There is the notion that informal learning is directly related to the experience of lived reality – the 'lifeworld' (see Glossary). At the same time there is a separate (but connected) notion that relates informal learning to the discursive production that constitutes it.

This distinction is important to this book. It has a direct bearing on how managerial, HRD and education practices related to informal learning are formulated and implemented, raising critical questions: 'Should informal learning be structured or organised in new ways to *enable* the recognition of informally developed skills?' 'If so, in what ways?' 'How might informal learning connect with competency-based standards?' 'Should "recognised" informal learning be accompanied by correlative new reward systems?' Or, would such moves represent the 'colonisation of lifeworlds'? Among others, Welton (1995) argues 'lifeworlds' may be better left alone rather than turned towards new capitalistic corporate endeavours. Indeed, 'should one adopt definite standpoints on informal learning?'. Or might this lead, as Usher and Edwards (drawing on Foucault 1977) suggest, to an intensifying of surveillance through making it possible 'to qualify, to classify and to punish [establishing] over individuals a visibility through which one differentiates them and judges them' (1994: 103)? Chapter 2 continues this discussion about the different meanings and perspectives on informal learning, and Chapter 3 unmasks the rhetoric about work as a learning environment.

Note

1   A discourse in Foucault's sense (in Lee 1992: 10) is a particular way of organising meaning and hence of ordering the world. Different 'institutions' (forms of social organisation, such as workplaces) produce different discourses which set up positions for individuals to occupy – things they can and must say and do, and things they cannot and must not. Hence, discourses are forms of regulation of social meanings and social actions. Given that the world is governed by a multitude of often competing and contradictory discourses, individuals are positioned in complex and multiple ways, some of which may be traced at particular moments (through analyses of these discourses).

2 Theorising informal learning

Introduction: the main theories of informal learning

In this chapter I distinguish 'learning informally' from 'informal learning'. This may sound a little spurious, but informal learning is one of the circulating discourses about work-based learning. It is a topic that is written about, talked about and theorised – often in terms of how to 'enhance it', how to mobilise it in ways that will 'empower' self-directed workers, and for 'assessment' purposes. In some instances this is to align informal learning with competency-based standards. There is therefore a discourse of informal learning that intersects with those government and industry discourses seeking an alignment between industry demands for efficiencies and productivity, and education goals for self-directed learners, and, indeed, new markets. Learning informally has another connotation that relates to one's spontaneous experience in everyday situations. In making this distinction I am alluding to some of the definitional problems that accompany such a complex phenomena. And some of the narrow ways the definitions are used in contemporary managerial discourse warrant problematising.

A number of the contemporary definitions of 'informal learning' discussed in Chapter 1 owe a philosophical debt to Dewey's views on experience and education. He claimed that experience and education cannot be directly equated to each other:

> Any experience is mis-educative that has the effect of arresting or distorting the growth of further experience. An experience may be such as to engender callousness; it may produce lack of sensitivity and of responsiveness. . . . But there is another aspect of the matter. Experience does not go on simply inside a person. It does go on there, for it influences the formation of attitudes of desire and purpose. But this is not the whole story. Every genuine experience

has an active side which changes in some degree the objective conditions under which experiences are had. . . . When this fact is ignored, experience is treated as if it were something which goes on exclusively inside an individual's body and mind. It ought not to be necessary to say that experience does not occur in a vacuum.

(Dewey 1938: 39–40)

Dewey's notion of active learning (and progressive education) has become a popular discourse in adult education and on the job training, but it has often been misinterpreted to mean 'vocational education' – learning about the job from *doing* it. Informal learning certainly has something to do with experience, but what exactly is the difference between learning from experience and experiential learning? Learning from experience happens in everyday contexts and is rarely recognised, whereas 'experiential learning' is a key element of a discourse which has this everyday process as its 'subject'. This discourse is influenced by the circulating discourses such as competency-based education and training (CBET) and recognition of prior learning (RPL) that construct 'informal learning' in a certain way, even though it appears to be merely a term that describes the process.

But it is not 'simply' a process because accounting for informal learning is, of necessity, discursive – cast in and communicated through language and understood by us through our discursive frameworks. The discursivity of accounts and the discursivity of our interpretations of, for example, competency-based standards, or the recognition of particular competencies attained, are generally given virtually no weight.

I am also discursively representing what informal learning might encompass and thus what might be excluded. The point of this is that the *discursive construction of informal learning* has tended to fall out of view in the drive to 'mobilise' it into observable and measurable performance. When it is observable and measurable it can be marshalled in certain ways, often through well-intentioned staff development approaches seeking to empower 'self-directed' learners. It is subject to the ensemble of government policy directions in VET and it is subject to the managerial discourses that pursue 'learning organisations'. In these ways, what is learned informally at particular work sites can be 'seen', rendered 'visible', 'utilised' in the desired government and corporate ways.

Why has informal learning become so important?

Informal learning fits very well with new forms of work organisation and new types of management, and has the potential effect of breaking the power of the formal education system. This may sound a dramatic claim, but contemporary uses of informal learning are clearly located within broader discourses of economic, workplace and education reforms. The 'informalisation' of learning is associated with a 'vocationalising' of education, which, in turn, is characterised by the promotion of work-based learning curricula and assessments. Wexler (1993) refers to these reforms of workplace and education as a 'corporatist reorganisation' of higher education and training. Notable in this reorganisation are the new 'partnerships' of the state, business corporations and significant groups of educational professionals which are effecting change in the infrastructure, implementation and rhetoric and, ultimately, the meaning of education. The human capital view of informal learning is a feature of this discourse that seeks to align education and work. In part, this alignment is why interest in informal learning, particularly in the workplace, is growing quite dramatically.

Informal learning is, however, never neutral. It is never independent of sociality and, as such, learning will be influenced by a person's social positioning at work or indeed anywhere. Social positioning will influence access to and experience of learning opportunities. It will shape one's identity, leading to different knowledges of 'reality'. One's conception of 'reality', one's 'experience', is not simply a 'given', and can never be read as unproblematic. As Usher and Edwards argue:

> there is no single ordered view of the world to be imparted, but multiple 'realities' to be constructed through an already interpreted experience. Our knowledge and understanding of history and the present are relative and partial, dependent upon the meanings we take and which regulate and construct our experience.
>
> (Usher and Edwards 1994: 199)

Much of the HRD, management and adult education literature has been framed, historically, by the contributions of 'individual actors' being emphasised, or overemphasised; or important insights into the intersubjective character of human discourse, the 'big' factors, being given pre-eminence, or not sufficiently taken into consideration, depending on one's perspective. Adult learning literature for instance tends to privilege 'the individual' as being at the very centre of knowledge production (and acquisition), *or* privilege social/structural context. And it is a particular kind of individual – the unified, sovereign subject whose experience provides a window on to the world – that is given primacy.

The following sections explore the relationship between experience and learning. This relationship is often analysed with learning being contingent upon experience; that is, explanation about what is learnt commences with experience. Yet it can also be argued that 'experience' is precisely that which is in need of explanation. Any approach to using experience for learning will generate its own representations of experience and thus what is being constructed and recognised as 'learning'.

Much of the writing on informal learning takes three main perspectives: informal learning as a valid form of knowledge acquisition; how people learn from experience; how learning from experience can best be facilitated and assessed. A postmodern critique of experiential learning has also emerged which challenges the arguments of each of these perspectives, asking 'Why has this form of learning become an important discourse at this particular historic moment?'. In the following sections of this chapter I will briefly consider the underlying assumptions of these perspectives. These sections are: the prevailing views of informal learning; experiential learning; reflection and the autonomous subject; the politics of learning from experience; and postmodernism and informal learning. I identify how experience can be constructed discursively, how interests frame learning, and how it is often assumed that individuals frame their 'own' experiences.

Prevailing views of informal learning

Contemporary views of 'informal learning' frequently rest on human capital theory for justification. This theory is interested in how to make informal learning effective – deliberately encouraged – referring to its processes such as mentoring, networking, working in teams, receiving feedback, and trial and error to show *how* it can be enhanced. Marsick and Watkins, who represent this perspective, argue that

> informal learning can be deliberately encouraged by an organisation, or it can take place despite an environment not highly conducive to learning. Incidental learning on the other hand, almost always takes place in everyday experience although people are not always conscious of it.
>
> (Marsick and Watkins 1990b: 12)

This definition acknowledges environmental barriers which are not 'conducive to learning', but it has an underlying instrumental interest. The ways this interest is being used in organisational development have major implications for HRD practitioners' roles, purposes and assessment procedures. Employees now frequently desire to have their informal learning 'recognised' so that it can be credited in formal courses. In some instances it can translate to extra remuneration.

Paralleling the discourse on workplace-based learning is a body of research (frequently funded by government and/or sponsored by industry) and theory within education, sociology, cognitive psychology, cultural psychology, ecological psychology and anthropology. Lave and Wenger (1991), Billett (1992) and Stevenson (1994b), suggest that 'authentic settings' such as the workplace provide a basis for rich learning experiences which have the potential to be robust and highly transferable. Stevenson (1994b) suggests that the key to the transferability of work-based learning resides in the rich base of higher order procedural knowledge.

A key assumption about informal learning in the workplace in much of this research is that it has something to do with individuals (subjects) apprehending experience, reasoning, or logically thinking through their direct experience and giving that experience 'meaning'. Much of the research on work-based learning fails to acknowledge the representational effects of its own theorising – 'authorising' particular types of experience and 'framing' what constitutes an 'authentic' setting. For example, a cognitive science conception of the optimum path to transferable work-based learning will inevitably posit higher order cognitive functions as a 'truth' about experience. This discursively produces experience in a very particular (scientific) way. It is a 'truth' framed by the assumptions of cognitive science that include an 'objective' reality independent of the (subjective) knower. This is a notion that is very useful to the contemporary management of the workplace, with proof of an objective reality in relation to an individual's on the job learning relying on the observable and measurable. Skills training for job requirements and transferable work-based learning, including higher order cognitive development, are emphasised in this discourse.

Subjective experience is not, however, an incontrovertible starting (or concluding) point in any analysis or theory of what has been learnt from experience. The notion one holds of 'subjectivity' is important here. As Heidegger[1] puts it:

> knowledge and understanding are not the product of deliberate, conscious and methodological acts of the ordinary subject but an encounter and engagement with the world where pre-understandings constitute a structure of intelligibility, an 'absence' which is yet the condition of knowing anything.
>
> (Heidegger 1962, cited in Usher 1992: 205)

In formal learning, this 'absence' is (theoretically) addressed by prede-termined programmes where subject experts, curriculum designers, teachers, academics and bosses construct desirable knowledge. In the prevailing (dominant) discourses of informal workplace learning it is operational knowledge that is privileged. This type of knowledge attempts to align personal staff development with job-related require-ments. Observable skills and competencies are made 'present' through direct accounting for everyday learning events. This is partly why 'check-lists' of competence are now commonplace in many industries throughout Europe and other OECD nations. The human capital perspective on accounting for informal learning is that the 'everyday focus' of informal learning offers possibilities for improving the learning capabilities of complex organisations. Such possibilities are inextricably linked to organisational competitive interests and economic performance.

Mechthild Hart argues from a critical/feminist perspective that the contemporary valuing of workplace knowledge through skills and competencies is 'oriented towards maintaining or restoring the economic status quo [and this] can undermine the critical intent of education by blocking a fuller understanding of the cultural dynamics behind destructive and divisive economic and social arrangements' (Hart 1993: 19). She is concerned that what happens in individuals' engagement with their problems, tasks and dilemmas at work is funda-mental to learning about much more than merely work tasks. What happens in the objectification of skills through competency-based approaches to learning at work is that professional and personal iden-tity, gender relations and what constitutes 'worthwhile' notions of progress are affected and the processes involved in dealing with the apparently trivial tasks of day-to-day living become important themes for 'learning'.

The pedagogies of the everyday will be variously affected by *the atmosphere* within which people work, *conflict* between people, *work organisation*, individual *personality* and indeed the way training is theorised and conducted. Informal learning cannot be simplistically defined by a set of curricular aims. It is worth asking therefore what is being privileged when the talk is about 'informal learning'. What discourses are holding sway? Is it social/cultural context *or* individual autonomy that the talk is theoretically indebted to? Are concerns primarily about the structures and purposes of workplaces? Is it about organisational narratives or managerial story-telling? Is it about how to design work to be an 'educative environment'? Does the corporate talk accept the ideas of human capital theory as 'given'? And how are people portrayed when engaged in day-to-day situations and interventions, trying to make sense of their lives?

These questions represent cultural forms that remind us of the reflexive nature of social life – that social life has the capacity to change as our knowledge and thinking changes. HR managers, practitioners and educational thinkers must cope with this *reflexivity* (see Glossary). Their practices need to be seen as located in particular historical circumstances, discourses and social contexts. Cervero notes that current researchers are not the first to observe that learning from experience is a central way that people create their world and give meaning to it:

> John Dewey most recently made this point and David Hume before him and Aristotle before him. . . . However, for the better part of this century, our society has given legitimacy to knowledge that is formal, abstract and general, while devaluing knowledge that is local, specific and based on practice. . . . For this we owe a debt to Plato and Socrates, who believed that for something to count as knowledge it had to be de-contextualised, generalised and abstracted to cover a range of situations.
>
> (Cervero 1992, cited in Beckett 1993: 4)

Marsick and Watkins draw on Dewey's experiential learning orthodoxy to argue that 'learning takes place through an ongoing dialectical process of action and reflection' (1990a: 8). But to use reflection for learning, one must consciously become aware that one is actually learning. This implies intentionality, resting heavily on a paradigm of consciousness and the following section critically examines the place of 'intentionality' in experiential learning theory.

Experiential learning

Experiential learning or experience-based learning is based on a set of assumptions identified by Andresen, Boud and Cohen (1995: 207–8) as:

- experience is the foundation of, and the stimulus for, learning
- learners actively construct their own experience
- learning is a holistic experience
- learning is socially and culturally constructed
- learning is influenced by the socio-emotional context in which it occurs.

Some powerful tensions exist within and between these assumptions – for example, that learners 'actively construct their own experience' whilst, at the same time, 'learning is socially and culturally constructed'. An individualistic-humanist discourse of adult education seems incompatible with a critical social-transformation practice, but both hold meaningful ideas about work purposes for many HRD managers and practitioners. On the surface these assumptions appear to represent a dichotomy; important differences exist between adult education as practised within an individualistic discourse of personal empowerment, and a pedagogy of critical social theory. That both are assumed as underpinning experiential learning is intriguing as they carry such different implications for practice. For instance, the humanistic theory of experiential learning, common in management and HR practices promoting 'self-directed learners', presupposes a great deal about individual autonomy.

Adult learning theory within the discourse of 'personal empowerment' holds that learning can become most effective in overcoming barriers or blind-spots if personal emotions are addressed in the learning process. This 'humanistic' position, shared by many HRD practitioners and adult educators, holds that individuals may be most productive when they feel that work is personally meaningful and not simply an instrumental means to another end. What is personally meaningful is thus critical to learning, and problematic to any reconciliation of the above assumptions.

Andresen, Boud and Cohen cite the words of Mao Tse Tung (1968: 20) to illustrate both the importance of personal meaning and ideology in learning:

> all genuine knowledge originates in direct experience . . . human knowledge can in no way be separated from practice . . . practice is higher than (theoretical) knowledge. Whoever wants to know a thing has no way except by coming into contact with it, that is, by living (practising) in its environment . . . practice, knowledge, again practice, and again knowledge . . . such is the dialectical-materialist theory of the unity of knowing and doing.
>
> (Andresen, Boud and Cohen 1995: 212)

Here I am using Mao's elevation of 'practice' over 'theory' to highlight a deep irony. He espoused the importance of personal experience to knowledge formation, but he enacted such oppressive events as the 'Hundred Flowers' campaign, the Cultural Revolution, and ideology-led practice on a grand scale.[2] Ideology-led practice, or as Lather (1986) puts it, 'adopting an openly ideological stance', can be seen as simply leading to a new form of oppression – rendering the notion of any 'truly' liberating education very dubious.

One attempt to construct a framework for making sense of experiential learning is Weil and McGill's (1989) idea of 'villages'. They view experiential learning as 'a spectrum of meanings, practices and ideologies which emerge out of the work and commitments of people' (1989: 3). In this spectrum they discern four emphases on experiential learning, each the basis for a cluster of interrelated ideas, concerns and values which they refer to as 'villages'. They include:

- the assessment and accreditation of prior experiential learning experiences
- experiential learning and change in higher and continuing education
- experiential learning and social change
- personal growth and development.

Weil and McGill hold that a person or organisation which knows only their own village, cannot understand it. It is through 'dialogue across villages that we are enabled to consider what we intend and what we do from new perspectives' (1989: 4).

Boud (1989: 40–3) points out that approaches of each village can be located within the main traditions in adult learning, which include:

- training and efficiency in learning
- self-directed learning (and the andragogy school)[3]
- learner-centred and humanistic education
- critical pedagogy and social action.

He adds that 'at the heart of the main traditions is *the role of autonomy*, and the variety of approaches which might promote the individual's autonomy' (Boud 1989: 40). These traditions highlight the main conceptions of experiential learning, sharing *autonomy* as a central notion. Usher problematises this notion in his influential postmodern critique:

> adult education works with an ethics of personal empowerment and autonomy. In this sense, adult education is part of the educational project of the Enlightenment and because of this is cast in and expresses itself through a discourse of individual agency.
>
> (Usher 1992: 201)

This 'Enlightenment' theory of experiential learning (see Glossary) falls within the humanistic discourse of reflecting on and learning from experience. But to know and understand one's experience from reflection requires the acceptance of the assumption that 'the subject, through conscious awareness, can be both the source and shaper of its experience' (Usher 1992: 207). Usher's point is that the taken-for-granted presuppositions about 'reflection' ought to be problematised as one's social relations – how one is positioned within social hierarchies (and the effects of this positioning on emotions) – will grossly affect the subject's 'reflections'.

Reflection and the autonomous subject

As we have seen, it can be argued that experiential learning theory presupposes too much about individual agency. Proponents of the humanistic adult education theory argue, however, that it does not. They claim that reflection is the bridge between experience and learning. Boud, Cohen and Walker, for instance, say that

> reflection consists of those processes in which learners engage to recapture, notice and re-evaluate their experience, to work with experience to turn it into learning . . . through entering into a dialogue with our experience we can turn experiential knowledge, which may not be readily accessible to us, into propositional knowledge which can be shared and interrogated.
>
> (Boud, Cohen and Walker 1993: 9)

This definition implies making inferences, generalisations, analogies, discriminations and evaluations. It also requires feeling and remembering, using beliefs to make interpretations, analysis and judgments, however unaware one may be of doing so.

As Mezirow points out,

> if reflection is understood as an assessment of how or why we have perceived, thought, felt or acted, it must be differentiated from an assessment of how best to perform these functions when each phase of an action is guided by what we have learned before.
>
> (Mezirow 1990: 8)

He is making a distinction between action and reflection. Action can be a creative process that involves our prejudices and distortions but reflection requires conscious attention to those distortions in our reasoning and attitudes. Attending to our reasoning and attitudes requires what C. Wright Mills called:

> a quality of mind that will help . . . [people] to use information and to develop reason in order to achieve lucid summations of what is going on in the world and what may be happening within themselves. The sociological imagination enables its possessor to understand the

larger historical scene in terms of its meaning for the inner life and the external career of a variety of the individuals . . . the sociological imagination enables us to grasp history and biography and the relations between the two within society.

(Mills 1970: 11–12)

Virginia Griffin (1987) uses just such an imagination in relation to her home town in her research paper on the 'autodidactic or self-directed process of learning'. She identifies five dimensions of learning, sometimes operating individually, sometimes together:

- the rational
- the physical (or physiological)
- the emotional
- the relational
- the metaphorical (or intuitive).

She argues that there is constant shifting between, and interaction among, these dimensions, which in turn are perceived through 'valuing and judging systems'. What is missing in Griffin's analysis however is a more comprehensive critique of the overall social and economic context within which this 'self-directed' experiential learning occurs. It could be argued, for instance, that particular types of discourses, social conditions and context can (and do) systematically exclude some groups from learning and developmental opportunities. Nonetheless, Griffin's findings suggest a picture of enormous complexity and unpredictability in adult learning and constitute an important hypothesis about the non-linear nature of learning. Subsequent studies have refined this hypothesis. Taylor (1987: 183) identifies four phases of self-directed learning – detachment, divergence, engagement and convergence. Taylor argues 'the four phases occur in a consistent order around a particular learning theme or problem being worked on':

- Disconfirmation (phase one): a major discrepancy between expectations and experience
- Disorientation: a period of intensive disorientation and confusion accompanied by a crisis of confidence and withdrawal from other people who are associated with the source of confusion
- Naming the problem (phase two): naming the problem without blaming self and others
- Exploration: beginning with relaxation with unresolved issue, an intuitively guided, collaborative and open-ended exploration with a gathering of insights, confidence and satisfaction
- Reflection (phase three): a private reflective review

- Reorientation: a major insight or synthesis experience with a new approach to the learning (or teaching) task
- Sharing the discovery (phase four): testing out the new understanding with others
- Equilibrium: a period in which the new perspective and approach is elaborated, refined and applied.

In this case, the theory represented is that of an individualistic social-psychology consistent with the traditions of the 'humanistic discourse'. Taylor's hypothesis firmly locates reflection within a psychologistic discourse. The conception of 'subjects' is in terms of linear temporality, and experience, although presented as a helix-like cumulative progression, reflects rather than challenges the research's founding assumptions.

This discourse celebrates experience and learning through experience as means of individual empowerment. It is a discourse whereby learners actively define their own experience by attaching meaning to events. As Boud *et al.* put it, 'we may use language and ideas to express meaning, and in the process use externally defined objects, but only the person who experiences can ultimately give meaning to the experience' (1993: 8). It is this meaning-giving status accorded to the person which postmodern views of experiential learning seriously dispute (Usher, Bryant and Johnston 1997). They draw upon Foucault's 'counter history of ideas' to refute the idea of individual 'agency' and thus the status of 'meaning-giver'. Foucault (1982: 208) views the subject 'as an effect of . . . historically located, disciplinary processes and concepts which enable people to consider themselves as individual subjects and which constrain them from thinking otherwise'. On the following page he writes 'we have to know the historical conditions which motivate our conceptualisation. We need a historical awareness of our present circumstance' (1982: 209).

Foucault's influential notions of 'historical situatedness' and the 'disciplinary processes' inherent in power/knowledge formations, seriously challenge conventional adult education theory based on personal empowerment and autonomy. For instance, Foucault (1982: 210) warns of the dangers inherent in attempting to 'rationalise' without investigating the links between the rationalisation and power. Commonly, reflection is seen as taking place when we look back on something and question the assumptions which guided it. Reflective practices are generally less concerned with the question of 'what cognitive processes are operating' and more with the interplay of the individual and influential social forces. But there is no clear way to determine at any point the ways in which external authority shapes the mind (Lacan 1977). Nor is it always clear what one's 'true' interests might be – a primary goal of reflection.

Linking reflection to 'transformation' is important to mainstream theories of experiential learning in that they claim that learning does not entail 'teaching' or transmitting a body of knowledge to a passive learner – 'knowledge is something created in the learning process where teachers, learners, bodies of knowledge and experiential meanings interact' (Usher 1992: 211). Experiential learning theory is premised on the idea that all parties to the transaction are affected, and to varying degrees, 'transformed'.

In the discourse of experiential learning are questions seldom addressed about whether 'emancipatory intent' and so-called 'liberating' reform processes merely lead to other forms of control. For example, what are the goals of empowerment underlying learning at work? What are the ethics of 'other directed' experiential learning activities *set up* by trainers, line-managers, coaches and mentors to be 'experiential'? A serious consideration of the ethics of 'other directed' experiential learning events at work is relatively undeveloped in the literature. But experiential learning in organisations, defined in often well-intentioned humanistic terms, might ultimately be disabling rather than enabling – even though most staff developers, learning facilitators and HRD practitioners would most likely dispute this. Such an analysis can have demoralising effects according to recent empirical work on training practices in multinationals (see Boje 1994; Casey 1995; Garrick and Solomon 1997). Each suggest that experiential learning techniques are embodied in the new corporate language and practices of 'enabling', 'self-direction', 'teamwork' and 'learning organisations'. These techniques however represent forms of discursive 'persuasion' whereby workers are no more 'empowered' than before and are, in effect, often required to work longer hours and become more efficient.

Ontological assumptions about organisations, the 'authentic settings' prized by the research referred to earlier in this chapter, are thus important to a coherent theory of experiential learning. For Greenfield, organisations are not objective, 'but a social phenomena, subjective in nature . . . organisational reality, as experienced, is thus like a cultural artifact' (Evers and Lakomski 1991: 96). There is a paradox of educational thought in this that relates to the significance of 'human dynamism' in 'creating' the 'cultural artifact'. Drawing on Aristotle's theory of causation to explain:

to create something means to make it non-technically, but yet consciously and voluntarily . . . it should be clear that when we speak of an artist making a poem, or a play, or a painting, or a piece of music, the kind of *making* to which we refer is the kind we call creating. . . . These things are not made as a means to an end, they are not made to any preconceived plan, they are not made by imposing form on a given matter. Yet they are made deliberately and responsibly, by people who know what they are doing, even though they do not know in advance what is going to become of it.

(Beckett 1992: 140)

Using Aristotle's conception, experience in organisations relates to hierarchical constructions of knowledge which give rise to dualisms such as theory and practice, thinking and doing, facts and values, mind and body. Such dualisms are inadequate for making sense of life as, inter alia, there is always some form of politics accompanying experience.

The politics of learning from experience

Knowledge acquired from experience is far from unproblematic even though much of the current research on workplace-based learning tends not to acknowledge this. Research theories frame conceptions of experience through their epistemologies, language, and ontological assumptions about so-called 'authentic' workplace settings. Subjective 'everyday' experience contains innumerable normative interpretations of 'reality'. The 'common sense' that is prized in the workplace is, as Berger and Luckman put it, 'the reality par excellence [where] the everyday appears already objectified . . . ordered by a variety of cultural instructions as to how things should be done . . . involving a complex set of personal and social values' (1981: 35).

This section is not going to be turned into a political science treatise, but the tensions between the values of individuals and the ideologies of their workplaces require scrutiny. For instance, looking at what managers *actually do* rather than what they hope to do can be a useful exercise. How do organisational contexts frame outcomes of learning and of practice? What conditions promote 'meaningful' practices? How does corporate philosophy actually affect practice? Beckett (1996) suggests that explicitly surfacing managerial processes is a key to further learning, and can be examined through three deceptively simple questions: What are we doing? Why are we doing it? What comes next? For HRD managers, answers to such questions can be accompanied by tensions related to 'bottom line' requirements and organisational rhetoric about promoting 'learning organisations' and 'critical thinkers' who can generate innovation.

Underlying these tensions are personal and professional beliefs, convictions and values. These are influential factors on individuals at work and Brookfield (1991) describes some of the strategies used to deal with everyday tensions and dilemmas: 'the distinction between a practical discussion and formal theoretical discussion is somewhat spurious and demands a critical self-reflexivity to clarify what we are bringing to the discussion ourselves' (1991: 1).

Precision about 'what we are bringing to the discussion ourselves' is problematic. There are multiple perspectives on this, such as liberal, behaviourist, progressive, humanist, radical and postmodern philosophies, discursive, 'andragogical' and 'pedagogical' orientations. Indeed, HRD practitioners and learning facilitators have theoretical orientations in their everyday practices whether they realise this explicitly or not. In adopting a postmodern perspective, however, 'individuals' are not actually viewed as 'meaning-givers' but meaning-takers. Usher, Bryant and Johnston (1997) explain that this is 'where the meaning of experience is not conferred exclusively or authentically by individuals . . . [but] the place of language is a key issue'.

Making sense of what to do in the face of conflict and ethical dilemmas at work can highlight how problematic meaning giving can be. It is sometimes completely unclear as to 'what one ought to do', which in turn illustrates the importance of self-reflexivity in making sense of one's informal learning. But this is not a purely internal psychological process. Reflexivity is like language itself: an historically embedded social process shaped by dominant discourses, personal and political ideology. So, how is one being influenced? What discourses are shaping the decision-making processes at work? How is power functioning among the relationships involved? How are you being affected? These are the types of questions that can help in our attempts to unmask informal learning.

Workplace learning can very easily reproduce the dominant values HRD practitioners and educators sometimes purport to challenge, particularly when they are responding to managerial injunctions to 'facilitate' change. If learning is to be a meaningful workplace purpose, an examination of the values held by individuals and how these can clash with workplace ideologies at both macro- and micro-levels is essential. Ideology is often used as a person's or group's general social and political world view. The various political philosophies like liberalism, capitalism, feminism, socialism and so on offer their adherents cogent (but different) explanations of the causes and nature of social problems. They provide blueprints for social and political change, according to the principles valued most highly by each particular 'ism'.

The grand theories can give rise to significant clashes between personal perspectives and work requirements: for instance, by HRD practitioners disagreeing with corporate strategies related to 'downsizing' – how many workers are to go, from what sections, through what processes – or 'image-making' and so on. The alignment (or misalignment) of work contexts with the individual's values is a critical ingredient of the tensions and ethical dilemmas experienced. For managers and HRD practitioners, workplaces are not always conceptually malleable or as flexible as their rhetoric might suggest. Work imperatives can, at times, fully test ideological resolve and there is no easy answer. If one adopts a conceptually malleable position, one runs the risk of being viewed by some other employees, managers and colleagues as uncommitted to anything (i.e. becoming pragmatic); or worse, of becoming an untrustworthy tool of management. The 'ideologically committed' run the risk of an inflexibility, or dogma, which can also lead to oppression.

Usher claims that a central problem with a critical pedagogy is that it is itself a part of a discourse which counters individualism by theorising 'the subject' as a construction rather than an originary point. This subject is generally regarded as an exploited object of 'false-consciousness'. The exploited subject has their experience:

> rendered inauthentic by distorting ideology and oppressive social structures . . . [and] without some sense of agency and a notion of a contested and always 'in process' subjectivity, social empowerment easily becomes oppression in another guise.
>
> (Usher 1992: 203)

Many experiential learning theorists hope that critical reflection will help resolve the binary, and in spite of postmodern scepticism, draw on Habermas's (1978) critique of instrumental reason – in which 'subjectivity' is shaped socially by structural and political forces – to base their practices. This influential theory is based, however, on the binary of social construction versus individual agency. Usher asserts that a problem with Habermasian theory is that 'it is itself part of a [hegemonic] discourse whereby its subject tends to be the exploited subject of "false consciousness", deprived of agency and posited as a social victim' (1992: 203).

HRD practices that are based on the binary opposition of individual–social are problematic, particularly as practitioners today face the daunting task of helping bridge the gap between the workplace-based learning and formal education institutions. Schön adds that this can include dilemmas about 'professional knowledge and the expectations of the workplaces they are serving' (1983: 15). HRD personnel are expected to complement the drive for competitive workplaces, improved productivity, worker empowerment and worker satisfaction. This is why many organisations have, over the past few years, attempted to introduce reforms based on notions such as 'the learning company', 'learning organisation' and 'quality circles'.

Many HRD personnel have actively promoted such concepts, often taking them up without calling into question their underlying values and epistemologies. Such notions, particularly in contexts of profit maximisation, can simply become the new forms of strategic control over workplace processes related to 'worker interests', 'company good', fairness and ethics. Awareness of strategic control brings HRD personnel face to face with dilemmas such as 'Who owns the HRD practitioner?' and 'What ought one to do when faced with crises of allegiance?'. In conditions of postmodernity crises of allegiance are likely to occur quite frequently.

Postmodernism and informal learning

Burbules summarises the postmodern critique of education in this way:

> postmodernism is said to be the rejection of the Enlightenment; it is about the infusion of power into our theories of knowledge, language and ethics; it is anti-rationalistic; it offers a radical social constructivism; it privileges difference over commonality; it is the discursive constitution of social (and natural) reality; it stresses a decentred view of the subject and the 'fungibility' of identity and so on.
>
> (Burbules 1995: 2)

But such a neat summary (as Burbules acknowledges) is precisely that: too neat. 'Postmodernism' is not a specific theoretical position itself, but an intellectual trend that comprises several quite different theoretical or philosophical theories. These theories are particularly indebted to the European philosophers Foucault, Lacan, Derrida, Lyotard and Baudrillard. More recently, their writings have been applied to the philosophy of education by Burbules and Rice (1991), Lather (1991), Usher (1992), Usher and Edwards (1994), Boje (1994, 1995) and Burbules (1995). For Usher and Edwards, postmodernism encompasses:

> trends of interdisciplinarity and experiential approaches to teaching

and learning [that] can be seen as changes taking place under the impact of the postmodern and therefore very much part of it. In other words, there is no uniform, unified postmodern discourse of education. However, it is through these [types of] changes that the Enlightenment tradition and the place of education within it is increasingly questioned, exposing the certainties and 'warranted' claims of educational theories and practice to a critical examination, a shaking of the foundations.

(Usher and Edwards 1994: 25)

Informed in large part by Foucault, Derrida and Lyotard, Usher and Edwards indicate the centrality of discourse, the importance of deconstruction (see Glossary), and the validity of assessing local (power) networks rather than 'universal' or large abstract social 'systems'. The story-teller, for instance, is positioned in relation to events (and other selves), and an identity conferred. Stories, although unique to individuals – in the sense that each tells her/his 'own' story – are at the same time culturally located. As such, stories are 'transindividual'. Postmodern writers therefore search for local/cultural conditions that produce 'knowledge' and recognise the plurality of knowledges. In this way, discourse displaces knowledge as *the* object of study. In turn, this allows a freeing of linguistic meanings from the determinism of structuralist definitions, and a viewing of 'actors' as participants in discourse rather than central to the process of signification.

Openness to knowing is thus a central standpoint of postmodernism which, in relation to informal learning, assumes engagement among persons and between persons and the adoption of certain stances while maintaining a 'sceptical distance'. A postmodern position would thus hold that educators and trainers should not take themselves too seriously (hence Baudrillard's statement: 'forget Foucault, forget Baudrillard'). This lack of 'unreserved commitment' particularly upsets those committed to socialist and Marxist positions in adult education. Anyon (1994: 115) asserts that there has been 'a retreat of Marxism and socialist feminism in the face of postmodern and post-structural theories in education'.

Anyon's perspective is interesting in part because of her personal history as a feminist-Marxist contributor in the early 1980s.[4] She points out that a binary opposition (of Marxism to postmodernism) does not aid the struggles for a more equitable society. The idea of a binary opposition between worker and capitalist, suggests Anyon, is limiting and 'to some scholars has become the quaint remnants of the Marxist metanarrative' (1994: 116).

She is also critical of aspects of postmodernism, arguing that there is an often obscured meta-narrative of postmodernism which describes a universal Truth:

> this is a metanarrative of indeterminacy; a metanarrative about *the certainty of uncertainty*. Arguing that meaning is always indeterminate seems no less a deterministic and universalising view than the Enlightenment narratives such as the orthodox Marxist view in which capitalists are 'always' expropriators, and workers 'always' righteous.
>
> (Anyon 1994: 122)

She concludes that an essential characteristic of a socially useful theory is that it contains theoretical recommendations which are capable of enactment. Thus 'a theory that urges the integration of theory and practice must develop types of praxis that exemplify this: a theory that [does] not oppress others' (1994: 129).

The range of claims for postmodernism has given rise to the criticism that it is too relativistic (Mongardini 1990; Mestrovic 1991; Himmelfarb 1994). Mongardini goes so far as to argue that postmodernism is:

> the last ideology adopted by modernity to save itself. . . . Like it or not, postmodernism marks the end of the old order. Postmodernism aestheticises modernity's unqualified glorification of change, the engine of an economistic mentality and *values that Marxism did not annihilate*. The effect is to continue modernity's economistic and rationalistic reduction of culture to privatism, fragmentation and neo-romantic exaltation of momentary experience. What is lost finally is not only the individual to the 'fetishism of objects', but also the moral passions, religion, solidarity . . . and a spiritual culture, life-giving tendencies, and symbolic structures . . . to a rationalism that has become excessively abstract, but in itself does not produce anything more than primitive forms of fantasy, magic, regression and negation of history.
>
> (Mongardini 1990: 53)

Mongardini argues that postmodernism generates a crisis of identity which passes from the level of the individual to the entire culture. This criticism may be rather extreme, however, as Foucault rejects the notion of a monolithic discourse (of postmodernism), and Burbules (drawing upon Derrida) argues that:

> our practices of communication, explanation, justification, truth-telling and so on are always partly expressions of the particular

language or languages we have. But because our languages are diverse and noncongruent, there will always be a limit upon any particular discursive system as a standpoint, in a place and time, within which one can try to describe all matters of truth, value and so forth; such matters will always be to some extent the expressions of *this* language, and *this* place and time.

(Burbules 1995: 6)

For Latour (1993), however, the postmodern critique does not go far enough, because it accepts and defines itself against the problematic category of the *modern*. The 'crisis of modernity' is not that circumstances have changed, which suddenly throw modernist hopes into doubt, but that modernism was always self-deceived about its capacities to carry through on its (Enlightenment) promises, and has only recently become aware of it:

postmodernism is a symptom, not a fresh solution. It lives under the modern Constitution, but it no longer believes in the guarantees the Constitution offers. . . . [He adds that] Modernity has never begun . . . hence the hint of the ludicrous that always accompanies postmodern thinkers; they claim to come after a time that has not even started.

(Latour 1993: 46–7)[5]

Concluding comments

In this chapter I have identified the dominant discourses that give form to our understandings of what informal learning is. To draw some conclusions about the various perspectives I am briefly returning to, and problematising, the four 'villages' of experiential learning referred to earlier. The villages are underpinned by a conception of learning *as a process* whereby: 'people individually and in association with others, engage in direct encounter and then purposefully reflect upon, validate, transform, give meaning to and seek to integrate their different ways of knowing' (Weil and McGill 1989: 248).

A number of problems exist with this conception. First, there is the issue of the integration of different ways of knowing. Jansen and Wildemeersch assert that for any 'framework of understanding to transcend the mere exchange of everyday experiences a balanced combination of informal theories [taken-for-granted understandings of reality] and formal theories seems necessary' (1992: 6). They are concerned that the villages do not adequately address this 'balanced combination'. The conceptual pathways within and between the villages are relatively undeveloped, leaving the notion of experiential learning as a collection of ideological standpoints rather than a coherent theory.

Second, a concern of postmodern philosophy about the villages is that, in the latter, 'subjects are not the authors of their own "texts", but their identities are being constituted and reconstituted by the forms of life, the lifeworlds or linguistic contexts in which they find themselves' (Jansen and Wildemeersch 1992: 6).

Notions of community action and social transformation (the third village) have become increasingly problematic as radical frameworks have become increasingly fragmented. As Acker, Barry and Esseveld (1983) and Ellsworth (1989) point out, an emancipatory intent is no guarantee of an emancipatory outcome. This gulf between intents and outcomes is further articulated by Lather as a consequence of the 'enactment of power relations, with research practices more as inscriptions of legitimation than procedures that help us get closer to some "truth" that is captured by language' (Lather 1991: 14). The implication of this for practice is that research needs continually to demystify the reality of its own practice, or, as Edwards and Usher (1993) suggest – texts are always open to challenge.

Postmodern concerns about 'orthodox' theorisations of experiential learning highlight the importance of the views one holds on 'objectivity' and 'subjectivity', and about authorities' claiming power to define 'truth'. These concerns will depend substantially on one's philosophical and epistemological position on what it means 'to know'. For Foucault:

> truth isn't outside power or lacking in power: contrary to a myth whose history and functions would repay further study, truth isn't the reward of free spirits, the child of protracted solitude, nor the privilege of those who have succeeded in liberating themselves. Truth is a thing of this world: it is produced only by virtue of multiple forms of constraint. And it induces regular effects of power. Each society has its regime of truth. Its 'general politics' of truth: that is, the types of discourse which it accepts and makes function as true; the mechanisms and instances which enable one to distinguish true and false statements, the means by which each is sanctioned; the techniques and procedures accorded value in the acquisition of truth; the status of those who are charged with saying what counts is true.
>
> (Foucault 1988c: 131)

Certain dynamics of power can distort and compromise even the best of human intentions. In the current world, technical systems of surveillance, manipulation and control are increasingly widespread and subtle. 'We inevitably participate in these, consciously or unconsciously, nearly all the time' (Burbules 1995: 6).

The main problem with the 'villages' is that all their theorisations of experience, despite their differences, fail to recognise adequately that, in theorising experience, they discursively reproduce power relations. Even with an emancipatory intent, they can end up having oppressive effects. Nonetheless, experiential learning, as exemplified through the villages, has been shown to have an important philosophic role in bringing together (as a core concept) various approaches to 'experience'. The philosophies of experience-based learning are now being applied to work contexts and, as Hart points out, this 'current debate on work and education contains suggestions that are important and useful' (1993: 33). The marshalling of informal learning contains potential for the experience of some marginalised groups to be formally recognised and accredited.

But this 'applied' role is not without philosophical problems. Postmodern perspectives problematise 'orthodox' ideas about 'the subject', autonomy, gender, local conditions, language and discourse, power/knowledge formations, and the relationship of knowledge and experience. As Foucault suggests, 'the theory generated thus far is not indispensable ... the task of "truth" is now linked to the challenging of taboos' (1990: 130). Based on a Foucauldian reading, one would need to be deeply sceptical of the purposes of structuring and 'using' informal learning in workplaces – irrespective of the village to which one believes (or at least feels) they belong. It is precisely this doubt about structuring and 'using' informal learning in workplaces that is explored in Chapters 3 and 4.

Notes

1   The nature of 'being in the world' ('dasein', as Heidegger (1962), put it), is such that already knowing something is a condition of knowing anything. The world, and the structure of knowledge that goes with it, already exist and therefore there is no Archimedean point from which we can know the world by standing outside it – hence situated selves. But this pre-knowing is never an explicit conscious knowing. It is therefore always an absence – yet because it is the condition of knowing, it is also present – hence it is an 'absent present'! This is not a binary logic, however, as it is not an either/or – the present is defined through absence – both are equally necessary to one another. (See also Glossary of terms.)

2   Jung Chang's autobiographical account of Mao's role in ideology-led prac-
    tice claims 'Mao's ignorance of how an economy worked, [his] almost
    metaphysical disregard for reality . . . might have been interesting in a
    poet, but in a leader with absolute power was quite another matter. One of
    its main components was a deep-seated contempt for human life' (1991:
    293).

3   Andragogy, according to Knowles (1980: 39) is premised on at least four
    crucial assumptions about the characteristics of adult learners that are
    different from the assumptions on which traditional pedagogy is premised.
    These assumptions are that 'as a person matures:

- his (sic) self-concept moves from one of being a dependent personality
  towards one of being self-directed;
- he accumulates a growing reservoir of experience that becomes an
  increasing resource for learning;
- his readiness to learn becomes oriented increasingly to the developmental tasks of his social roles; and
- his time perspective changes from one of postponed application of
  knowledge to immediacy of application, and accordingly his orientation toward learning shifts from one of subject-centredness to one of
  problem-centredness.'

4   Anyon's (1983) analysis focused on a critical theory of accommodation
    and resistance, public/private discrepancies, gender and class issues, class
    difference and the contradictions of modern living.

5   Latour advocates a 'nonmodernism' that interrogates within the modern
    the 'always present hybrids and oppositions that belie its categories and
    boundaries' (1993: 47).

3 Work as a learning environment
Unmasking the language of HRD

The condition of learning at work

The postmodern condition of work is characterised by restructuring, dispersal and fragmentation. It is affected by volatile labour markets, fast switches from one product to another, niche marketing, ever-increasing consumer orientations, new patterns of management, new technologies and global interconnections. These characteristics have reduced the need for manual labour, promoting the need for a 'flexible' yet specialised labour force. Increasingly the possession of transferable skills is viewed as vital to workers who are to service and expand the market economy. Learning at work has become a highly desirable 'commodity'. Contemporary approaches to the organisation of work contain much rhetoric about education and training. In this rhetoric, learning and work are inseparable, an effect being the privileging of workplaces as sites of valid 'education'.

The transformation of education and training makes it important to distinguish between the language about how training will benefit workers, improve worker conditions and prospects for advancement, on the one hand, and corporate realities in which knowledge about worker competencies informs decisions about downsizing and redundancies on the other. At the same time, the notion of 'cybernetic capitalism' has resulted in some postmodern theorists becoming increasingly sceptical of workplaces as learning environments. Indeed, Baudrillard asks to what extent the cybernetic revolution has 'blurred the distinction between man and machine?' (1993: 170–1).

Many views and theories exist about work as a learning environment. Zuboff (1988) for instance presents an influential argument about modern technology in the workplace, suggesting that unprecedented developmental opportunities now exist for workers. She argues that the new communication and computer technologies allow for more intellectual activity and therefore superior forms of work. It is proposed that 'cybernetic workplaces' allow for direct, sensual involvement, thus presenting new opportunities (and problems) for work design.

Hart (1993: 32) is critical of Zuboff's argument, claiming that it leads towards 'Orwellian solutions'. Hart cites new 'sensing technology' as an example of these 'solutions', as a worker's body can, for example, be connected to the plant in such a way as to become a cybernetic extension: 'her body would shake with plant vibrations reduced electronically to a human scale, and she would feel warmer or cooler as the factory temperature changed. Pressure and sounds could be similarly transmitted' (Hirschhorn, quoted in Hart 1993: 32).

Hart correctly points out that the challenge for the worker is partly to 'distinguish her own internal body cues from the messages of the plant . . . a model for educative work? I believe not' (1993: 32).

From the many divergent views about work and its educative effects I shall address three broad approaches to *the organisation of work*. Each offers powerful conceptions that have direct bearings on how one might view learning at work. I will then draw on Foucault's ideas about power/knowledge formations to review these perspectives. From a Foucauldian perspective we can say that the ways in which we talk about learning at work reflect certain kinds of dominant interests. Terms such as 'flexibility' and 'skills' symbolise power formations or 'regimes of truth' that involve discourses which a society accepts, the mechanisms by which people discern true and false statements, the techniques for acquiring truth which are accepted as valid, and the individuals and institutions which are able to define 'truth'. The approaches to work organisation considered are:

1 'Taylorism', which is an approach to work organisation based on standardisation of tasks, specialisation of workforce skills, close supervision and a hierarchical management structure. The propositions raised are that this remains a prevalent curricular structure, with de-skilling the pre-eminent method for workplace design (Boje and Winsor 1993: 57).
2 'Flexible specialisation' is now a prevalent occupational condition that emphasises the interaction between socialisation and work organisation (Casey 1995). The proposition here is that one can no longer talk of a unified type of rationality that organises and governs the spheres of work. There is no overriding claim as to how work should be organised in the face of constant and rapid change, but to survive in competitive markets the rhetoric holds that the

workforce is required to be highly skilled, flexible, innovative and mobile.

3 A 'learning organisation' is the approach sought by many corporations as they require 'a highly skilled workforce, modern technology and an appropriate structure and culture' (*Harvard Business Review* July–August 1993: 78). This notion holds that workplaces can and should be designed to enable learning experiences, enhance worker motivation and awareness of technological advances, and 'improve' labour processes and modes of production. That this designing is correct – a 'given' – underpins contemporary discourses of learning at work and is becoming very important in determining what is accepted as 'valid' knowledge.

Is Taylorism alive and well?

Boje and Winsor (1993: 57) argue that Taylorism is being given a new vitality and respectability by a re-packaging 'masquerading under a costume of worker development, involvement and empowerment'. Their thesis is that activities such as total quality management have been positioned as a carefully engineered set of technological process modifications that promise a range of efficiencies and competitive advantages, but they are actually resurrecting Taylorism. Watkins's earlier (1986) study of high-tech industries also led him to the view that Taylorist principles are still being applied in a variety of ways. Not all high-tech industries operate with high-tech occupations – 'women and minorities are frequently hired to perform repetitive, low-wage tasks . . . some high-tech corporations simply shift their assembly line work to countries like Taiwan and Hong Kong' (1986: 23). He argues that:

- the labour market is highly segmented (for example, between elite technicians, managers, sales personnel, those performing creative conceptual work and unskilled service workers)
- it is a myth that advanced technological workplaces require more highly credentialled and qualified workers, claiming that a de-skilling process is operating for most workers
- contemporary labour conditions propel a numerically small elite into the post-industrial future, polarising the labour market – with most working under essentially Taylorised conditions.

Watkins's claim that Taylorism is alive and well owes a theoretical debt to Braverman's (1974) influential 'de-skilling thesis'. Braverman was never convinced that learning can be plausibly applied to the workplace, claiming:

the unity of thought and action, conception and execution, hand and mind, which capitalism threatened from its beginnings, is now attacked by a systematic dissolution employing all the resources of science and the various engineering disciplines based upon it. The subjective factor of the labour process is removed to a place among its inanimate objective factors. To the materials and instruments of production are added a 'labour force', another 'factor of production', and the process is henceforth carried on by management as the sole subjective element. This is the ideal towards which management tends in pursuit of which it uses and shapes every productive innovation furnished by science.

(Braverman in Welton 1991: 16)

However, a notion central to Marxist sociology, that labour is *the* fundamental social fact, is now being radically questioned. Contemporary philosophers including Foucault, Barthes, Touraine, Gorz and Toffler no longer treat labour, and the position of the worker in the productive process, as the chief organising principle of social structures. Arguing from different theoretical premises, they hold that the industrial form of rationality – linear, logical, scientific – no longer offers social development that will free workers from the conditions that fundamentally constrain them. Indeed, the post-industrial changes in production and consumption – from mass production, mass market, machine-paced systems – to the production of specialist, niche and luxury goods as well as production systems based on information technology, have led to new forms of economically active labour: flexible, but specialised.

Flexible specialisation

Hirschhorn argues that the technologies of the cybernetic workplace offer 'developmental' opportunities for work, based on principles of integration and flexibility: 'the principle of flexibility creates a conception of work in which the worker's capacity to learn, to adapt, and to regulate the evolving controls becomes central to the machine system's developmental potential' (Hirschhorn 1984: 58).

He claims that the new workplaces require a 'culture of learning, an appreciation of tacit knowledge, a feeling for interpersonal processes, and an appreciation of our organisational design choices' (1984: 169). Increasingly labour is required to have specialised yet highly transferable skills, hence flexible specialisation. It is ideas about 'developmental possibilities' – through critical reflection and transformative action – that are seized upon by proponents of the flexible specialisation argument and by advocates of the new vocationalism.

In the post-Fordist context,[1] the vocationalist discourse personalises economic competitiveness by stressing the need for individual employees to be motivated and continually up-skilled or re-skilled, and made more flexible. This 'development' provides a meaning which aligns skill and knowledge development to economic competitiveness. For Usher, Bryant and Johnston (1997) this meaning is one-dimensional. They point out that the new attitudes and competencies required by employees change the relationships between pedagogy, knowledge and labour processes. What is foregrounded in the drive for flexibility and continuous learning, they argue, are social skills and flexible competencies rather than subject-based knowledge.

'Learner-centred' developmental possibilities and cybernetic work environments are also questioned by Lee and Zemke. They suggest many work environments are now characterised by 'high levels of stress, insecurity, tough decisions and sixty-hour working weeks', adding that although

> you might expect a resurgence of a management model based on Machiavelli's Prince . . . or some other Theory-X icon, instead there is a string of scholarly articles and books trying to make sense of the chaos by proposing management and work organisation models based on heart and soul.
>
> (Lee and Zemke 1993: 22)

Exemplifying their point, DuPree – chairman of a major American furniture manufacturer – surmises that participative management is the most effective contemporary practice. As Lee and Zemke point out, DuPree's version of participative management ends up 'in a place where leaders create covenantal relationships – bonds that fulfil deep needs and give work meaning for employees – with the purpose of the corporation redemption, not profit' (Lee and Zemke 1993: 23).

Braverman would be sceptical of DuPree's interpretation of leadership. He argues that to maintain control over the labour process, capitalist operations de-skill work and limit worker discretion on the job, with new technologies being a potent example. Berryman points out that this de-skilling theory was based on the existence of:

> a trade-off between skills and control of the work process and implied a deskilling direction as a by-product of the capitalist drive

to control the labour process. Thus, [Braverman] replaced a techno-logical determinism with an organisational determinism that emerged from the fundamental characteristics of capitalism.

(Berryman 1993: 353)

The power of Braverman's argument, suggests Berryman, lies in its theoretical underpinning. In conjunction with Watkins's argument that Taylorism is still prevalent, the de-skilling thesis remains pertinent despite data on the persistence and growth of high-skilled production jobs. For instance, the 1990 Commission on the Skills of the American Workforce largely adopts Zuboff's (1988) argument that new tech-nology leads to more rewarding and challenging production jobs, but only if the employer organised work to take advantage of those skills. That is, skill requirements are a function of the way that work is organised rather than of the technologies used.

This focus on 'determinants of the choice of work organisation' (Berryman 1993: 354) theoretically underpins the 'flexible specialisa-tion' of Piore and Sabel (1984) which emphasises the interaction between socialisation and organisation in shaping behaviour of workers. This emphasis accepts phenomena (such as human emotions and desires) generally ignored, or treated as anomalies by economic theories. Table 3.1 briefly summarises the main points in the deskilling and flexible specialisation theories.

A key analytical implication of these two perspectives is that how workers, managers and firms conceive of their strategies of *work organisation* and *workplace socialisation* are very influential in shaping how workers and firms respond to market conditions. This viewpoint underscores most of the HRD literature on 'the learning

Table 3.1 Analytical implications of the two perspectives

	De-skilling	*Flexible specialisation*
Long-term skill trends	Dynamic of de-skilling	Dynamic of upgrading and multi-skilling
Structure of control	Based on Taylorist ideas and techniques	Career structures and internal labour markets for core workers
Employment relations	Minimum of interaction model of least commitment of employer to employee/worker to company	Worker commitment plus core/periphery labour market structure

organisation', resulting in interpretations of workplace learning that 'confirm' cultural re-design and re-engineering processes.

The learning organisation, or a new operationalism?

Recent studies of 'the learning organisation' (Senge 1990, 1994; Ford 1993; Kasl, Dechant and Marsick 1993; Watkins and Marsick 1993) have argued that more effective and productive organisations have cultures that provide structured and active learning environments for employees at all levels. What 'effective and productive' means, however, can be problematic in workplaces as there is a complex interplay of physical, technical and social forces in the constitution of skilled work and workers:

> The more deeply we scratch the surface, the more difficult it is to find a line where one begins and the other ends: it is a seamless fabric. Indeed, this seamless quality is precisely the way that power struggles at work are experienced in the ordinary routines of everyday life.
>
> (Jackson 1991: 17)

Schultz illustrates these everyday forces, quoting from a woman worker in an Australian steel mill:

> they put me on one job for six weeks cutting steel. You had to pull a grid out. It was a real struggle every time. After six weeks, when they told me the knack, with a twist and a flick of the wrist, it was easy, but they only showed me after they decided that, 'yeah, she can do it'. There was always a knack.
>
> (Schultz 1985: 170)

With today's workplace restructuring, HRD practitioners are widely used as a medium for promoting organisational re-design. Workplace learning initiatives are being used to reorganise trade work and multi-skilling and job enhancement programmes are being introduced. Training is also used to introduce management philosophies stressing new corporate cultures – flatter hierarchies, work teams and quality circles – largely inspired by Japanese models of industrial relations.

Senge (1990) and Ford (1993) follow Japanese managerial concepts which assert that individuals, teams and enterprises are continually learning to meet internal and external changes. This is an important goal of workplace reform in most industries, but few organisations, according to Ford, have fully achieved continual learning. Ford (1993: 11) claims this is partly because such an achievement requires conceptual innovation by the enterprise and a high degree of workforce participation in critical aspects of organisation development, including the development of skills. In practice this means that all members of the workforce share in some or all of the following:

- enterprise strategic planning
- enterprise conceptual and cultural changes
- workplace reform strategies
- skill formation practices, including the preparation of learning materials
- development of new work organisation.

A key term associated with these practices (and thus the 'learning organisation') is *empowerment*. The term empowerment implies, according to Welton, that 'all employees of the enterprise, especially those at operative level, are given more power and choice in the work of the enterprise and greater opportunities for learning. It means more autonomy for individuals and teams, and greater individual and team responsibility for production, construction, quality and safety objectives' (Welton 1991: 37).

Kornbluh and Greene (1989: 259) argue that people in organisations must be enabled to move from 'learned helplessness to empowered actors' by four central themes about worker empowerment:

- unlearning their deference to authority and understanding the social and political processes within the organisation that negatively affect their lives
- being nurtured in this process by a mentor, coach or friend
- exercising their new understanding and competencies through progressively increasing responsibility
- learning within a supportive organisational framework of interdependence and mutuality.

Empowerment has deep political implications. As Jackson points out: 'such changes invariably undermine the existing organisation of job categories and thus the organisational cohesion and power of the unions' (1991: 28). This is one reason why trade unions can have, on occasion, vested interests in preserving the Taylorist status quo. Newman shares this concern, although he strongly asserts that trade union training is very important for workers to 'protect themselves and others from exploitation, improve working conditions, make workplaces safer, contribute to the development of their enterprise and make their voices heard on industrial and economic matters – through their trade unions' (Newman 1993: 162). Rainbird (1990) asserts that unions increasingly regard training issues as central to their own interests. These issues include not only technical upgrading to protect current jobs and clarify career pathways, but also longer-range policy issues like plant-based involvement and worker participation in job design and labour force planning.

Stressing the importance of 'shared vision and anchoring vision in a set of governing ideals to an organisation's learning', Senge argues that a 'commitment to "the truth" amongst all levels or workers is essential' (1990: 223). For Senge 'truth' is directly linked to 'openness and honesty' which underpins team learning and aids local decision-making. Senge fashions his arguments from organisations that operate within the commercial market place, but his idealism is not tempered by the day-to-day realities of competitive work practices, conflicts, gender, politics and power issues.

Not surprisingly, the notion of 'the learning organisation', coupled with Senge's focus on the roles of managers as 'leaders', has been accepted by many contemporary managers. Senge's words – 'systemic thinking is critical to a learning organisation' – strike a chord with corporate managers. These words are derived from the total quality movement in Japan which Senge describes as 'the first wave in building learning organisations'. Systems thinking is now the *fifth discipline*, the other four 'disciplines' being:

- developing personal mastery (emphasising a personal vision)
- having mental models (which test assumptions)
- building 'shared visions'
- understanding the influence of 'team-learning'.

Senge's theory does not fully acknowledge the problematic nature of the notions involved. For instance, 'shared visions' can easily become rhetoric for masking underlying conflict, or a way of obtaining compliance – through 'belonging' to the shared vision. His arguments about 'team-learning' also place ultimate responsibility (and power) for any radical change with the executive staff of the organisation. Senge dresses up the conventional management notion of 'management's right to manage' in the liberal-humanist language of adult learning in the workplace. Set against postmodern conditions, including increasing social fragmentation and global market competitiveness, this language increasingly appears to offer more refined technologies for engineering an economically active, smiling, but politically passive (compliant) workforce, rather than its promised autonomous self-directing, empowered workers.

Discourses of competitiveness

As society becomes more complex its professional labour becomes more differentiated, more fragmented, more subject to change. A significant aspect of the processes of unpredictable change is 'de-differentiation', or the breaking-down, blurring and increasing permeability of boundaries.[2] In the period of 'de-differentiation' the cognitive demands upon workers correspondingly alter. No longer are the pools of knowledge and expertise acquired in initial education sufficient for the new order. What are now required are the abilities to put that knowledge and expertise to use in unfamiliar circumstances; and so we find demands for 'flexibility', 'communication skills' and 'teamwork'. Barnett goes as far as to assert that:

> Also required are the abilities to jettison that learning over the lifespan, to be prepared to take on new forms of experience and knowledge and to develop these skills anew. In other words, the regeneration of capital requires not knowledge per se, but abilities to exploit, and if necessary, discard knowledge. We are in a throw-away society, cognitively speaking.
>
> (Barnett 1994: 15)

Germany, the USA, Canada, the UK and Sweden have all recently initiated major change in their vocational education and training systems as a strategy for increasing their international competitiveness. Indeed, OECD reforms commonly include improving the training opportunities for adults.[3] This involves improving the training of trainers and integrating education and training by such methods as assessment of prior learning, articulation arrangements, setting competency standards for general education and developing new models of formal education which link industry and education more closely. The notion of skill formation is central to this transformation, and HRD personnel are thus located strategically in a discourse about economic competitiveness.

It is not only employers who are urging a stronger relationship between industries and education. It is on the agendas of big business, unions and governments. Such agendas favour forms of knowledge which are 'useful'; that is, instrumental and operational, exemplified by a key question from employers to prospective employees which is not so much what do they know, or understand, but rather *what can they do*?

OECD nations are currently considering changes required to work organisation to be competitive beyond the 1990s. For manufacturing, Bolwijn and Kumpe (in Hayton 1992) describe a four-phase model, outlining structural and cultural requirements of each phase (see Table 3.2).

Bolwijn and Kumpe are promoting a discourse of industry competitiveness that encourages workplace cultures based on participation and democratisation. Their theory holds that people in the innovative firm need to be *empowered* to take responsibility and set organisational goals (see Table 3.3).

Bolwijn and Kumpe, in line with many other post-Fordist writers, interpret current changes in the workplace as part of a widespread trend towards flatter management structures with greater autonomy and responsibility being given to trade and non-trade (operative level) staff. Their model, although useful for clarifying conceptual elements of work organisation, does not distinguish the organisations' everyday cultural, social and industrial relations features from structural, organisational and administrative arrangements.

Maurice, Sellier and Silvestre's influential study of French and German work structures points out that

> compared with the state-run general education system in France, it may appear that German employers lay a heavy hand on the German (occupational training) system, particularly in the light of the frequent protests aroused in France by any attempt to bring occupational training into closer association with industry.
>
> (Maurice, Sellier and Silvestre 1986: 65)

Table 3.2 Efficient firm model – structural and cultural change pathway

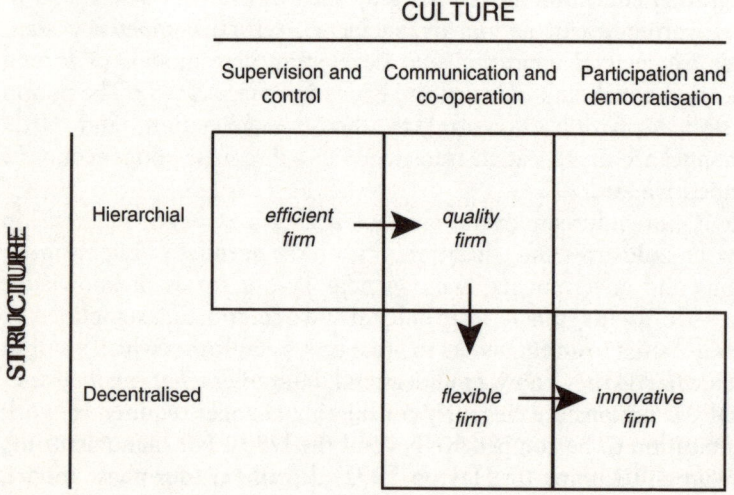

Table 3.3 Descriptions of the four phases of organisational development

Efficient firm	Quality firm	Flexible firm	Innovative firm
In the `efficient firm' all efforts are directed at reducing costs. The firm specialises in a narrow range of products or services. Work organisation is based on standardisation of tasks and specialisation of labour. Management's role is mainly planning, control and supervision.	All efforts are directed at the pursuit of quality while recognising the still necessary efficiency improvements. The many changes necessary to achieve this are a cultural shock to the efficient firm. Many firms are pursuing this through the total quality management strategy.	As well as cost reduction and quality improvement, efforts are directed at increasing speed. This means faster delivery of service, faster adaptation to market changes, and offering greater variety in services. To achieve this a flat management structure is used and most work is carried out by small multi-skilled teams.	The team-work concept is used to its fullest extent to tap the creative abilities of the workforce. There are few distinctions between managers and workers. The innovative climate is maintained by the employment of `mavericks', an open-door policy, and promotion of diagonal communication.

Source: Bolwijn and Kumpe 1990, in Hayton 1992

They add that in Germany, the fact that many social institutions – unions, churches, and towns – have established their own occupational training programmes 'reveals a fairly broad consensus about the value of acquiring professional skill'.

The point they make is that the development of skills and the organisation of the 'actors' within a firm or enterprise are heavily influenced by the broader social and institutional links formed by industry–government arrangements and national accreditation systems. This has major implications for any long-term trend of skill upgrading or multi-skilling, and for programmes seeking to recognise informal learning. It also raises some fundamental questions about:

- the affects on workers of becoming more flexible
- how workers are 'being made' more flexible
- how new skills are being acquired
- how new skills are recognised and reflected in reward systems or wages structures

- HRD functions including the 'informalisation' of skill acquisition programmes.

Critical social theorists including Habermas (1987); Rainbird (1988); Pateman (1989); Welton (1991); Wexler (1992); Hart (1993); Horkheimer and Adorno (1993) and Casey (1995) have variously observed the effects of the authority *structure of institutions* on psychological qualities and attitudes of individuals. Drawing on de-skilling concepts developed in Braverman's (1974) *Labour and Monopoly Capital*,[4] Rainbird argues that:

> in a period of high unemployment, when workers themselves are under the threat of redundancy, pressures to adopt flexible working practices can be intense ... companies rely on the fear of the workers that if they don't adapt and exhibit 'flexible attitudes' and abilities of their own innovation then they are ripe for selection for redundancy. Incredible pressure is being placed on [those aged] 45 or so who dread what's happening and the indications suggest that older people are accepting more menial tasks to avoid being trapped by the constant changes.
>
> (Rainbird 1988: 174)

It has become increasingly clear that major and rapid economic and social change characterised by cyclical, temporary unemployment has given way to structural and ongoing unemployment. Flexible speciali-sation is resulting in core and periphery workforces with the growth of an 'underclass' (Galbraith 1992). Because of this, contemporary Marxist scholarship which addresses structural deficiencies and the theme of alienated labour in the context of technical change retains analytical power. Welton (1995) and Mezirow (1995) both emphasise that human beings can learn to be helpless when confronted with structures that block scope for their imagination or action.

Work-based learning is now firmly on the political agenda and is viewed as a way to promote workplace communicative processes. Feminists such as Pateman (1989: 217) see some value in this. Pateman says 'women's speech [in the workplace] has been persistently and systematically invalidated'. She claims it is precisely the socialisation dimension of workplace learning that has never been fully appreciated by political theorists. Mechthild Hart, however, is very sceptical of the effects of training, claiming that 'evidence abounds that sexism and racism remain a primary organising factor in distributing and struc-turing work', viewing up-skilling 'opportunities' for women, minorities and immigrants 'as a lever for greater economic exploitation' (Hart 1993: 28). She adds that despite the so-called revolution of the smart-machine (of Zuboff 1988), work remains propped up by 'a very unrevolutionary industrial division of labour' (1993: 28).

Unions and management frequently engage in negotiations about extending worker skills so that workers can undertake a wider range of tasks. Multi-skilling is an essential part of the workplace reform strategies of many organisations. The popular rhetoric about multi-skilling is that it enables small teams of workers to be largely self-sufficient in carrying out a range of production or service functions. It is thus associated with structural changes in work organisation, involving a move away from centralised to decentralised management and the formation of supposedly semi-autonomous work teams. This usually means broadening each worker's skills. Communication skills and inter-personal skills are held by senior managers to be increasingly important to decentralised work organisation structures. In particular, abilities that contribute to team-building and participation are prized because they promote 'self-directed' and 'team-based' learning. Team building symbolises a movement away from the traditional separation between working and learning, with learning becoming increasingly integrated into a person's work life.

Learners are now required to adapt, in increasingly subtle ways, to the competencies needed for optimal capital efficiency. Postmodern theorists Usher, Bryant and Johnston (1997) link this phenomenon to a 'vocationalist pedagogy'. In a vocationalist pedagogy, learning means proceeding to the correct answer in the most efficient way. This in turn means that adaptation and application provide little space for experimentation, open-endedness and unforeseen outcomes. Experience at work is only valued if it contributes to learning about the most efficient outcomes being sought. If it does not, it is discounted. Thus experience has no inherent value other than as a tool for enhancing motivation and achieving behavioural competencies, even though, in the post-Fordist context, skills are meant to be empowering. Experience and knowledge of learners and knowledge arising from this becomes a device, a means for best achieving a pre-defined end. Learner experience *appears* to be valued, but its use is instrumental, selective and at best illustrative.

The vocabulary of the 'learning society' with its notions of skill formation, competence, outcomes, problem-based learning, experiential learning, transferability and TQM alters traditional understandings of knowledge and reason. Traditional emphases on language, formal subject and discipline-based conventions and critical enquiry provided outcomes which could be tentative, ambiguous, uncertain, contradictory. The new terminology suggests that knowledge is related to observable outcomes, the doing, the actions and transdisciplinary forms of skill. Employers want to be more certain of what their workers now do. This new vocabulary is not 'linguistic window dressing' (Barnett 1994: 71), but represents major epistemological changes in the character of what counts as valid knowledge.

Aligning educational goals with industry needs

The beliefs that knowledge is no longer the special province of formal institutions and that learning in the workplace is valuable and assessable, form an overarching rationale for national reforms of education and training. Modularised and 'flexible' training packages, designed to assist workers to achieve the necessary standards required for optimum enterprise efficiency, have become convenient to HRD practices and central to market-driven approaches to adult and higher education.[5] Participants in workplace training activities desire – indeed expect – to have their experiences validated in the form of competencies. Big business and unions support them in this. Workers and others within many sections of industry assume that competencies assessed in the workplace are (or at least should be) automatically transferable to courses within formal institutions, and more generally recognised by employers. Such assumptions are aligned with successful movement in a flexible labour market. More radical 'readings' of the education reform process, such as that by Usher and Edwards, suggest that 'the social system is going "nowhere" even as it changes; it is "simply" being driven to maximise its efficiency' (1994: 176). Proponents of the reforms, however, argue that there can be no objections in principle to the application of competencies and work-based learning outcomes to educational processes.

New partnerships between education and industry are evolving in a direction which Wexler (1993) refers to as 'educational corporatism'. In this corporatism, specific mechanisms such as skill-based pay and embedded training – doing by learning – will supposedly increase the amount of learning at work. Ethically and epistemologically, however, the point of the 'doing' or 'doing by learning' appears to be to increase practical knowledge to boost short- and medium-term productivity. Purposeful human activity calls for goals beyond the practices of merely boosting economic competitiveness or being more 'work-smart'. The notion of a work-smart or clever country, founded on economically competitive practices, has important ethical dimensions. For instance, will the new conceptions of knowledge, education and training reward human capacities that improve economic competitiveness – at the expense of other kinds of virtues such as friendship, altruism, kindness, ethical concern, generosity, cultural understanding and so on? What form of society might the valorisation of instrumental knowledge lead to? Will the reforms widen our sense of rationality, or lead to new forms of epistemological closure?[6]

Competency-based training

Definitions of competence are located in a particular discourse related to 'performance outcomes'. To describe a person as 'competent' in this discourse is to say that their actions are being performed to prescribed standards. The standards may be either difficult or easy to attain. For example, performance at 'level one' of an industry's competency-based standards usually implies the ability to perform routine, predictable work. This work is judged, usually with the aid of a standardised checklist, and forms a basis for progression. 'Level four' might imply a greater complexity in task performance, a greater degree of responsibility or personal accountability, perhaps the supervision of others and so on. Supporters of the notion of competency-based standards argue that

> outcome statements can be created for all learning which is considered important or for what people want . . . after all, if you cannot say what you require, how can you develop it and how do you know when you have achieved it?
>
> (Jessup, cited in Barnett 1994: 72)

What counts as 'skill' and what is translated into training activities is often linked with industrial power-plays. Acker (1989) claims there is an ample body of evidence to show that without the presence of a strong union, the procedures that recognise and value worker skills will represent capital interests. She further asserts that the training of workers has most commonly been formalised where unions have a strong hand. Rainbird agrees:

> skills are more likely to receive recognition in the wages structure if unions effectively claim and defend them. The problem is that management may impose new skills on workers and resist acknowledging their existence if training is very short, or if informal training takes place outside the ambit of union control and initiatives.
>
> (Rainbird 1988: 176)

Paradoxically, unions are being encouraged to enter into co-operative training arrangements, either with individual employers or enterprises, under the sponsorship of government instrumentalities. The contradictions inherent in these arrangements, suggests Jackson, 'will surface over time since the fundamental interests which unions and management have in organisational design are not the same'. She cites an Oregon Equal-Pay Project which saw conflict emerge over the technical details of training policy and practice as it became clear that the 'readily available, and even readily imaginable models of training are deeply embedded in the existing power structure' (1991: 29).

In many countries, including South Africa, Canada, New Zealand, Australia and parts of Latin America, the restructuring of industrial awards is intended to provide for the establishment of skill-related career paths. Major unions argue that skill-related career paths give employees incentives such as increased pay, more satisfying jobs and clearer career pathways. The provision of vocational education and training at various levels is required to support this argument and trade unions demand that education and training opportunities are provided for workers. A central mechanism underpinning contemporary vocational education and training approaches is competency-based standards. The 'standards' are meant to be 'objective'. The idea of an objective approach to workplace training and worker development schemes is appealing to the agendas of both business and trade unions. But the notion of objectivity in recognising and promoting workplace skills and learning warrants interrogation.

Conventional trade union theory has been based upon the distinction between 'labour' and 'work' which comes from Marx. Habermas (1978, 1987, 1991), Bernstein (1991) and Wexler (1993) variously assert that if labour is envisaged as a set of competencies, of performance to a prescribed (external) standard, then the person is diminished. Their argument is that for work, issues of ownership, authenticity, care, craft and identification are of critical importance. Without these elements, labour faces alienation, estrangement and commodification.

It is therefore curious that trade unions have combined with business over competency-based standards – because the standards are defined externally (by others) and have a tendency to *reduce* the authenticity of human actions. By definition, competencies require a degree of predictability (they have to in order to be prescribed, observable, assessable standards). The idea of a competence which is unpredictable is ultimately incoherent. Thus the standards prescribe what is 'right' in the workplace.

Supporters of competency-based training usually argue that when fully implemented it will impact significantly on entry-level training such as trade apprenticeships. It dispenses with the notion of 'time serving' in trade training and will change the way 'competence' is defined and assessed. Defining competence in a broad way, assert these writers, should allow a wide variety of delivery mechanisms, in particular skill formation in workplaces, to be made more systematic and accredited.

Competency-based training and assessment is, however, a slippery notion. Hager and Gonczi (1991: 30) identify three broad approaches to conceptualising competencies:

- analysing work in terms of roles and thence tasks and sub-tasks. This focuses on the performance aspect of a competent worker.
- analysing the knowledge, skills and attitudes required by the worker. This focuses on the attributes of a competent worker.
- analysing knowledge, skills and attitudes in the context of the performance of realistic tasks. This integrates attributes and performance into a single framework.

The third approach – the most holistic interpretation – offers the strongest conception of competence, argue Hager and Gonczi (1993), as all occupations involve performance of generic tasks such as planning or contingency management in addition to specific tasks. Tasks might include performing in accordance with an overall conception of what one's work is about, working ethically, and so on. Just as abilities or capabilities are necessary, but not sufficient for competence, so the performance of tasks is also necessary but not sufficient for competence. Thus, they argue, any satisfactory account of competence must include both attributes and tasks.

Hager and Gonczi (1993) show how 'competence' is relational: it links together two disparate phenomena. Only by recognising the relational nature of knowledge, attributes and task performance can competency standards capture the richness of work. Any approach which ignores this will lead inevitably to impoverished competency standards.

This 'holistic' notion of competence has a humanistic appeal. It provides a 'human face' for what might otherwise be an overtly regulatory, hierarchical and unattractive systemic approach. With their concentration on outcomes, and essentially performance outcomes (rather than inputs and processes), competency-based approaches tend not to differentiate workers on the basis of any characteristics other than what workers are capable of doing. Age, gender, cultural and ethnic background are irrelevant in the determination (and assessment) of competencies. But of course these factors will be highly relevant to the processes leading to the achievement of competencies.

It is precisely this lack of differentiation, claim supporters of the competence movement, that makes the application of standards essentially democratic. But this so-called democracy does not address the issues of control, management and integration of workers into the production process. The surface appearance of objective competencies conceals the ways power functions in the construction of competence. For instance, drawing on critical social theory, there is substantive documentation of the increased exercise of control over workers' productive activity and work habits in the cybernetic era. Aronowitz follows Marx's labour theory of value (in which value is measured by quantities of labour time to produce commodities) to argue that under the new technological changes, production becomes 'more and more based upon technocratically-controlled systems of knowledge organisation rather than the control of labor' (Aronowitz 1981: 86).

Thus questions of how to assist people of varying age, language, gender and experience to achieve the relevant occupational competencies foreground issues of domination and control rather than of civil liberties and individual opportunity. Although labour time remains a key aspect of production, it is the new knowledge which becomes an increasingly significant productive force. As a result, workers are increasingly observed and monitored through the mechanism of 'objective' workplace competencies.

Further, there is conflict between linking the acquisition of competencies with remuneration and employer desire to keep production and labour costs to a minimum. In some organisations this can easily result in the wish not to recognise and reward skill development. Indeed, 'what counts' as learning in a competency-based system can have major career and remuneration consequences indicating that discourses of competence are most certainly sites of power. However, as Foucault (1980a) reminds us, powerful discourses do not talk *directly* of power. If competency-based education and training approaches are to work they have to be both subtle and appealing – to 'construct' autonomous self-directed learners.

Without 'definite' conclusions

Contemporary theorisations of workplaces as learning environments have paralleled historical changes to workplaces from scientifically-managed 'Taylorised' workplaces, to 'flexible specialisation' and then to cybernetic 'learning organisations' and enterprises. These are not necessarily mutually exclusive as approaches to the organisation of work. What is significant is that there are very important links between the ways in which work is organised, the content of work, and 'opportunities' for employees and learning. Recognition of these links corresponds to a re-configuration of the meaning of knowledge in society. Contemporary knowledge, in the context of workplace and education and training reforms, is being re-moulded – increasingly aligned with the skills and assessments of competent performance – to pre-specified industry standards.

'Human resources' are very costly and on the job training is one of the central mechanisms used to 'manage' these resources. This is, in part, why competency-based systems have proved to be so popular. Mistakes made by employees can be expensive, and expensive mistakes contradict market demands for ever-increasing efficiencies. This translates to the need for skills to be pre-defined and for knowledge to be packaged to meet the demands and desires of the consumer age. Such are the cultural shifts within which HRD practitioners are required to perform.

A centrepiece of contemporary vocational education and training reforms has been shown to be 'competence', and there are different versions of what this can mean depending on one's standpoint. However, the connection between professional power, knowledge and control is apparent. On this reading, competencies can be viewed as a fairly prescriptive technology for getting workers to perform to pre-defined standards. From the perspective of the various governmental and industry regulatory authorities, however, competency-based standards are a useful embodiment of instrumental reason. The competencies provide a blueprint of industry standards (and thus training regimes) which are intended to promote internationally competitive economies.

While there is much ambiguity and confusion between the perspectives of 'the authorities' and a Foucauldian reading of competence, underlying interest in competence appears to be practical in character. But this shift has important epistemological implications. For instance, what increasingly counts is 'whether competence has the desired outcome – does it work?' Barnett (1994: 101). I have argued that the reforms of education and training – based upon competency-based standards – are intended to serve workplace and industrial efficiency. The justification of such reforms is grounded in human capital theory and its accompanying economic rhetoric. As rhetoric frequently conflicts with individual experience, critical questions are raised about the underlying links between competency-based standards, the exercise of power, and learning in the new work order.

Inevitably, this raises further questions. How does the implementation of competency-based training affect 'learning' at work? Do competency-based frameworks offer suitable approaches to understanding and assessing workers' learning about their practices? Does the discourse of competence marginalise knowledge and understanding unrelated to workplace performance? Might competencies represent relatively benign manifestations of attempts at industrial relations harmony between unions and business? Are competency-based standards representations of 'ever and more subtle refinements of technologies of power. . . . Power exercised in the search for normalised and governable people?' (Marshall 1989, in Edwards and Usher 1994: 6).

These questions have a direct bearing on how informal learning is conceived of, and in turn, how it might be 'talked about' and researched. Ideas about how informal learning is talked about and actively promoted by managerial attempts to 'construct' autonomous, self-directed learning 'teams' are examined in Chapter 4 with illustrations from various corporate settings. Chapter 5 then goes on to explore how such discourses and the exercise of power affect individual HRD professionals performing their daily roles in the context of the Sydney 2000 Olympic Games construction sites.

Notes

1 Fordism may be viewed as the application of 'Taylorist' principles to manufacturing, with the added features, exploited by Henry Ford, of continuous flow line production and mass marketing.

2 Demarcations have always been contested in various ways but significant questions arise from de-differentiation. Shifting boundaries, changing values and purposes of work and learning are also related to modern forms of governance. Within education, for instance, the structuring metaphors of 'discipline', 'subjects', 'fields of practice' and so on are becoming problematic. In the state of de-differentiation, the metaphors of markets, competence, quality, and the management of learning, which their proponents argue transcend boundaries, are providing the language of practice, policy and study.

3 As capital becomes more internationalised and the globe more integrated into market mechanisms (globalisation) new problems of advanced modern capitalism are emerging. Increased flexibility is now held by influential commentators (see Reich 1993) to be an essential labour form to match the requirements of capital accumulation, but the trends for flexible labour are not experienced evenly across the globe (Edwards 1994: 162). The OECD nations, and in particular the United States, are actively supporting 'flexible' solutions to the problems of capital accumulation – flexibility of labour and of capital are thus intimately connected.

4 Braverman argues that the development of the productive forces under capitalism requires constant technical innovation whereby management

seeks to extend managerial control over the labour process by separating conception from the execution of work.

5   This phenomenon is common to most modernised Western countries (e.g. see the British National Council for Vocational Qualifications; Human Resource Development, Canada; the Australian National Training Authority; and similar bodies throughout the OECD nations). Flexible and distance training packages are now being aggressively marketed by Western universities and technical education systems to most developing nations.

6   For Aristotle, the purpose of practical wisdom was eudemonia, the well-balanced life of well-being. Practical wisdom – phronesis – became wisdom once the ethical (virtuous) purpose had evolved for an individual. Ensnarement in a rationalised, social-economic lifeworld, devoid of deeper ethical purposes, represents a part of the social emptying – the absence of the social and 'the commodifying of human relations' (Wexler 1987).

4 The hidden curriculum of learning at work

The strategies of post-industrial workplaces

That people learn in the course of being at work seems to be a common sense view that implies a 'curriculum' exists in everyday activities. Discourses on industrial work have long held the belief that there are many processes that socialise people at work. Yet we know little about the socialisation effects of post-industrial work. Professional identities are shaped within new waves of communication devices such as 'learning organisations' self-directing teams, empowerment strategies, quality circles and so on. These are both symbolic and practical tools of communication in many post-industrial workplaces and can be described as discursive institutional practices.

To examine the effects of these discursive practices, this chapter draws on Foucault's (1988b) theorisations of technologies of power. This theory enables the unmasking of ways employees can be seduced by corporate reward/punishment systems. It is argued that contemporary corporate reward/punishment systems do contain hidden curricula – and this often entails a disciplinary agenda. It is therefore essential to ask whether it is possible for managers and HRD practitioners to resist oppressive disciplinary agendas and if so, what sorts of strategies can be effective in ensuring that power is always productive, 'not merely repressive of culture' (in Du Gay 1996: 63).

Theorisations that generalise about contemporary workplace learning can be problematic. Deliberate or overt educational activities at, or for, work only comprise the manifest curriculum of work. There is always much more to learning than that which is directly observed or stated:

> corporate educational activities include the collection of deliberate learning activities that the company or company approved educators provide and in which workers participate knowingly for the

perceived advantage of both themselves and the company.

(Casey 1995: 78)

This manifest curriculum is always accompanied by the hidden curriculum of work that socialises and shapes workers. The shaping of worker identities requires compliance with corporate objectives and directions, but a compliance that involves active subjects making choices and decisions about their place in the new corporate culture. Professional identities are being formed in the new managerial language of 'competitiveness', 'self-direction', 'TQM', 'competency-based education and training' (CBET), and measurable performance indicators. Organisations now operate in contexts of such rapid change that decision making is often uncertain, feeding corporate desires for firm (decisive/rational) outcomes that are subject to these types of binding corporate/managerial discourses.

High-tech corporate workplaces are facsimiles of these post-industrial conditions. They are commonly organised to 'facilitate' learning. At least that is how the rhetoric has it. Learning at work does more than 'simply' up-skill workers. It includes a socialisation that enables new ways of performing. But a hidden part of the learning curriculum for post-industrial work is its rarely surfaced disciplinary agenda. This involves a set of practices in the design of corporate culture that utilise 'choice', 'empowerment' and 'self-development'. Such terms are thus set against a highly problematic social backdrop.

The analysis acknowledges that structures of power and dominance are always contested, with new alliances forming to challenge existing ones. Discourses of workplace reform and workplace learning arise in specific political contexts and do not 'simply' reflect those contexts as if they were pre-given. These discourses actively create new ways for people *to be* at work. Indeed, 'all actors – workers and managers – participate in a dialectic of control that allows them at least the power of defiance' (Whittington 1992: 695). As there is an active component to the human technologies and techniques of 'developing staff', it is important to ask whether the activities *designed* to boost learning at work can offer something beyond an alignment of workers to the new competency requirements and languages of workplace performativity.

'Developing' staff

Theorising the development of staff as 'a technology' may sound a little extreme, but as Casey (1995: 80) points out, contemporary emphases on team building and 'family' style participatory structures acculturate employees into the company. Workers *learn* productivity, not just the skills and competencies necessary to perform the job. Drawing on LaBier's (1986) studies of the psychological effects of stressful corporate work on the emotional lives of company executives (and the emotional lives of their employees) Casey makes a convincing argument that the informal learning experiences of employees deeply affects their working and emotional lives. With workplace strategies for obtaining greater efficiencies and competitive advantages extending more deeply into 'the person', critical analyses of the deliberate corporate fashioning of employee identities are needed. This analysis centres on workers being seduced by (inter alia) four complementary and interrelated 'technologies':

- the language of *difference* – the promise of valuing diverse knowledges, skills and experiences
- the language of *empowerment* – the corporate promise of participation in decision-making processes with an accompanying sense of 'ownership'
- the promise of *belonging* – the construction of a sense of teamwork, community and 'corporate-family' bonds
- the promise of *reward* – the alignment of promotion and wages with skill levels, work-titles, image and status for increased 'flexibility' and productivity.

These technologies are not merely repressive and it is precisely their positive aspects which make them appear so plausible, so seductive. Indeed, the seductive power of these four technologies is compounded by their overlaps, their interrelationships and their connectedness to workers' conceptions of who they are, what they may be able to do, and become. To illustrate how the technologies work I have integrated extracts from interviews with six corporate HRD managers into the text. For the sake of the narrative I have located the interpretive methods of this aspect of the study in the Appendix. The extracts presented here provide data on their professional roles, critical incidents they had experienced, and, consequently, a range of workplace influences on their own informal learning. The six interviews were with (pseudonyms):

- Maria – HRD manager at the Sydney head office of a multinational small goods and soft drink manufacturer and distributor
- Christine – HRD manager of a national financial institution

- Simon – national HRD manager of multinational commerce and financial management consulting company
- Michael – HRD practitioner in a multinational aerospace engineering corporation
- Vinod – HRD manager of a high-volume aluminium products manufacturer
- Jodie – HRD practitioner in an Australian legal institution.

Their descriptions frequently objectify the ends/goals/visions of their organisations. They operate within discourses of 'quality', 'empowerment of workers', 'learning cultures' and 'competence'. Yet many of the practices that 'objectify' these so-called visions remain firmly in the hands of an elite group – often financial controllers, management experts and consultants. HRD personnel are charged with implementing the ideas of these leaders, who Gee refers to as the 'new organisational priesthood' (1994: 11).

Metaphors and metonyms for power relations at work are sought, and in several instances, dramatic gulfs between the stated ideals of management and actual workplace practices are revealed. That such gulfs occur when training others can provoke ethical tensions for the trainers, as Vinod pointed out:

> There is a goods train line which runs between the workshops and the administration office where the top-brass sit. This symbolises the divisions which still exist between the workers and managers. There is still us-and-them thinking that is difficult to get rid of. My mission is across the track. Getting total quality management while such a division exists makes the talk of TQM more like rhetoric. This poses an additional challenge for trainers like me – we need to facilitate a more trusting environment.

Postmodern ideas about trust, truth and being 'true to yourself' as well as to others suggest that these noble intents can be more problematic than they might sound. Foucault (1980b) offers a way of analysing 'trustworthiness' in contemporary workplaces, with which I sympathise. This approach acknowledges that practice is governed by an ever-moving agenda to which one contributes. But this ever-moving agenda can never be solely one's own. Foucault argues that truth, or more precisely, 'regimes of truth' are central to modern forms of governance, and that power-knowledge formations have been cloaked in the 'objective' knowledge of expertise and the humanistic discourses of helping and empowerment. The humanistic discourses of helping and empowerment are influential in the descriptions of the HR practitioners' work. Each of them referred to the need for *greater trust*, but achieving this was sometimes difficult, exemplifying Foucault's above point, as Michael explains:

> The retrenchments and other things which management did undermined some of our [training] initiatives. You need much more than a 'stated' shared commitment. The culture of this place is, in fact, very hierarchical and the moves to change that are still fairly much on the surface. It was frustrating in a way.

By 'very hierarchical', Michael is referring to management's control over decision making despite the company's rhetoric about team approaches, autonomy and empowered workers. Attempting to build a 'learning organisation' against a background of retrenchments compromised Michael's credibility with shop-floor workers as an HR practitioner despite his best intentions to serve 'worker interests'.

Jodie's credibility partly rested on how she addressed the issue of dealing with difference and diversity in the HRD programme. She made a particular point about the importance of this terrain for the success of her professional practice. Although 'difference and diversity' represents corporate rhetoric, it is a rhetoric that she said she was happy to support:

> I think there are areas of court operations which are close to the raw emotions of the clients. There is a natural scepticism on the part of those closer to those emotions about how objective the system can be. I would like the [Court's] training program to offer an avenue for all staff to express their experiences, but this is not always easy. . . . Dealing with difference and diverse needs requires creativity and this requires resources.

The corporate rhetoric that accompanies the 'celebration' of difference is not as innocent as some might hope. The rhetoric translates to a range of practices that require active participation, and as the following section explains, a willingness to 'buy into' the rhetoric.

The language of difference

The process of globalisation, involving the dismantling of national and trade borders accompanied by the growth of multinational companies and movement of people for work or migration purposes, has heightened the need for 'valuing difference' within workplace cultures. Globalisation can also be seen to fuel a homogenisation of values, organisational cultures, languages and work practices, producing unified and integrated common cultures. Paradoxically, globalisation has, at the same time, strengthened the processes for establishing and maintaining local cultures and local differences. This illustrates the coexistence of seemingly contradictory processes. However:

> what does seem clear is that it is not helpful to regard the global and local as dichotomies separated in space or time: it would seem that the processes of globalization and localization are inextricably bound together in the current phase.
>
> (Featherstone 1995: 103)

In other words, global economics and communication are connected with local diversity. Despite the movement towards a global culture, local differences are becoming increasingly defined. Nation states, regions and organisations are constructing boundaries and images defining their uniqueness, but at the same time it is precisely through attempts to define uniqueness that cultural complexities can be highlighted. This is illustrated in workplaces as they compete for a market share – to meet the particular needs of niche consumer groups. Boutique services replace mass production, and servicing this shift are employees' cultural and technological knowledge and skills – a relationship well 'appreciated' by human capital theory. Increasingly, the relationship between production and inter-cultural marketing involves dialogues across national and local borders.

Such dialogues pose critical questions about the degree to which the development of workplace cultures based on increasingly systematic/standardised training (and credentialling) can coexist with different cultural experiences and skills of employees. For instance, are the systematic and standardised training nomenclature actually recognising different knowledges and values? Or do they have the effect of homogenising? Do management, work and training practices realise, or conflict with, the rhetoric of valuing difference? And to what extent is corporate culture incorporated into the employees' personal identity?

As 'industry-driven' vocational education and training systems increasingly frame workplace competencies, the training and credentialling of learning outcomes become part of the technologies for developing values around cultural differences: in knowledges, experiences and identities. Yet industry competency standards, a key technology for the construction of skilled workers, prescribe singular ways of performing. They provide templates for training that will regenerate the same ways. In the call for standardisation and 'benchmarking', the strict boundaries around *units of work* and *units of learning* render invisible the overlaps and the complex relationships that allow for different and competing workplace practices. The 'outcomes' focus of the standards also makes invisible the cultural knowledge that underpins worker skills.

Recognition of prior learning, heralded as one of the key conceptual shifts that acknowledge and accredit learning outside formal institutions, potentially provides the opportunity for giving space and reward for individual's diverse knowledges, experiences and skills. But when this meaning is recognised and assessed it is being framed within monocultural classifications of competence. In this way 'each [person] can only be understood in terms of sameness and conformity' (Michaelson 1996).

In the rhetoric of workplace culture there is much promise of recognition of diverse experiences and knowledges. Yet contemporary corporations promote 'culture' as people sharing the same 'visions', common goals, *doing* common tasks and working towards predetermined workplace standards.

This is reinforced in a number of workplace practices. Increasingly, job application processes include personality tests, even extending into family interviews, reflecting a further blurring of public and private domains. Accompanying these processes are recruitment practices and criteria that reflect very specific kinds of attitudes and values – those that match the imaging and reproduction requirements of the corporate culture. Applying Foucault's (1988b) theory of technologies of power, these corporate practices are associated with a certain type of domination. Each practice implies 'certain modes of training and *modification of individuals*, not only in the obvious sense of acquiring certain skills but also in the sense of acquiring certain attitudes' (Foucault 1988b: 18). This was evidenced in Christine's learning from experience in her corporate environment:

> The organisation is very hierarchical and the ownership of training has included major political battles. You have to observe the hierarchy to get things done. This is very political and carries with it a real tension. Our immediate managers are very supportive, but further up the line there is a 'bean-counting' mentality which does not necessarily see the value, in terms of money outlay, in training or organisational development. With the hierarchy, I have learned to ask a lot of questions to ensure the design of new programs clearly reflects developmental expectations.

Christine's words about her need to 'ensure the design of new programs clearly reflects developmental expectations' illustrate how practitioners can be subtly defined and 'governed'. Her professional practice is inscribed in a never ending process to which everyone at work is, in some way, a party (even if it is oppositional). With this analysis, 'the hierarchy' she refers to is not simply a top-down pyramid with a single authoritative source at its peak. Rather, it is an apparatus that does not have an identifiable locus of control. Although in most cases workplaces will have a 'boss', or board of directors, 'in charge', the point is that in shaping and reproducing practices we all directly contribute to our own particular forms of workplace governance.

Simon's understandings of what 'really drives' his corporate role illustrate a further aspect of governance at work:

> The *dollar* sign is the only thing which drives this organisation. Not so much in terms of the overall training program, as this is a cost centre rather than a profit making centre. But the whole thing which drives this is the dollar sign. You hear terms such as utilisation rates, how much billing have I got, how much time is chargeable, numbers of clients, getting fees – you're talking about a firm of accountants, for heaven's sake. That is what it is all about.

Of his purpose as a national professional development manager, he said:

> Our mission statement says we have to develop our people, but that means nothing to the partners really. But if you describe the training philosophy as: impact and performance-based training where the training value ratio equals fees generated as a result of this training, plus cost savings divided by the cost of the training – they think that's terrific!

He suggested that this principle is:

Training value ratio = fees generated + cost savings – cost of training

> I understand this requirement. In this environment you can't afford to be too humanistic although I would hold that I am [humanistic] and that the professional education program really needs to be for it to work. But you have to understand and respect the culture of the organisation for it to move towards a learning environment.

Simon characterises the HRD function as seeking to maximise bottom-line productivity. What is being learned informally is, in part, how one's personal values align with those of the organisation. Indeed, the corporate sphere is penetrating more deeply into all aspects of employees' lives. Management practices suggest a triumph of the hierarchy with decisions continuing to be made by the same decision makers even within the 'flattened hierarchy' (Brooks 1994). Furthermore, employees are often locked into particular ways of working by accounting practices and total quality management (TQM) requirements designed to ensure uniformity and compliance to rigid standards.

Communication systems and practices, motivated by the need to improve information flow, are being standardised. While the standardisation of modes and formats can assist in both the giving and receiving of information (by increasing reader predictability and by 'scaffolding' writing tasks), it can also limit new meanings, for example, document templates ensure particular constructions of texts.

At the same time as the increase in written documentation, spoken information continues to be communicated through powerful informal networks. In team meetings voices that use the 'appropriate' language and communication strategies are listened to. Communication training thus tends to focus on individual language skills that empower, rather than examine the power relations within the organisation that empower some while disempowering others. Indeed, training sessions which seek the narrow promotion of 'cultural capital' resources can lead to losses of dignity and sense of self-worth.

Cultural knowledge is frequently utilised for productivity purposes. This is illustrated by the cultural knowledge of migrant employees that is often drawn upon in shaping and producing products (and services) for local or international niche markets and for communicating with multinational partners as well as the local community. However, if the value of the 'human resource' doesn't have a direct relationship with the capital product or service being developed, it has little or no place. Subsequently, individual initiatives in meetings and other decision-making forums can be withdrawn. At other times overt or covert racism can silence employees who no longer feel willing or confident about what they can contribute – thus diverse contributions become invisible and/or inaudible.

Much of the rhetoric around difference is about obtaining compliance with corporate objectives and production imperatives. Valuing diverse knowledges and skills contradicts the organisational culture in which pre-defined values, beliefs, attitudes and behaviours (sameness) are rewarded. Training programmes, rather than developing diversity and innovation, are framed by singular, compliance-seeking structures and technologies – including the language of 'empowerment'.

The language of empowerment

Along with the new global markets, flexible accumulation of capital, volatile labour markets, quick switches from one product to another, niche marketing and ever greater levels of consumerism (postmodern society) come new patterns of management. The new forms of post-Fordist management are technologies designed to transform organisational and corporate cultures in order to capitalise on global conditions of competitiveness. With reduced need for manual work, social labour requires *intellectually trained* workers who possess both specialised skills and the 'flexibility' to perform as required by their corporation. In order to fully utilise its flexible specialists – compete successfully – contemporary corporations have developed a rhetoric about 'worker empowerment'. Empowered, self-directed workers are meant to reflect the flat/lateral work hierarchies that characterise post-Fordist workplaces. They are a part of an economic/managerial formula that rests on a re-configured form of human capital theory.

The re-configuration assumes worker autonomy, dynamic decision-making and more democratised work arrangements. Workers are *trained to be empowered*. Trainers are thus temporary sources of the empowerment text. They 'direct' a few moments in the corporate participation process. The message of training is, however, one that seeks compliance. In so far as the trainer's message is one of change, trainees rarely take the message very seriously. HRD practitioners are not empowered to demand any significant changes. They are meant to convey to trainees the importance of attaining 'shared goals' or work towards the 'total quality' required by the corporation. In a large-scale manufacturing environment, this, for Vinod, meant learning 'contextual skills':

> Developing listening skills, particularly with line managers, and questioning skills to ensure there are no gaps in my understanding of what needs to be done . . . when it comes to senior managers it becomes a question of appropriate assertiveness . . . when to ask your questions or raise issues which probe at what has been said . . . learning the contextual skill of when to be assertive has been very important to me.

This 'informal learning' resulted in changes to the way Vinod worked:

> I now have what I call a strong customer focus. I now apply these people skills to identifying what customers want. Not so much how to satisfy the customer with methodologies but to go the step further and sell our training. This is exciting for me in so far as I have been successful at it. Not so long ago I don't think I had these skills.

The communication practices at work here are expressions of corporate requirements for HRD generally and the behaviour of trainers specifically. Vinod's words indicate that he was able to accommodate much in the drive for a 'strong customer focus'. He was 'empowered' to go 'the step further' and sell the company's training. He was successful at it, but this experience of success required that he learn 'appropriate assertiveness' and know his place in the corporate hierarchy. In Vinod's example, triggers for his learning related to corporate imperatives for training, and for him to impress on workers the need for a 'strong customer focus'. Although it was a corporate requirement, Vinod says it was also 'exciting' to develop new communication skills. Drawing on Foucault's *Technologies of the Self*, this illustrates one of the ways we 'constantly reshape our past creations to conform to our present creative needs [representing] a paradox of the human condition: we are beings that create forms which ironically imprison our creativity' (Foucault; in Hutton 1988: 137).[1]

Concerns about the language of worker empowerment is not so much that it is illusory, but more about its seductive power. Many HRD practitioners have taken up the idea of worker empowerment following popular books on 'The Learning Organisation' and other HRD glossies that promise greater performance outcomes. There is a belief amongst many new wave managers and HRD practitioners that empowerment offers greater worker freedoms, more rewarding/satisfying work environments and the seduction of unprecedented opportunities for personal and professional advancement. Those who argue against this 'logic' may be painted as 'negative' at best. This happened to Michael whose words illustrate how he had been seduced by corporate rhetoric that failed to live up to its promises:

> My values were actually aligned with the rhetoric of the workplace reform – to promote self-direction, participation in decision-making and team-work. But management were unwilling to relinquish tight control. The reality was their words were complete and utter bullshit. My one regret is that, before I left, some of my work colleagues may have associated me with the cynicism of the corporation.

In Michael's HRD role he had been required to establish counselling and disciplinary procedures to help facilitate a 'restructure'. Elements of this requirement had made him 'very angry':

> I knew that my anger needed to be channelled appropriately, otherwise it could make the situation worse. The situation had to be diffused. If my anger contributed to my retrenchment then so be it. I have no regrets about being a person who stood up for what I believed in. But I don't think it was the reason. It was more

economically based and training might have been politically easier to cut that somewhere else.

Questioning must take appropriate forms or it is rendered inappropriate, thus attracting corporate sanctions. Pure positivity has become the corporate rule-game, with knowledge no longer possessing the 'shadow-side' which always demands a cost. As Letiche (1990: 237) puts it, training becomes 'a product of this epistemological shift in values ... with the goal of training to convey purely positive knowledge'. The denial of negativity is meant to offer new forms of liberation for workers. It rests upon a logic of human consciousness that is purely positive.

The new knowledge of the learning organisation does not contain its own negation. Even though the corporate construction of 'worker empowerment' is highly dubious, it does not face serious criticism. Some resistant trainers will doubt the message, of course, but when training jobs are scarce or being 'devolved' to other workers, such as line-managers, peer coaches and mentors, it is easier to play along. Besides, the rhetoric is easy to play along with – it contains the humanistic qualities that have, in the past, motivated many corporate trainers. It also contains a rhetoric derived, ironically given its location in high-capital, from socialism – about working more co-operatively in teams – becoming more a part of the corporate family.

The promise of belonging

Planned training activities that take place at work, or for work, comprise what Casey (1995: 78) calls 'the manifest curriculum of work'. This is accompanied by the hidden curriculum that socialises adult workers. Much more is learned than the material and physical acts of *doing* work. Workers are being trained to speak up 'appropriately' in the new 'empowered', self-directing corporate team context. But this can be problematic, as Brooks found in her research on collective team learning in organisations:

> for many of the team members the ability to contribute was related to the amount of formal power they had relative to others on the team and to whether they had enough power to collect data and attend team meetings.
>
> (Brooks 1994: 21)

Signs of resistance can be punished rather than rewarded unless they result in outcomes that contribute to the company's performance objectives. Resistance in the new workplace has shifted significantly away from union-based opposition to managerial directions towards a simulated solidarity based on corporate teams. Unions are being increasingly marginalised and in some industries are virtually powerless. Simultaneously, belonging to a team is now a career prerequisite.

A range of standard training practices teaches employees the competencies necessary to perform in their team situations. These practices are manifest at the professional level, where managers and team leaders are being trained in valuing diversity, how to work in teams, how to communicate and negotiate more effectively. But this training reduces these skills to the competencies required to perform work *tasks*. This may offer superficial advantages for workplace communication, but there is much more to 'knowing' about these topics than narrow skills-based training entails. Knowing, or understanding, may well be unvoiced. As Beckett (drawing on Aristotle's *Ethics*) argues, what is at the core of professional practice is: 'the expression of the judgment of understanding [which] gives practicality to the wisdom ascribed to someone who has acted rightly, or as Aristotle says, "soundly" or "well"' (Beckett 1993: 10).

The expression of professional judgment is not, however, immune from the powerful lure of belonging. Workers are now 'encouraged' to belong to their corporate family. This is symbolically represented in the proliferation of logos and corporate images that are embedded within all written documentation and realised in the selective use of democratic language such as *we, our, shared*. This helps to foster a sense of community with its accompanying, yet perhaps mythical, characteristics of belonging and security. Furthermore there are increasing opportunities for workers to participate in share schemes which not only motivate the link between the individual employee's work with productivity, but also reinforce the illusion of *our* company and *our* business. This is strengthened by the 'public' display of company profits and turnovers on notice boards and company newsletters.

The corporate family with its multiple and complex levels, departments and relationships may capture a sense of an extended family. But workers also belong to teams, a tighter nuclear family equivalent, and these teams are sold as autonomous units, promising a kind of boundary, belonging and protection from the potentially chaotic, dispersed, fragmented workplace in which flexibility, changing roles and responsibilities result in unpredictable social relationships. At times the result is a decentring of one's self. 'Belonging' is therefore a powerful lure.

Belonging to the corporate family and to the team rides on the notion of reciprocity where employee commitment to the new part-nering and team arrangements result in increased participation, energy and output, rewarded by whatever the organisation has to offer, in this case a sense of autonomy, protection, responsibility and financial rewards.

However, such reciprocity has its costs. There are problems with the protection offered by the promise of belonging. How does protection figure in a workplace where information technologies monitor input and output on an individual basis? How does protection figure where your colleagues are assessing your competencies? And how does protection actually work against a backdrop of large-scale downsizing or company re-engineering as illustrated in Michael's earlier words?

Even with the competency-based approach to training and assess-ment, workers are learning more than the skills and competencies that are necessary to perform the job. They are experiencing the 'normal' stresses of the new corporate-partnering and team requirements. The new 'corporate family' has an emotional effect on the lives of workers and on the broader community. Contemporary management and training and development literature continues an almost exclusive coverage of building learning organisations and family-style participa-tory structures, glossing over deeper issues such as the *emotional toll* upon selves. The new partnerships, the family-style learning organisa-tions, seek to absorb more and more of the worker's self into the organisation – the organisation which, above all else, must perform competitively – at peak efficiency.

Jodie's story illustrates how the promise of belonging influences her interpretations of events in the organisation:

> Our collective experiences are valued within our own unit. The training unit functions as a team, and teamwork is being promoted throughout the corporation. It is a part of the new corporate language associated with becoming a learning organisation, in efforts to be more efficient and competitive. The idea is that team-work will make work more rewarding.

Christine referred to her experiences of working in teams in a corpo-rate banking environment and the need to 'feel comfortable with other team members':

> Other people's perceptions and ideas help to redefine your own ideas and also identify constraints and considerations. Getting other ideas helps you to step back and think about where you are going. This has been one of the most important impacts on my learning at

work – involvement with small groups with a project team approach.

As a result of her informal learning in teams, she cites as important 'assessing the bigger picture before establishing the nuts and bolts'. In the process of being exposed to a 'bigger picture' through team involvement, she again highlighted the issue of trust. Trust is being promoted in each of these corporations through new organisational structures based on teams and corporate 'families'. The team to which one belongs is promoted as family-like and it is essential to trust your team members. Sporting metaphors are also quite common in this team promotion – such as 'hitting home-runs'.

The notion of corporate team is a convenient cultural formation. It is now a common corporate script for obtaining the desired sensibilities in employees. Sensibilities are monitored through competencies which will promote greater involvement and productivity. This corporate script is reflected in each of the interview excerpts in various ways. Simon addressed it directly:

> Doing your job is not enough in this organisation. You have to be seen to be doing a good job. You don't have to be too overt about it, but you have to make sure that you are recognised for what you are doing, and trusting people is important. When you delegate, you have to trust people. I think if I respect and trust my staff, work hard and am honest with them, we can feel as though we are doing something worthwhile. I now believe that being honest both to yourself and others is fundamental to one's learning – it is one of the things which is most important.

Belonging to a team or network is stressed by Simon, who links 'belonging' to:

> Knowing who holds power whether it be formal or informal. . . . Knowing about the interplay of personalities, networks and informal channels of communications. Working the network matters. I now make sure that my staff are involved in the outplace [networks external to the corporation] as well as on a range of internal committees. This helps with developing a collective team approach as well as giving the individuals on the team a profile and network of their own. I don't want people to interpret this as an attempt to manipulate the system. It comes back to honesty. You have to be honest about who you are and what you are doing.

Simon's descriptions – 'being honest about who you are and what you are doing' – actually illustrate some very complex processes. Borrowing the language of Foucault, knowing oneself and what one is doing is entangled with power and control. These terms have, simultaneously, an active and a passive sense. Usher, Bryant and Johnston argue that this is the sense of:

> being a subject and of being subjected, of a body of systematic knowledge and of a system of regulation and control, of being authorised and of knowing and affirming oneself. This is not just a matter of language per se but of discursive practices. Practitioners find themselves at the very centre of these ambiguities and forced to act within them.
>
> (Usher, Bryant and Johnston 1997: 83)

The idea of 'knowing oneself' is related to what Foucault calls 'technologies of the self' and in particular it is a confessional practice that is part of self-governance. Here, people are not so much regulated through objectifying power/knowledge discourses, but regulate themselves through a subjectifying discourse that emphasises the need to talk about and know oneself. According to Rose (1994) this talk, where the autonomous self becomes the normative centre of attention and the focus of activity, becomes the means of empowerment. Usher and Edwards (1995: 9) further argue that guidance and counselling are forms of confession where the meanings ascribed to self are already effects of power – that is, people have already accepted the legitimacy and truth of confession and the meanings this evokes, including knowing oneself for both personal and economic reasons. In Simon's case, his confessional practices also helped with 'developing a collective team approach as well as giving the individuals on the team a profile and network of their own'.

Individual notions of success, failure, the hidden agendas, emotional experiences at work and career motivations all impacted on these trainers' informal learning. Learning experiences were associated with major successes, crises, jolts, perceived threats, fear of failure or coming to terms with major change. These day-to-day events shaped the nature and extent of the learning. From the comments of these trainers, informal learning was intimately connected with a constant defining and redefining of their informal theories that applied to their organisations, their roles and purposes within them, and their required task performance levels.

The social structuring of work – the new designer work-culture – is significant for psychological functioning as it profoundly affects people's views of reality. There are reciprocal relations among work, occupation and personality. This reciprocity is exploited in contemporary corporate practices through 'real world' corporate and industrial practices and discourses, and results in individual tensions, including conflicts between personal values and professional demands. What people do and learn in their work carries over into other spheres of their lives. Their cognitive functions, values, priorities in life and conceptions of themselves are a part of the 'lessons' of work.

In order to belong, designer work cultures seek a precise alignment of a person's values, attitudes and abilities with the needs of the organisation. Any traits that might impede work, or are unnecessary, are suppressed or eliminated. Corporate talk about a 'celebration of difference' is purely that: talk. Rather, attributes of toughness, aggressiveness, decisiveness and individual competence are truly prized. And corporate reward systems, as the following section explains, tend to deliver on this promise.

The promise of reward

Workplace reward systems are normally accepted as givens. They are often exempted from critical scrutiny due to powerful interests vested in them. Corporate reward systems can, however, be read as 'technologies of power' in which individuals submit to certain ends in order to be rewarded. It is the dialectic of submission/reward that is scrutinised here. To understand this dialectic, corporate reward systems need to be viewed as tied not only to power, but also 'technologies of sign systems' (Foucault 1988b: 18). For corporate learning facilitators and trainers this technology can be expressed through processes of 'designer learning' and training. They are in positions of trust. Contemporary corporations stress the issue of trust. It is a part of the 'belonging' to which the previous section referred. In turn, this is a reward for 'fitting-in'.

Increasingly, but not conclusively, the new corporate culture's effort to establish team bonds and emotional commitments among team members is effective in obtaining this compliant fitting-in. As Lasch (1984) argues, 'the team-family culture bolsters a fragile corporate self formed under the influence of traditional hierarchies and weakened by the cultural narcissism of advanced industrial society' (in Casey 1995: 150). The point is that belonging to a corporate family, complying with its processes, such as feedback, recognition and reward systems, provides a compensatory effect to the 'acutely ambivalent and conflictual self' (Casey 1995: 150). That the employee feels valued and belongs to a major organisation with the promise of career paths and salary packages helps promote commitment and thus reduces active resistance.

Maria's story indicates that there are intrinsic rewards that accompany key features of corporate HRD work. She is a cheerful advocate of the new 'synergistic' learning corporation, asserting that the organisational characteristics which promote 'synergistic' learning include:

> Cooperative participation amongst all staff including senior management; open-mindedness and a preparedness to experiment with what can be done, or is achievable; innovation; an atmosphere which encourages continual learning; and financial support for innovative training measures.

Maria also stated that workplace projects, and trial and error learning, are directly connected to the company's formal training programme:

> They supplement, refine and ensure appropriate feedback-loops between the training-room and everyday informal learning processes. This promotes a situation in which people are reasonably unified in their approach, and who share goals and objectives.

Such an approach embodies corporate desires to create learning organisations, and a point of interest here is Maria's ready incorporation of corporate rhetoric into personal discourses. This is something Casey refers to as the 'corporate colonisation of the self' (1995: 138). But this interpretation does not sufficiently acknowledge Maria's personal contribution to the push for a desired corporate culture. She believes in it and feels rewarded by its active promotion. It is the subtle power of the reward system which helps maintain a corporatised self.

The subtle power of the reward system extends to the promise of a future gratification – sometimes directly connected to one's *image*: 'the sign form has appropriated labour in order to empty it . . . and to absorb it in the process of its own reproduction' (Baudrillard 1988: 130).

The 'emptying' process encompasses titles, money, the car (and where the car is parked) and status. These remain powerful influences in the modern workplace. The promise of future gratification; the promise of *being someone* in the hierarchy continues to count. It is important to one's identity and identification with work.

Being someone in the corporate team is, however, a convenient cultural formation. It is corporate script for obtaining desired sensibilities in employees. 'Being someone' holds a presupposition: that is, *knowing* about the interplay of personalities, networks, formal and informal channels of communications. Without this 'knowledge', corporate design for team-families is vulnerable. It is vulnerable because the team structures are orchestrated through communication patterns based on artefacts: images of the desired corporate employee.

The 'teams' are not based upon the spontaneous creation of groups of workers who wish to establish a community together. They are based on corporate work and the vulnerability indicates the fundamental importance to the corporation of reward and punishment systems.

Foucault (1977, 1988b) argues that the methods of discipline and punishment used in Western cultures have shifted dramatically over the past several hundred years, from ritual punishment delivered publicly by the sovereign, to an internalised, self-monitored technology of the self. Within this self-technology, individuals discipline themselves – in accordance with workplace norms. As Foucault explains, 'normalisation occurs through comparison, ranking, judging, measurement, differentiation and setting the limits in relation to the "Norm"' (Foucault 1977: 183).

HRD practitioners' 'performance' is increasingly measured in dollars and cents terms. This 'examination', which Foucault refers to as an instrument of discipline, combines the techniques of surveillance and normalisation. Examinations of professional performance take the form of a corporate 'ritualised ceremony of power which claims to establish an objective truth about the individual' (Foucault 1977: 183). Financially-based instruments for assessing the performance of HRD practitioners and managers do not, however, accurately reflect the elusive yet critical aspects of teaching and helping others to learn. Read from a Foucauldian standpoint, such professional practitioners are thus subjects of (and subjected to) the disciplinary regimes of the corporation. Panoptic group norms[2] and corporate technologies for regulation are exemplified by fancy job titles, financially-based performance reviews, participation in corporate profit-share schemes, and hyper-male culture in which the message of valuing diversity is one of the technologies of compliance. How the panopticon can actually work in practice is examined in detail in the following chapter.

Concluding remarks

In the post-industrial scenario the systematic fashioning of Western workers' learning is associated with a range of strategies that actively create new images, cultural values, work and social expectations. Workers can come to identify themselves and conceive of their interests in terms of the words and images that accompany the re-fashioning of the new learning workplaces (Rose 1996: 130). Du Gay (1996: 53) further argues that an effect of this identification 'actively transforms meanings and realities of work', but with an effect that workers are increasingly bound into the required productive ways. Boje chillingly describes some of the implications of this so-called 'humanisation of work' (for learning) as including:

> a seamless web of instructional apparatus where we are taught to be 'politically correct' bureaucrats. The learning occurs in the minute-by-minute interactions and the spaces along the hallways, lunchrooms and e-mail networks. The iron cage of the bureaucratic teaching machine is so ubiquitous and [seemingly] benign that the prisoners of modern learning no longer see the bars, the gears, or question the learning agenda.
>
> (Boje 1994: 447)

Boje's 'bureaucratic teaching machine' can readily be linked with Foucault's ideas on the exercise of power, which is not 'a naked fact, an institutional right, nor is it a structure which holds out to be smashed: it is elaborated, transformed, organised: it endows itself with processes which are more or less adjusted to the situation' (Foucault 1982: 224). 'The situation' under scrutiny here is related to the technologies of compliance in training which systematically produce instrumental outcomes whereby 'learning' no longer requires critical distance, dialogue and critique. Here the goal of training is the conveyance of a certain type of knowledge – instrumental knowledge; that which is needed to 'fit-in' with the team and get the job done – as distinct from a questioning knowledge which may contain its own negation.

What can sustain trainers and adult educators more generally in the face of such power? Perhaps problematising 'truths' about workplace learning and its purposes through deconstruction, in which reflection, doubt and questioning are central, would help. Contemporary work-based learning strategies rarely deal in self-criticism, paradox, irony or doubt, yet it is precisely these qualities that give substance to learning. Conclusions here centre on this 'lack'. If conceptions of training are to be better, they will have to take seriously the contested status of knowing/knowledge and include the characteristics of self-negation, irony and doubt. This means a high degree of tolerance for unanswered questions, uncertainty, ambiguity and difference. By definition, therefore, some problems will never be fully resolved, indicating new demands upon mental life. Further, more research and theoretical development is needed on the dialectical interaction between oneself and social formations. This includes the need to examine ways in which professional identities are developed in and through experiences of work.

Some of the concerns about contemporary approaches to HRD generally and training specifically stem from their location in a society of performativity. The drive to align training (and learning) towards enhanced production, more competitive outcomes and greater efficiencies is very powerful. Human resources planners and managers will inevitably ask 'Will this get us anywhere?' 'How does this relate to workplace "realities"?' and so on. They are looking for techniques that will improve the quality and efficiency regimes of their organisation. Baudrillard (1993) is less hopeful, asserting that a deep level of knowledge within contemporary organisations is impossible and there is no choice but to become an apologist of performative reality. This may sound a little harsh, however, as, in problematising the disciplinary effects of 'developing' staff and surfacing the ways work socialises people, openings can be created for different dialogues and different kinds of outcomes. Learning at work can include a recognition of the crisis in purpose which characterises contemporary (postmodern) society and radical analyses of corporate work/life. This approach does not deny instrumental learning in organisations, but it does require an unprecedented self-reflexivity of the 'authors' of corporate training, staff development and business learning.

Notes

1   Vinod resigned from the company six weeks after this interview, citing 'an atmosphere of repression' as one of his main reasons for leaving.
2   Central to Foucault's conceptualisation of the workings of power is the 'panopticon' – a technique of surveillance which sustains power relations *independent* of the personnel who exercise it. What is important about Foucault's panopticon for theories of learning within power/knowledge formations 'is that the subject of surveillance disciplines *himself*' (Lee and Taylor 1996: 67). In the context of this chapter, 'group norms' are posited as a form of panopticon. Corporate norms for team or group behaviour involve subtle techniques that impose strict codes of conduct, surveillance and 'self' discipline.

5 Professional identity and self-regulation at work

Corporate storytelling

This chapter will use Michel Foucault's (1977) idea of the 'panopticon' as a central metaphor for examining corporate language about worker empowerment, self-directed learning and identity. Foucault described 'the panoptic gaze' as 'multiple, automatic, continuous, hierarchical and anonymous power functions in a network of relations from top to bottom, from bottom to top, as well as laterally, to hold an enterprise together' (1977: 175). The panopticon is a form of surveillance in which workers think they are being observed and thus actively behave in ways desired by their organisation. Foucault's theory is applied to practices of workplace learning using the narratives of HRD practitioners in an organisation to demonstrate that experience of such surveillance is indeed a lived reality.

The panoptic gaze can be embodied in language use in relation to 'team-work', 'empowerment' and 'self-direction' and is aptly illustrated by the new 360 degree performance appraisal mechanisms being adopted by many organisations and companies. This 'gaze' results in the internalising of control, imposing forms of 'self-regulation'. Through the narratives of the principal HRD practitioners – at what I shall refer to as the 'Phaedrus' company – it is argued that the language of empowerment and self-direction is a part of *corporate storytelling* where staff development and training activities can be read as technologies necessary for the achievement of this corporate outcome.

The Phaedrus Construction Company

Phaedrus is one of Australia's largest construction companies. Phaedrus's parent company, which I refer to as 'Head Office', has a multi-layered international group profile involving various life and general insurance groups, a building society, asset management, project financing and a range of development and management divisions. 'Head Office' is one of the largest independent managers of property in the world, having recently acquired one of the largest real estate investment advisers in the United States. The total value of real estate under its US management operation alone is over \$10 billion. The corporation acquired its US investment adviser to form a global property investment and asset management group with operations in North America, Europe, South-East Asia and Australia. It has recently commenced operating in Europe.

In Australia, Phaedrus won construction projects worth over one billion dollars in 1994–5. Its Olympic constructions are estimated at about \$300 million. Phaedrus is one of the principal contractors and project managers of major components of the construction of venues for the Sydney 2000 Olympic Games. Construction began in 1992 and will continue until 2000. Work at the Olympics site is divided into project areas such as roadworks, building, landscaping and cleaning. At peak times, the site has employed around 400 people; 100 of these are involved in design, engineering, project management, clerical and administrative work. The remaining 300 carry out work in the field involving trades, labouring, driving and cleaning work. Phaedrus estimates that 40 per cent of the construction workers are from non-English-speaking backgrounds. All but three of the construction workforce is male. Most of the construction work is undertaken by subcontractors who are managed by personnel from Phaedrus's direct labour pool. These overseers manage project area teams responsible for specific areas such as roadworks or building. Team membership varies from three to thirteen people. The average size of a team is four or five and typically includes a project manager, a site engineer, a leading hand or foreman and one or two directly employed construction workers. Teams are not fixed or mutually exclusive, and some individuals can be members of several teams. Not all teams are active on-site at any one time. Promoting team work was central to the roles of the HRD practitioners at the site. Their brief, in short, was to 'build' a learning organisation (Watkins and Marsick 1992) – design, conduct and evaluate training activities that would foster team-work and self-direction in an environment characterised by constant 'flux', powerful corporate interests, and powerful trade unions.

Methodology

A Foucauldian analysis is used for this chapter and its interests are both empirical and critical. It is less concerned with interpretive accounts of experience and of how one story may reflect social reality, and more concerned with how discourses *produce* social realities. As discourses are organisations of knowledge, this analysis is interested in how these are linked to power, how they are embedded in social institutions and how they produce ways of understanding. The field study is briefly introduced at this point with a full discussion of the research methods, process and style of the analysis located in the Appendix.

Empirically, the two principal HRD practitioners – Marta and David (pseudonyms) – at one of the Sydney 2000 Olympic Games construction sites were interviewed over twelve months. They were asked about their job, its challenges and the dilemmas they sometimes faced. This generated descriptions of their lived experience at work, providing the texts for the following analysis. Marta and David were responsible for setting up a work-based learning programme for all personnel involved in the construction of some of the major sites for the forthcoming Olympic Games. Both had many years' experience in HRD although it was Marta's first 'excursion' into the construction industry. David had come through construction ranks after having started his early career as a qualified tradesman. Although not reported here, the research was further informed about contextual influences on the site by interviews with a cross-section of personnel (eighty).

This Olympic site presented many advantages for the research. The local excitement (and scepticism) generated by Sydney's hosting of the Olympic Games for the year 2000 has translated to extensive media coverage, some related to training. The Games also offer prospects for ongoing construction activities to the end of the century. Rare indeed in an industry of constant movement and change. It cannot, therefore, be regarded as a typical or ordinary project: it is a trophy project – one-off, and very high profile.

David and Marta's texts[1] provide insights into their informal learning about their professional roles, the interaction of corporate culture with their individual beliefs and values, and the subtle (at times stressful) influences of the hierarchies of work-power on their behaviour. A Foucauldian reading of their stories focuses on 'the multiplicity of sites through which power operates; and it does not posit a reality outside discourse, but rather looks to the discursive production of truth' (Pennycook 1994: 131). Through a discourse analysis of these texts, I seek to uncover the ways in which the mini-narratives tell of their learning and construction of professional identities at work.

The systems of surveillance of that work site are local realisations of larger contextual influences. The national training reforms which have industry competency standards as their centrepiece, are a technology for the centralised and regulated control of employees' work and learning. These reforms constitute a surveillance dynamic. Government policy, industry competency standards and competency curriculum together provide the framework for management, trainers and workers to link learning with productivity in terms of production processes and employee relations. The training discourse at the national and local levels, with its suggestion of 'user choice', the worker/learner as a consumer, sets up complementary relationships between centralised control, self-regulation and self-discipline. The worker/learner has a 'choice'; 'you will be empowered by taking up the company's training/learning choices and consequently will be rewarded with pay and portable qualifications'.

Surveillance is discursively produced and is illustrated through metaphors of *display*. These metaphors foreground the role of the *visible* as evident in much of the workplace learning discourse. For instance, competency standards are described as making *explicit* the nature of contemporary work; assessment is based on workers' ability to *demonstrate* competence. Workers learn, and are assessed on their learning, through *observation*; and we are told again and again about the significance of corporate *image*. This regulation of surface level activity and presentation encourages the display of certain ways of being at work – those that are valued and rewarded. This in itself results in the making 'invisible' of those things that do not 'fit'. Sameness is rewarded while difference is made invisible. *Display* becomes a technology that constructs performativity and therefore professional identity.

Discourse analysis has allowed me to gain a richer understanding of the way social and institutional practices shape and are shaped by discursive practices and the realisations of these influences in the texts of the practitioners involved. In my own discursive analysis I 'play' with metaphors used by David and Marta such as 'visibility' and 'invisibility' as my theoretical interest is, in this instance, in surveillance and the way workers construct and regulate their professional identities, working within and around the panoptic gaze. To do this, I draw on Fairclough's work on discourse analysis (1992) which provides a useful three-dimensional framework that sees any discursive event, that is, any instance of discourse, as being 'simultaneously a piece of text, an instance of discursive practice, and an instance of social practice' (1992: 4).

This view of discourse provides a more complete exploration of the broad and institutional social and cultural construction of texts as well as the processes for producing and interpreting texts. It takes into account the interactive processes of meaning-making and, in terms of the interests of this research, the subjectivity of workers, more particularly these two HRD professionals.

To understand the relationship of surveillance and subjectivity this discourse analysis focuses on inter-personal meaning as this 'provides a way of theorising how people position themselves through language in relation to each other and bodies of knowledge' (Fuller and Lee 1997: 7). The transcripts are used to understand how the HRD practitioners describe themselves and describe others.

The analysis is an exemplary one rather than an exhaustive one, acknowledging the site-specific conditions of this discursive practice. The focus is on particular language features:[2]

- nominalisation and the use of passive voice as a reflection of the way the subjects make themselves and their actions visible and invisible
- personal reference and lexical items as a reflection of the way the subjects distance themselves from the text that they are producing and from the 'action' in that text
- metaphors as realisations of transforming or transformed social practices.

(Fairclough 1992: 84)

The role of the researcher/researched relationship in the construction of these spoken narratives is acknowledged in the analysis and interpretation. What follows are a number of segments of transcripts which come from the taped interviews I conducted with the HRD practitioners at a major Olympic site. At the end of each segment an analysis is offered and italics are used in the interviews themselves to highlight the key textual features that have informed the commentary.

The discursive construction of learning at work

Establishment of a site-based training programme followed discussions and negotiations between the trainers, union delegates and site management. Marta (M) and David (D) suggested that these discussions exposed them from the outset to the power-based nature of work relationships. Positioning themselves, their professional HRD roles and training practices within the hierarchies of power – even though corporate rhetoric embraced the language of a team-based learning organisation – was both central to their informal learning and an outcome of it. The following comments from David illustrate this outcome.

Learning about the primacy of production: David's account

D: Learning now has to be woven so much into the production process that they [the construction workers] often won't even realise that they are learning. It took me a while to really learn about the primacy of production. Production is number one. That has to happen at all costs. No matter how important the training or learning is, it mustn't get in the way of that. If you [trainers] do get in the way or interfere, you cause organisational problems and I mean problems between people.

JG: You learned that on the site?

D: Yes. I really didn't know beforehand. You just have to experience it to know how important that is.

JG: I get the sense that you felt training and your role was getting in the way of production?

D: Oh yes!

JG: How was that made apparent to you?

D: They don't beat around the bush in this industry. You hear quickly and explicitly from a foreman, or even from the construction workers involved. They say things like 'I shouldn't really be here . . . I'm going to get my arse kicked for this'.

JG: How did you feel about this?

D: At the time, I had my own goals to push, and I was pushing site goals too – you know, the performance indicators the site had for training. The training program could have been done in another way – a more co-operative way that didn't affect production as badly. But the problem with doing it less visibly is that it is not obviously learning or training. It is like action-learning that we are really now moving towards.

JG: You have mentioned a number of times the importance of production and there was a period where you felt you, and the training role, were a little bit 'in the way'. It sounds as though there were some barriers you had to break through to be accepted in your HRD role at the construction site?

D: Yes, it was a bit uphill. But trying to get what we did at the Olympics site on other sites is absolutely impossible. You can't recreate it because subsequent jobs do not have comparable budgets. It has to be more *integrated and invisible* now.

JG: Invisible? Do you mean that the learning effort and the role of the trainer had to become less visible, less obvious?

D: Yes. Invisible and integrated . . . a part of the culture of the site. It's like a Catch-22 situation in some ways, as trainers need to be visible and have their offerings noticed, but at the same time be invisible.

The metaphor of 'invisibility' in part reflects a game of disguising power and power relations. The game works because the players involved believe they are engaged in meaningful actions – the actual construction of Olympic Games venues. The material construction itself is visible. But the discursive practices of the site, which are not, do represent complex power plays that establish, as David says, 'the primacy of production'. What he learned through the company's communicational practices was that, 'no matter how important the training or learning is, it mustn't get in the way of production'.

David's use of the pronoun 'you' (rather than 'I') highlights his construction of his professional identity as an invisible self. This reveals the relationship between the construction of invisible training practices and the trainer's identity. He is, to an extent, internally processing the in/visibility of training by distancing himself from 'the action' exemplified by his use of passive voice. This disguises his agency in the implementation of training. This disguise may be necessary because he does not want to present training as being as important as production. Rather, training needs to be seen as a means of aiding production. It could be argued that he wants to do his work surreptitiously, that is, he is accommodating himself to the prevailing culture (the primacy of production).

D: You can't look at learning or productivity without understanding what is going on around it. Skill development has become the bargaining chip in industrial relations negotiations. I'm between a rock and a hard place in this. For example, the union is asking the company for a site allowance plus a 10 per cent pay rise. Phaedrus are saying, 'no way, but we'll give you more education and training'. It feels like it's slipping to the old ways. Management is saying one thing – 'go to the next step in your training and learning plans' – but I can't. *I can't even set foot on the next construction site because no one will pay me.* Company structures are an impediment. The cost recovery thing is hugely problematic for the nature of my work.

'The cost recovery thing' means that for any training activity, including initial consultations and concept development time, the trainer's time (and overheads) have to be accounted for financially. This training framework brings with it an emphasis on financial measurement in which training philosophy is determined by the nature of its financial accountability. Trainers' performance is monitored by a financial graph published in-house. According to David this subverts the educational goals of training. It also effected a structural adjustment in the approach to training, as before it had been a corporate overhead with a justification couched in terms of its 'intrinsic worth' to the corporation and its employees.

David's struggle with the in/visibility of training and his professional identity is exemplified in his metaphor 'between a rock and a hard place'. This metaphor signifies two important meanings. The first signifies the way the company wants training to address union concerns about career pathways but is at the same time reluctant to pay for it. The second suggests an ambivalent place of training and the trainer in an organisation where the value of education and training is 'celebrated' but not necessarily rewarded by visible and tangible material and/or financial outcomes.

D: Through my training role I have been able to get to know virtually everyone in the company. One thing I have learned is that you can't treat learning separately from the culture and the politics. It's all interwoven together. You can probably remove a fair bit of the actual product from that – the actual building of the construction. But that too is affected by the culture and politics of the organisation. It will continue to be built pretty well regardless. But the development of the company is tied up with these complex issues and power plays.

David's learning in the workplace was affected by the workplace culture and politics as, by his own admission, the interests of the company were intimately tied to his own. For example, David visited the site from Head Office where career aspirations and abilities to serve the corporate philosophy are emphasised. But interpreting and implementing the philosophy at site level was sometimes problematic for the trainers. Head Office expectations and rhetoric were sometimes juxtaposed to site-based realities. Implementation does not 'simply' mean the promotion of skill-formation opportunities and clearer career pathways for workers. Training, with its close connection to corporate culture and management/industrial relations politics, has also developed a role in corporate imaging.

Training opportunities can at once provide both the chimera of career pathways, and the materialisation of skill-formation activities to progress. But progression within Phaedrus – once a major employer of direct labour – was becoming increasingly difficult due to its own employee reduction programme and turning towards project management as distinct from project building. The image of Phaedrus that training helps promote is therefore pertinent to the corporation, because for most workers, Phaedrus cannot deliver the promised career paths. Those who 'make it' in the new Phaedrus need to demonstrate corporate traits, attitudes and behaviour. David and Marta are, for instance, expected to train workers and indeed model the desired values of co-operation, team-work and 'appropriate' assertiveness. The relative industrial harmony prevalent is to an extent predicated upon the new flexible structures which require team participation and technical and communication skills such as map reading, writing and speaking up appropriately. Ascertaining the appropriate level of assertiveness may carry some risks, as is exemplified in Marta's account.

Turning 'invisible': Marta's account

For Marta, one of the three female professionals at a construction site with a workforce of 400 men, becoming 'invisible' was never an option. She is contracted to the site financially supported by a government grant, unlike David who is a Phaedrus employee. Her professional contribution as a trainer, however, did face the potential of *being made* 'invisible'. Her experience of the work culture and the hierarchies differed in several respects to David's. But it was also much affected by what she terms 'power bases' in the workplace. In the exercise of power, site managers would clearly state the principal aims of the project: to build the games project on or ahead of time, on or below budget, and to the satisfaction of the client. For unionists, the exercise of power was, in part, about maintaining a voice in the decision-making process and protecting members' interests – although against a backdrop of large-scale redundancies, dwindling union membership and diminishing influence, the exercise of union power at the Olympics site has been largely symbolic. Diminishing union influence had implications for Marta's informal learning:

M: I now believe one of the really important things for a HRD practitioner to do is work out where are the power bases in the workplace; like who are the informal leaders, who are the people that can get things done for you – how power works in an organisation. I was not only theoretically predisposed to this, it was through my own experience.

JG: Can you clarify for me how you did experience this?

M: When I started, I thought David was my power base on the site. The reality was that the Construction Project Manager was a key power broker. Working that out didn't take long – but it was important. Power is segmented. Some workers with tremendous technical skills have power and influence, but this is not necessarily manoeuvrable.

By 'not necessarily manoeuvrable' Marta is referring to an implicit politics of power. Even for those construction workers who possess prized technical skills, a fine line exists between exercising influence within their own sphere of competence and speaking up on broader site and industrial issues. Marta's constant internal negotiation between self and workplace culture illustrates the subtle power affecting her learning about the workplace. One manifest outcome of this negotiation is the attempt at a surface appearance of alignment between the employee and the traits the corporation deems desirable and useful. In Marta's words 'gaining credibility' was important to her; it was also 'a big personal achievement'. But to gain this credibility she first had to learn, as the following dialogue reveals, that 'production was all important, and that training was valued in the rhetoric, but not necessarily in practice'. To gain credibility she had to prove that she was 'useful'.

Usefulness implies not only the possession of technical knowledge and skills but, as Edwards argues, the 'real use value of knowledge is tied in increasingly complex ways to optimising the efficiency of the "system"' (1994: 167). In the postmodern condition, optimising the efficiency of 'the system', includes producing the image of an appropriate fit between the worker and work culture, particularly on a high-profile site such as the Olympics. Some of the effects of this link between 'really useful knowledge' and image were particularly pertinent for Marta:

JG: Do you think the company might have used you and your role for its own imaging purposes?

M: If they did, I don't think it was exploitative. There was an agenda there: 'how can we [the company] demonstrate that we are a "learning organisation"?' But this was an agenda that I was not unhappy to play along with. I felt, in terms of language and literacy, I had a limited impact. But there were changes in other ways.

JG: Can you tell me a little more about those changes?

M: I was organised enough to know that I was being used by the company for image reasons – to have a professional female at the site promoting a 'learning organisation' – but I did not feel exploited. I didn't mind; I just knew it was happening. . . .

Anyway, I feel that the discourse precedes the change. Many have said the learning organisation and training of staff is given 'lip-service', but then what happens is people realise they need to make it work, or that *'lip-service' simply looks ridiculous*. Gaining credibility, in what was for me a fairly alien culture, was a big personal achievement. But I feel as though I could have done more, technically and professionally, but training was not particularly highly valued at the site. *Production was all important.* Training was valued in the rhetoric, but not in practice.

JG: Can you clarify what *you* mean by this?

M: Sometimes workers in industry see the skills of educators as too invisible – you can't see their product. Construction workers, for example, will say – 'we have built this and as such it represents our skills, but we can't actually *see* what educators *do*'. What counts is intimately connected to what society values and how that is translated through the system you are working in. It is also about *what is visible*.

Marta's comment – 'I feel that the discourse precedes the change' – partly reflects her theory about training needing to focus on language and communication practices as a commencement point for change. For instance, her experience of workers telling her 'the learning organisation and training of staff is given lip-service', has translated to the observation that 'then what happens is people realise they need to make it work, or that "lip-service" simply looks ridiculous'. Nonetheless, what is 'seen and valued' can vary considerably when one looks more deeply into public comments and compares them with private thoughts. 'Invisibility' was a recurring metaphor in Marta's story. Marta defines success beyond the traditional financial and directly observable achievement-oriented 'performance indicators'. Her personal definitions relate to the alignment of her inner beliefs, values and standards of ethics with her learning and competence in the role. This is not unusual for successful women in organisation development roles argues Kaplan:

> what the popular literature does not address are the multi-layered aspects of success within the context of a field in which successful women – socialised not to brag or compete with men – admit to difficulties identifying and giving themselves credit for their contributions. In addition they have ambivalent feelings about getting recognition for their work.
>
> (Kaplan 1995: 68)

Marta believed her contribution to the construction site was through relationships, through the support she could offer colleagues and the service she provided to those who needed language, literacy and computing skills. What is being argued is that there is a range of modes for 'being visible', and a range of dimensions to 'being useful' in construction contexts. That Marta may be comfortable with a 'support role' played out behind the scenes does not make it less useful or less valuable. What should be at the forefront is not so much the trainer, but one-dimensional views of what is important and what constitutes 'really useful knowledge'. It is the symbolic and communication patterns within Phaedrus which can marginalise Marta's type of contribution, again bringing into question the discursive practices of the corporation and personal adaptations to them.

The way Marta 'tells her story' also reveals significant differences from the way David tells his. The differences signify that both her gender and contractual relationship with the company influence the way she describes her training practices and her identity as a professional HR practitioner. In sharp contrast to David's presentation of self, the use of the first person pronoun 'I' in Marta's text reveals her sense of agency/self-regulation. While her text reveals similar experiential meanings to David's about the subordinate role of training relative to the primacy of production, Marta's frequent use of 'I' suggests a different construction of her professional identity.[3]

Nevertheless, both David and Marta 'play' with issues of visibility and invisibility of training in their stories. Each is attempting to come to terms with the compelling value and valuing of 'concrete' products within the construction industry compared to the unseen characteristics/products of education and training illustrating an effect of the panoptic gaze on one's professional practices.

Self-regulation: visibility and invisibility in workplace performance

Personal adaptations and resistance to the discursive practices of the corporation are present in informal workplace learning in some form at all times. Some of these adaptations are characterised by discrepancies between public behaviour and private thoughts. Identification with and internalisation of the corporate culture is always incomplete. Internal processes of resistance, not generally observable, remain a critical part of the trainers' response. Personal adaptations to the requirements of construction site culture included a range of strategies for self-survival: both outward expression and internalisation of the organisations' values related to a flexible no-demarcation, team and 'partnering' environment. But the processes of adaptation are riddled with conflict, intra- and inter-personal influences, autobiographical influences, local level politics and gender issues. The distinction between public and private thinking and behaviour is not so 'distinct' and subject to subtle discipline at work.

A feminist in macho-land

M: I've learned [about] the workplace culture here. . . . My values had to adapt. Gender issues, racism issues . . . things that might have been important to me . . . I had to develop a detached position in relation to these. . . . Why I was there was not to impose my value system on that place.

JG: Detached?

M: I think I was compromised a bit in what I believe. But part of being a professional trainer is that you learn to separate your own values from those you are working with. You have to have a public face and private thoughts that can be quite different. I would say that over time the things I believed in came to the fore.

JG: Could you give an example of that?

M: I brought in a 'Nelson Mandela cake' one day. I was making a statement against racism, although people may not have known what I had thought on this earlier. Also before I came here I had been working with women for many years. I have fairly radical ideas on gender equality. I have values and opinions which would be threatening to many men on the site. I am a strong feminist and many of the blokes here would see that as threatening. I've never said anything about that here. It is a question of professional distance.

Marta uses the metaphoric distinction between 'public face and private thoughts' as a justification for her apparent compromises. It is an example of self-regulation but also a means of constructing a kind of resistance which may well be very effective given the perceived constraints of the workplace. The Nelson Mandela cake was also a form of symbolic resistance to some of the workplace practices she opposed. The cake was shared with site managers in their shed. She viewed direct opposition or confrontation to be quite difficult and perhaps counterproductive. Celebrating symbolically the achievements of Mandela was intended to generate questions about unacceptable workplace practices, but it was also non-threatening, both to herself and the staff who were present. Through it she felt she had made a statement about things which really mattered to her. And she had learnt that this symbolic approach was tolerated by senior personnel.

The 'question of professional distance' was also the territory of tensions and dilemmas. Balancing what is important to oneself with what is required at a particular site gives an ethical dimension to informal learning – what ought one to do if one wishes to resist something? Marta's balancing, in other words self-regulation, is described by Marta explicitly and seemingly unselfconsciously. Balancing (self-regulating) her feminist values with corporate values and cultural practices was an important element of Marta's site-based learning:

M:　My feminism is something which doesn't have to be explored in my role. If I was trying to get ahead in the company, that might be very different. I think it would be more of a problem. But I've been able to 'skirt' that problem!

JG:　So, you've come directly from working virtually exclusively with women [in a previous job] into the construction industry.

M:　Yes, it was a shock. It was dramatic.

JG:　Could you tell me a little more about that shock?

M:　The shock was behavioural. How do you behave here as a woman? When I get up in the morning I wonder what I should wear because I don't want to look like a dag, I don't want to look too sexy, I've got to look professional, but I'm running around a construction site. So, you are constantly finding a line between being a woman in that role; relating to a lot of men that are not used to relating to women and I'm not really used to relating to men because of my background. You have to play certain games for a while. You have to be very careful because you don't know how your behaviour is going to be interpreted. You have to be very careful about how you go about presenting yourself in this context.

JG:　Given there are 400 men and three women involved in the actual construction, one could be forgiven for assuming this [gender imbalance] has had an effect on how you would be seeing yourself here.

M:　I see myself, in my own terms, as not having been very successful. I don't think that I have achieved the things I could have achieved in terms of range, numbers . . . like getting to a greater number of people. Then I began rationalising that one person in a context like this can only do so much. . . . There have also been incidental benefits to the company of me having been here. You can't always predict what the impact of an educator's role will be. I haven't been able to directly impact upon a lot of people here. My role has had indirect effects, simply by me being here. I think having me here represents a changed reality for many of the men. To have a woman on the site who is a language and literacy teacher is new for them. I've been able to be here, get involved with them in a learning capacity without them being threatened by it; without it changing their lives too drastically and without me thinking it might affect them drastically. The role has had pay-offs, not so much in a formal educational sense, but in changing their realities at work. . . . I've had frustrations and personal non-satisfaction about what I wanted to achieve, and I've had confusion. But it has not really been difficult. Aspects of it have been personally difficult such as having to deal with racism or gender discrimination which are covert rather than overt. But I was never unhappy. I knew the potential was there for me to be looked upon as a joke; I knew that it would take time. I knew that my success was dependent upon factors outside of my control.

Marta's text demonstrates the effects of self-regulation but it also shows that this regulation has not been entirely successful. Marta has not aligned her beliefs and values with those of the corporate culture. Her overt self-regulation and 'visible' practices around the gendered ways that have been institutionally constructed are exemplified throughout her narrative. Of particular interest in this text is the way Marta's explicit construction of her professional self is realised linguistically through the frequent thematisation of 'I'. This contrasts sharply and significantly with her shift to 'you' when she describes normative organisational behaviour – 'you have to be very careful because you don't know how your behaviour is going to be interpreted. You have to be very careful about how you go about presenting yourself in this context.' This shift to 'you' is suggestive of the tension she experiences in relation to the agency of her practices given the power of the 'other' in the construction of her work and thus professional identity.

A significant difference in the way Marta describes herself and her work is the minimal amount of con/textual reference compared to David's. Marta tends to construct her professional identity as separate from the production processes while David sees himself in relation to production processes. Perhaps this is a consequence of the difference in their employment contracts. But in Marta's self-analysis she ascribes (and then describes) her agency in the construction of her professional identity whereas David's professional identity is described by him as 'constructed' by production processes.

The exercise of power at the site and the notion of a panoptic gaze were certainly factors outside of Marta's professional control. A major effect of the panopticon, according to Foucault (1977: 201) is to induce a state of conscious and permanent visibility that assumes the automatic functioning of power. Although Marta is not a prisoner at the site her performance is constantly observed (and she acts accordingly). It would be naive not to realise that the professional women at the site face both overt and covert scrutiny of their clothing and appearance every day. Women in the Australian construction context remain few. Their on-site presence is a novelty; a novelty managed by Marta through careful attention to her presentation of self in everyday work life. Goffman referred to this as an art of 'impression management; a performance best understood as a protective practice' (1959: 208). A protective practice that cannot be divorced from the exercise and distribution of power relations throughout the site.

Performing competently under the gaze

'Success' for David also depended on many factors outside his control. For instance, the training unit was set up to be a cost recovery, or profit-generating company (as distinct from a corporate overhead), but a lot of time is spent convincing people about the sort of money required to simply recover costs. David finds that about 40 per cent of his time goes on marketing and administration. What this does is force the hourly rate up to $150 to $200 per hour just to recover costs. A Foucauldian reading of this practice is that David's informal learning is being disciplined. He is being 'trained' to perform in quite specific ways. In this context, hierarchical observation and normalising judgment are combined in a procedure that demands measurable 'cost recovery' from training activities. Also, his experience depends on corporate storytelling related to the need to present the 'correct' corporate image mediated through the way training is carried out.

Within conventional HRD practices, the worker is often presented as 'foremost', a social being seeking fulfilment of his or her need to 'belong' to the group relations or workplace 'team'. David, while complying with the corporation's culture and expectations, points out that 'group norms' can be a real problem in the company – working long hours and weekends. Working long hours and weekends, up to sixty or seventy hours a week, was fairly typical within Phaedrus. Many of the workers commenced at 6.30 or 7 a.m., and continued until well after 5 p.m. Some construction workers were paid overtime allowances; others were not. But being conspicuously dedicated to the job by working long hours was a part of the company culture. It is highlighting the corporation's hold over the behaviour of staff. If you do not work the long hours you can be accused not so much of letting the corporation down, but of the far worse offence of letting down your own team, your own mates. This panoptic gaze is a part of a collective (corporate) story that ensures individuals comply with group norms, and exemplifies a deterioration in industrial conditions.

A part of David's adaptation to the panoptic gaze of the site entailed what he describes as his 'phantom-like' approach to the role. Becoming a 'phantom' at the site suited the arrangement of work with its personal and inter-personal tensions. For instance, there was 'the cost-recovery thing' (David's words) in relation to his consulting time; there was his sense of not wanting to 'get in the way of production' and there were the purposes for which information about workers' competencies were being used:

D: I don't mind having a phantom-like role. Within Phaedrus I'm confident about this now as they are still using me. I don't get the credit for some things I facilitate, and nor should I, because all I might have done is provide the basics – the right people at the right time and the resources for them to use.

JG: Isn't there a skill in selecting the right people at the right time and in knowing the appropriate resources?

D: Oh yes, skill and a system. I have developed a skills database and I guess I can take some credit for that. The system works well. I try to make sure people know about this system. The system recognises their skills and they get paid for it.

JG: It seems ironic that *you* set the system up, but to be rewarded you really need to come from production and make use of the system to have skills noticed. In the meantime, *you* disappear, phantom-like, back into the corporation.

D: Yes, it highlights something which all salaried staff experience. When you negotiate individual salaries you are at a distinct disadvantage unless you are a real key person in the company, such as a key decision-maker, or if you happen to hoard a really key skill that no one else has. The same thing happens to managers who are on salary. . . . Who can really tell what the differences are between them [managers] – it is very complex. I'm not sure what the impact of the competency-based standards movement will be on this. I'm sceptical, for example, when it came to downsizing in

> our company, the Industrial Relations people began the redundancy program in the traditional way – tainted by who likes whom. Now they have much more information to base their decisions on.

JG: Are competency-based standards being used to assist decision-makers about who should be made redundant?

D: Yes. The information they now have – upon which to make decisions about who goes – is much greater than before. The information base for this purpose used to be quite shallow.

David's description of himself in the 'phantom-like' role is significant. When explaining this phantom-like role he shifts away from the 'you' – the 'other' – to the more personalised 'I'. In this shift his role analysis is within the safety of the phantom role enabling him to acknowledge his own agency in work practices. It is significant as David describes himself in a way that amplifies the power and influence of the panoptic gaze on the construction of professional identity, regulating the in/visibility of one's performance.

Becoming 'phantom-like' also indicates a self-strategy based on his experience of corporate change, the exercise of power and compliance-seeking processes such as salary negotiations: 'when you negotiate individual salaries you are at a distinct disadvantage unless you are a real key person in the company'; or downsizing: 'now they have much more information to base their decisions on'. What David learns informally encompasses an internal dialogue about his location within the corporate change process and about the role he is required to perform in effecting desired corporate changes. There is no finality to the meaning-making which comes from this internal dialogue. But there is an important challenge to the beliefs and values to which one subscribes. How much do you accommodate, how much do you resist? How much space for resistance is left? How does one go about resisting the panoptic corporate gaze?

Clarifying their own (values) positions in relation to competency-based standards (CBS) is a critical issue facing trainers and staff developers in many industries. Competencies *are* being used as data to inform corporations about their redundancy decisions. They can be readily theorised as an effect of the panopticon at work – a new form of surveillance in the guise of 'humanising' and objectifying performance. This sharpens the need for practitioners to clarify their own roles in relation to the development and deployment of competency-based standards. Without clarification, they can perform as clerks and technicians of corporate change, as the assessment of competence can become double-edged; it can cut one (or one's colleagues) out of a job.

Concluding comments

A contemporary human resource project for many employers and managers is to align productivity, efficiency and competitiveness with the 'humanisation of work'. Empowerment and self-direction are central methods of this project – manifest in the promotion of workplace learning. Chapter 4 examined how technologies to enhance workplace learning are subject to the micro-politics and power relations that 'educate' professional practitioners in their daily practice. This chapter elaborates this theorisation through the stories of Marta and David, that worker subjectivity and professional identity are subject to powerful discursive workplace influences and imperatives. I have focused on discourses of staff development, learning and training which construct and promote certain valued kinds of identity. It would be unusual for staff development and training not to be seen as serving corporate outcomes, but what has changed is that empowerment and self-direction are now seen as necessary to the achievement of corporate outcomes. These *are* now corporate 'group norms'. The stories told here, however, reveal that 'benefits' to individuals are partial and more complex than often implied.

Workers are active in their compliance with an ensemble of disciplinary practices that have significant implications for workplace learning, skill development and knowledge transfer. Experience of workplaces, power relations, 'group norms', team-work, shared e-mail systems, performance appraisal mechanisms and so on influence what/how performative knowledge is constructed by the learner. The stories of Marta and David illustrate quite graphically how professional identities are discursively produced within and against corporate power relations and how 'active subjects' self-regulate through personal adaptations to, and interpretations of, appropriate professional positioning.

Learning in this workplace was subject to a range of subtle, at times powerful forces – the hidden curricula of workplace learning. In adopting a post-structural theorisation of workplace learning, ways are identified in which the 'workplace curriculum' is developed through discursive corporate practices, power relations, gender, and image-making technologies that 'discipline subjects'. This should not be read as entirely deterministic. Corporations require active subjects, as active subjects can align their goals and aspirations to those of the corporation. Self-regulation doesn't work with passive subjects. Only active subjects can control themselves, and perform competently – an imperative linked to the disciplinary agendas of the workplace.

Performing competently and having the performance recognised is clearly effected by a panoptic gaze of contemporary workplaces – a gaze embedded in the dominant social discourses and cultural practices of the moment. At this moment such dominant social discourses and cultural practices include the alignment of formal educational goals with industry demands and workplace imperatives. It is an era of 'performativity'.

Notes

1   The term 'texts' here is used in the postmodern sense that knowledge of the real is textual, that is 'always already signified, interpreted or "written" and, therefore, a "reading" which can be "rewritten" and "reread". Hence there is neither an originary point of knowledge nor a final interpretation. . . . Readings of the postmodern "text" are thus subject to contingency and the historical moment in which it is read. Given that the object of research is open to contest, all claims to presence, to an unmediated self and an unmediated knowledgeability, are always problematic' (Usher, Bryant and Johnston 1997: 207–8). Also see the Glossary for a brief explanation of 'deconstruction', 'hermeneutics' and 'semiotics'.

2   I am indebted to Nicky Solomon for bringing this language analysis into the study. This chapter builds on some of our previous joint work including Garrick, J. and Solomon, N. (1997) *Learning at Work: Identity and Self-regulation.* Presented to the 5th International Conference on Post-compulsory Education and Training, *Good Thinking – Good Practice: Research Perspectives on Learning and Work*, vol. 1, pp. 53–66. Centre for Learning and Work Research, Griffith University, Brisbane, 26–29 November.

3   This analytical point was made by Nicky Solomon.

6 The performativity principle in informal learning

> Knowledge is and will be produced in order to be sold, it is and will be consumed in order to be valorised in a new production: in both cases, the goal is exchange. Knowledge ceases to be an end in itself, it loses its 'use-value'.
>
> (Lyotard 1984: 4)

The new links between industry and education

Lyotard is making the point that the nature of knowledge cannot survive unchanged within the context of the general social transformation he terms 'the postmodern condition', and that 'useful' knowledge is increasingly based on 'performativity'. In this chapter I draw on Lyotard's notion of 'performativity' to interpret changes occurring in the development of 'valid' knowledge and the new linkages between industry and education. Performativity follows the principle of optimal performance:

> maximising output (the information or modifications obtained) and minimising input (the energy expended in the process) . . . it is a game pertaining not to the true, the just, or the beautiful, etc., but to efficiency: a technical move is 'good' when it does better and/or expends less energy than another.
>
> (Lyotard 1984: 44)

For Lyotard, performativity is the best possible input/output equation, and this chapter uses narrative accounts from the Sydney 2000 Olympic Games developments to illustrate ways in which the state and private companies construct this equation through financial and production discourses. It is argued that the transmission of knowledge through work-based learning and formal education is grossly affected by the performativity principle.

The new linkages between industry and education centre on the technical-rational discourse of 'competence'. Competency-based standards are intended to widen the scope of vocational education and training and are now extending throughout national education systems. They even reach children in elementary school and are couched in discourses that use 'national interests' as their justification. Supporters of competency-based approaches to education and training argue that competencies do 'in fact' improve performativity by offering 'objective' criteria against which someone's output can be judged. For instance, workers or learners have available to them a centrally determined, pre-defined set of standards to work towards. The standards provide the technical criteria which influences (determines) the 'truth' about performance. They are a social framework for revealing workplace 'realities' in which the goal of learning becomes 'competence demonstrated in specific ways' (Usher and Edwards 1994: 115).

> The emphasis on performance is a part of the 'no nonsense' management style of discourse that has become so powerful since the 1980s . . . it does not make sense to be managed 'inefficiently' or 'ineffectively'. We require 'value for money' and 'quality' of goods and services. If this is obtained through effective and efficient management, then all to the good.
>
> (Usher and Edwards 1994: 112)

The HRD practitioners at the Olympics sites were on the front line of implementing competency-based training for workers and then seeking its formal accreditation. Their mini-narratives[1] can be read as symbolic of the industry–education interface.

Competence as a metaphor

Competency-based standards are not so much a metaphor for technical-rationalism but more a set of tools used by technical-rationalism to disguise and make more palatable some of its operations. Rational HRD practices rely on a range of means-enhancing devices such as psychometric analyses, technical competence, linear thinking and instrumental reason. Work-based learning and training can be viewed as delivery systems within which the worth of HRD operatives, or learning facilitators, is defined in terms of the skills, or sets of competencies, they possess that match the technical-rational systems procedures. This is a technical-rationalist picture that Parker (1997: 4) correctly observes 'is easily the most prevalent one on the market today. . . . Rationality is judged solely in terms of the efficiency of means in achieving ends'. This cultural context will be very familiar to many managers and HRD practitioners even though such a 'reality' may be unsettling. Competency-based standards disguise the ways power operates in particular sites and their implementation has some specific consequences for the ways practitioners operate. One consequence is that they can (pre)determine ways in which one sees others perform.

Aphorisms of competence

The stories of David and Marta from the Sydney Olympics construction sites make clear the complexities which surround the term 'informal learning'. Contested notions about the roles and purposes of HRD practice and the links between management, industrial relations, training and the broader industry–education interface are shown to directly impact on what practitioners learn through engagement with the job. Their stories also highlight the influences on informal learning of felt experience through personal goals, unconscious desires, motivations and autobiography. The search for a stronger definition of informal learning than currently exists reveals that there is no underlying 'truth' about it, no unifying or reducible pattern which might enable greater prediction or certainty. Nevertheless, one implication of this study is that HRD professionals need to acknowledge the extent to which informal learning is discursively constructed in particular work contexts and understand its depths and complexities in order to perform. This means more than aligning informal learning with the pre-determined competencies. Marta's (M) account illustrates some of the difficulties of trying overtly to connect informal learning with preset competencies. Her resistance to seeing others through the lens of modularised building blocks is self-evident.

Aphorism one: competence as 'non-judgmental'

M: [As an HRD practitioner] You have to *value what people do know, rather than judge* them on what they don't know. A lot of cross-cultural training has helped me in this. People always bring a lot into a learning situation. *You have to work from that premise.* . . . I think with learning and teaching there is always a temptation to use your knowledge as a power base. So, if people misspell something, for example, you do have the power to point that out to them. I think the way in which you do that indicates to the person that it is not necessarily a power differential. So I think they just know. To an extent you have to de-power the role of the trainer in order to empower the learner. I think this is a very important issue. People learn when they are motivated to learn, and they won't be motivated to learn if they are threatened. The predisposition to learning comes from people believing they can learn – which relates to how they are treated in the learning context. . . . People have to be trained in a certain way; *knowledge is transmitted in a certain way*. People however learn in different ways. *Formal learning is very rigid* in the way it deals with people's learning. It has to be tied to institutional requirements. You shouldn't place a judgment on how people learn. If you are looking for competencies there, you are looking for important approaches to *how people see others* who have not learned formally. There is a pendulum which swings between formal education and the informal learning which goes on at work.

'How people see others' and 'valuing what people do know' are nominalisms in Marta's account. They express a humanistic discourse in which subjects are valued for knowing what they want to learn and have natural tendencies towards self-directedness which can be inhibited by formal (institutional), teacher-controlled education, in her words – 'formal learning is very rigid in the way it deals with people's learning. It has to be tied to institutional requirements'. Usher (1996: 106) points out that such a 'humanistic subject provides a means for constructing and demonising institutionalised, provider-led education as the "other"' In contrast, competency-based training in the workplace can be constructed as the only means of providing the right conditions for releasing workers' natural tendencies to learn. It gains a 'progressive' learner-centred image which has been (and is) very attractive to employers and unions. It is attractive to employers for its links to performativity, and it is attractive to unions for its non-elitist image and accompanying rhetoric about clearer career and training pathways for workers in all industries.

In this front-line dialogue, however, Marta expresses concern about the inability of competency-based standards to promote and reflect diversity in learning and practice. She is particularly concerned about pre-determined goals framing the principal learning outcomes and that anything critical, theoretical, abstract or simply not directly applicable to immediate tasks is not particularly prized in a competency-based framework, perhaps inadvertently denigrated. Quixotically, she also makes a case that, in some instances, the codified, pre-determined approach to learning outcomes helps in the recognition of informally acquired skills. They can also serve institutional and company ends by clarifying where primary responsibility for learning resides – with the flexible self-directed individuals who now have the opportunity to see, rationally and 'objectively', what they need to do to progress competently.

JG: At this site, where do you see primary responsibility for learning residing – with individuals, organisations, formal institutions, your training program?

M: This might come back to the formal/informal learning thing. I know I've learned an enormous amount here. I've learned about the way people do things here. But I don't feel I've learned anything new. No, that's not quite right. It's more like the layers of learning were re-experienced . . . in a new cultural context. It was like re-layered knowledge. So, it was like 'here it is again', I've come across this before but in a different context. Like learning how to behave. You've learned it before, so it's not a new experience. It's a relearning of something you've actually known. It's not that the challenges were not great enough. Not at all. I've learned a lot about negotiation, about the company, about life on building sites. All that is new. But in the overall experience, I don't think there is anything about myself that it has faced me with. A lot of it has been relearning information about the way things work. It's re-applying strategies you already know, locating those strategies in a new culture.

From my experience I would have to say that industry can harm education if it is only an industry/production agenda which is being pursued. Many in industry think educational goals are *too social*, and often educators think industry is too focused *on production* and business bottom lines. Finding the right balance is important, but not so easy.

Marta's use of the metaphor 're-layered knowledge' – 'like the layers of learning were re-experienced . . . in a new cultural context' – is linked to her search for knowledge of herself and for self-regulation, as shown in Chapter 5. For Marta, a principal challenge of her learning was whether it 'faced her with anything new about herself'. A Foucauldian reading of this challenge raises the issue of the relationship between knowledge and power. Foucault seeks to show how the inculcation of a 'discipline of self-control' has generated an imperative to seek 'knowledge of the self' (Hutton 1988: 131). In Phaedrus, everyone is called upon to monitor her or his own behaviour. For Marta, the technologies of self-management related to 're-learning information and re-applying strategies you already know – in a new culture'. The re-application of self-strategies is redolent of Foucault's argument that 'we continually reshape our past creations to conform with our present needs, a pattern of creation and constraint that is ceaselessly repeated' (Hutton 1988: 137). For Foucault, past experiences are lost in the maze of formulas humans have created to classify them:

> we discover our identity not by fathoming the original meaning of behaviour precedents, as Freud taught, but rather by deconstructing the formalities through which we endlessly examine, evaluate and classify our experiences. . . . Whereas Freud asks 'how our past experience shapes our lives in the present', Foucault asks 'why we seek to discover truth in the formal rules that we have designed to discipline life's experience'.
>
> (Hutton 1988: 136)

The 'rules' at the Olympic Games site that had disciplinary effects on Marta are embedded in her comment: 'many in industry think educational goals are too social, and often educators think industry is too focused on production and business bottom lines.' In finding the so-called 'right balance', the trainers relied on the industry's competency-based standards to objectify what workers were learning. But as shown in Chapter 5, implementation of the standards was subject to an ensemble of industrial relations considerations. These were sometimes at odds with Marta's personal standpoints on education goals, which were related to notions of 'social justice', 'equality of opportunity' and 'anti-discrimination'. In her site-based training 'negotiations', such goals were overwhelmed by Olympic construction imperatives. Butler describes this aspect of performativity as the relation of 'being implicated in that which one opposes [which contains possibilities] for turning power against itself to produce alternative modalities of power' (Butler 1993: 241).

It is precisely these types of ideological and theoretical matters that are not adequately expressed in the language of competency-based standards, because, as this study makes clear, site-level interpretations privilege conceptions of knowledge and understanding equated to *getting the job done*. That is, according to common site rhetoric, '*done* on time, under budget and with the "quality finish" that will satisfy the client'. In this analysis, it is therefore little wonder that Marta senses the pendulum has swung in favour of work-based learning in the present (post-industrial) juncture.

Aphorism two: competence as part of the 'seamless web' of corporate learning

The power which technical-rationalism currently exerts over HRD and management can be judged by the extent to which a vocabulary of discrete competencies defines the concept of professional practice. For technical-rationalists, the curriculum is a cog in the delivery system, albeit a significant one. In workplaces, learning is currently packaged as a 'systems' issue. For the most part, what is 'right' is framed by the theoretical perspectives one holds, whether these perspectives are implicit or have been developed through formal education. As I have argued in earlier chapters, the prevalent theory of workplace learning rests on the assumptions of human capital theory and what Senge (1994), in his influential field book for building a learning organisation, calls 'systems thinking'. The power of such metaphors has consequences for the way in which we describe and construct our own practices. David's informal learning at the site, coupled with his formal trade background, exemplifies how this intersection of discourses led him to the conclusion that 'nothing must get in the way of production'. David (D) has a formal trade and technical and further education (TAFE) background. This has a direct impact on his theories about learning in the workplace. Briefly recapitulating his words:

> *Learning to me now has to be woven so much into the production process* that they often won't even realise that they are learning. It took me a while to really learn about the primacy of production. Production is number one. That has to happen at all costs. No matter how important the training or learning is – it mustn't get in the way of that.... *Training is [being] integrated into everyone's job.*

The corporation is devolving training functions 'into everyone's job'. This new, supposedly seamless web of corporate learning and training is coupled with the view that competency-based standards represent 'useful' knowledge. Ironically, David saw CBS as 'irrelevant' to him personally, partly because he doesn't see himself as a trainer any longer. In his words, 'I'm in a skills-management role and systems development really'. His argument that CBS may be 'useful to provide more of a focus [for the] boundaryless roles in the company' is common in the managerial discourse which supports competency-based standards as support for corporate emphases on team-work, peer learning, self-directed learning and the integration of training 'into everyone's role'. The 'usefulness' of the competency frameworks therefore extends far beyond the simple clarification of roles, occupational or career pathways and skill formation requirements. It begins to re-frame what is recognised as knowledge.

For Lyotard (1984: 51) the distinction between the modern and postmodern conditions of knowledge rests in the purpose of knowledge. Lyotard argues that, in modernity, the production and dissemination of knowledge was justified on the grounds that it contributed to the pursuit of truth and/or the liberty of humanity. In an era of postmodern doubt and uncertainty exacerbated by environmental degradation, nuclear testing, global warming and continued exploitation of developing countries, the 'metanarratives' which legitimated 'truth' and 'liberty' are unsustainable (Edwards 1994: 166).

The criterion of optimising the efficient performance of the system has thus become increasingly a basis for conceptualising what *is* important knowledge. 'The question (overt or implied) now asked by the professionalist student, the State, or institutions of higher education is no longer "is it true?" but "What use is it?"' (Lyotard 1984: 51). At the level of personal experience, David's mini-narrative exemplifies this precisely: 'nothing must get in the way of production . . . and training must become invisible, woven into production processes'. His story is steeped in the ideas and beliefs held within the organisation which are framed, at the macro-level, by corporate uncertainty. This macro-level framing of competency-based standards by major industry groups, big unions and governments presents them as a useful device for creating a sense of greater certainty, and developing new grounds for industrial relations negotiations. The use of competency-based standards and training as grounds for industrial relations is less volatile than conventional remuneration and hours/conditions bargaining that has previously characterised the building and construction industry. The connections between industrial relations and training are meant to clarify career pathways, skill formation processes and assessment procedures. Through these processes and procedures learning becomes an *observable commodity*.

A more observable, measurable notion of learning is meant to help the overall business environment. As a favourable by-product, competency-based standards are meant to assist workers to clarify what they need to learn to advance in their careers (or, at least, this is the line accepted by unions). Codified sets of standards, benchmarks and competencies are managerial answers to corporate dissonance in the context of the flexible accumulation of capital. They are artefacts in response to doubt and uncertainty, and in alignment with the discourses of performativity and economic competitiveness. The economistic drive to identify and label informal learning to boost its productive potential has been influential on HRD practices. As David put it, reflecting the corporate philosophy, the drive to have learning 'woven into the production process' and to have that learning formally accredited is powerful.

David and Marta were required to deal in some way with power relations at the site every day, with a never-stated coercion implied – if you don't like what you are required to do, then get out! Periodically, conflict between personal values and workplace directions resulted in Marta and David experiencing dilemmas and some desires for resistance. Desires for resistance related to opposing dominant workplace expectations of, and managerial purposes for, training. As Marta and David both say, it is a 'brutally honest' and at times ruthless environment in which resistance can quickly lead to the termination of employment – highlighting the need for HRD practitioners to be aware of what they are doing and why. The mini-narratives have illustrated how causes and effects of resistance produce strong emotional responses, and informal learning may be found within this terrain of 'dealing with' or reflecting upon emotional experiences.

Yet the links between dealing with emotional experience and the trainer's intentionality in their own learning remain cloudy. How much agency does a person really have? If any? At the level of individual subjectivity, reflexivity, emotions, implicit/informal theories held, one's formal education, capacities to interpret experience (meta-cognition), gender issues and personal beliefs affect informal learning. At structural levels, the organisation of work, the materiality of construction, the recognition, feedback and reward systems of the corporation apply. Informal learning is inseparable from the dialectical relationship between the social and the self. Following Lyotard, in the contemporary context of the mercantilisation of knowledge, a key question about informal learning becomes: 'Is it saleable?' And in the context of power-growth: 'Is it efficient?' In post-industrial workplaces having competence does seem saleable, but the direct alignment of informal learning with knowledge written in terms of clearly defined competencies remains problematic. The bridges between informal learning and competency-based standards are not so simplistic or definable. This becomes problematic because competencies are efficient and 'what no longer makes the grade is competence as defined by other criteria true/false, just/unjust, etc. – and, of course, low performativity in general' (Lyotard 1984: 51).

An implication of the dialectic of self/society in this story is that if informal learning is to have any influence on management and HRD theory and practice, it needs to be submitted to different forms of methodologies and critical review. As Chalofsky (1996: 292) points out, informal learning *is* important in organisations, but can entail 'antagonisms' – 'like the Chinese concept of yin and yang, everything . . . depends on opposite forces being in balance. . . . A dynamic balance, not a static one'. For HRD practices, this might mean addressing the antagonisms and power formations within workplaces and learning how to use the power relations to modify the organisation or system.

In this study Marta and David were required to attend regular meetings with both senior management and Phaedrus's foremen, who unequivocally spelled out expectations of compliance with production schedules. This had the effect of marginalising the voices of the HRD practitioners. However, the practitioner's voice is only marginalised if she or he allows it to be so. Modifying an organisation's culture, if that is the goal, does not always mean direct confrontation, nor can the practitioners ignore the organisation's goals. It appears that the HRD practitioners' voice will be discounted until they *show* they understand and *speak* the language of the organisation, understand how to leverage power (through developing strategic alliances and so on), and can *demonstrate* their worth to the company. How they play out their 'visibility' in particular situations has been shown to be a key in their learning from experience.

The notion of 'situatedness' and the critical role of emotion in learning highlight flaws in the current drive to account for and 'recognise' informal learning. For example, tightly bound, neatly compartmentalised, observable 'elements' and 'units' of competence – ripe for measurement and, as the study suggests, surveillance – are only one aspect of informal learning. Check-lists of competencies do not acknowledge their discursive construction. Nor do they adequately represent some of the principal characteristics of informal learning – individuals' abilities to 'adapt' to a site, the self-strategies of resistance and accommodation which accompany 'felt experience', negotiations of personal values with work requirements, and the presentation of oneself in the everyday. These relate to the shaping influences of workplace culture – its politics, power relations, the management of HRD functions, the links between training and industrial relations, the networks, peers and mentors, and the significations which come from recognition and feedback.

Networks, peers and mentors

Mentors, peers and networks are commonly cited as important in promoting learning from experience. A range of approaches to each of these is advocated, from formalised procedures to informal sponta- neous connections. This section focuses on how each of these terms – networks, peers, mentors – is used in HRD theory and practice. Some postmodern ideas about the 'technical' deployment of these strategies are considered, as 'helping' others to learn can, in various ways, conceal power relations and performativity imperatives. From the following vignettes, the position of mentors or peers in the work hier- archy is less important than their abilities to promote professional interests, ideas and plans. Sometimes this comes in the form of 'devil's advocacy', which came from surprising sources at the Olympics site. Construction workers employed in the first-aid hut were one such source for both David and Marta (and in due course, myself). But networks are not always reliable. Hearsay may be very influential in shaping situated or implicit knowledge/information held about work at a particular site, and dialogue too can have a down side if it creates what Boje describes as 'a unilateral consensus' (1995: 1029) – a consensus which silences marginalised voices.

The construction of 'bonds' that really bind

In the 'systems' approach to creating learning organisations, a desired corporate effect is for bonds that bind workers to each other and to the company. To an extent this reflects the origins of the Western appropri- ation of Japanese management and industrial relations concepts. Japanese productivity at a national level has been attributed (since Demming) to the existence of deep social bonds between Japanese workers and their companies. US and European companies have attempted to construct similar allegiances between workers and companies through devices such as 'coaches', 'mentors', 'peer instruc- tion' and so on. These are processes that extend into everyday activities. They are intended to be embedded in work activities in such ways that workers will not even notice that they are 'learning'. Yet these processes are a part of corporate discourse and design. In relation to the corporate desire to create binding bonds, I asked David about his own informal networks and how these had affected his own learning in Phaedrus. His comments are indicative of how powerful these constructed bonds can be:

D: Hearsay and informal networks are extremely influential. For example the other day, the Chief Executive – I can't say exactly what he said – but it related to the importance of immersing yourself in the culture; he mentioned we *might* be heading into China in the near future, and the sorts of changes the company may be heading into. There are dilemmas in shaping your own career – company strategic directions have a big role to play in this. . . . The network, the powerful hearsay . . . it's complex. I've begun to network with the powerful influences in the corporation – both inside and outside, in the community. This is partly a self-preservation thing. *But I don't mind this.* I'm starting to see that politics are bloody important.

JG: Have you ever had a mentor?

D: Yes, informally. . . . I've learned a lot from a few mentors in Head Office. They've helped me understand the culture. Understanding the processes of the culture has been really important in this. This has happened without any conscious effort. Where it happens overtly it has negative side effects . . . it feels patronising and turns you off. Well-worded comments from the Chairman also have a focusing effect.

Networks, peers and mentors have helped David to '*understand the processes of the culture. . . . This has happened without any conscious effort. Where it happens overtly it has negative side-effects . . . it feels patronising and turns you off*'. The incorporation of David into the corporate culture is reflected in his above comments. But he is, to an extent, a willing subject who wishes to participate actively in promoting the corporate culture. He wants to promote the new team focus, learning with and from peers and mentors. This narrative tells of a connection between the transmission of corporate culture and the reproduction of skills. David's role is a symbolic and material link in this transmission – through his education and training function. The corporation is not overtly dominating every facet of what is being learnt. Those who are promoting the new 'learning organisations' consider team and co-operative approaches 'good', containing transformative potentials for individuals and the deeper benefits of 'virtual' family-like bonds.

Deep paradoxes can be found within these constructed bonds. The overt domination of the corporation has shifted into the territory of covert shaping of internal staff relationships, including through mentoring, peer learning procedures and learning networks. Employees such as David, who willingly belong to these corporate networks, are now giving more of themselves to corporate objectives than before:

D: Events at home, your whole life impacts on what you are doing at work. I go to bed at about 12 and get up at 6 and don't take holidays any more. I don't have time to think about all this much. I've been feeling tired lately. I feel like I'm setting myself up for a disaster.

JG: Disaster?

D: I don't like to think about this at work. I reflect on the train, it's about a one hour trip; arrive at work at 7.50 [a.m.].

JG: Can you tell me a little about your train trip in to work every day?

D: I do two things. One of two. I either sleep, if I haven't had enough, or I plan what I'm going to do for the day. I find I can think more clearly on the train. That's why I suggested we meet here at the Olympics site today. We are relatively free of disturbances. We have an open plan office [at Head Office] which can drive me nuts. *There is no privacy* and constant distractions. When you are working under pressure this is a problem. It has its good points of course. In the team situation, *someone always wants you*. Five minutes here and there, all of a sudden you've lost an hour. *You often have to catch up at home on weekends.* ... With the open plan office, it's difficult not to be drawn into other conversations. The time to reflect on what is going on is not there. The train is very important in this. I recently drove in and lost that reflection time on the train and really felt the loss.

In the corporate drive for team-work and 'empowered' workers there is an accompanying simulated 'team environment'. The emphasis on team-work is related to the performativity criterion in knowledge:

> In general, teamwork does in fact improve performance, if it is done under certain conditions. ... In particular it has been established that teamwork is especially successful in improving performativity within the framework of a given model, that is, for the implementation of a task. Its advantages seem less certain when the need is to 'imagine' new models.
>
> (Lyotard 1984: 53)

The corporation's belief that team-work does in fact improve performance led to people actually being forced to communicate with each other by proximity. For David, this is exemplified in his comments that 'there is no privacy' and 'someone always wants you' with a result being 'you often have to catch up at home on weekends' and his sense of impending personal disaster. This is not so much a matter of his (lack of) 'time-management' skills but the corporate attempt to engineer a team environment and its reach into the personal domain. Away from Head Office, David had some breathing-space where he and Marta were quickly required to learn from each other. But they learned different things and in different ways. Marta's story suggests (prompted by my question about gender influences) that structural features of the workplace, although important, were not the principal effects on her work-based learning.

Learning about the 'dark side' (and situated ethics)

Marta's support network assisted her in dealing with some emotional aspects of the job – what she refers to as 'the darker side of life'. In responding to the darker side she was faced with ethical dilemmas about what she ought to do. Her strategies were based on separating 'the personal' from 'the professional'. What she terms 'supportive others' helped make this strategy work for her. Situated ethics, gender and 'networking' are themes reflected in her self-strategies, as the following dialogue illustrates:

JG: Has there been anything in this job which has drawn strong emotions from you?

M: Yes. I've encountered *racism* which has made me angry. But I have an understanding of why it exists, and the framework that it is within. So, it's not something that I have reacted to.

JG: You still sound angry about this. What have you done with your anger?

M: What *I* always do with anger, *I* would talk about it to other people who are sympathetic to this type of injustice. So, it doesn't help to react in a direct sense as a constructive way of dealing with it. This is a learned response because; two things – it's where *I'm* coming from, my values base; but *I'm* in a work situation. *I* don't necessarily have to work with such people for the rest of my life, so it is something *I* tolerate in a professional capacity much the same as a doctor might have to treat someone they don't particularly like. *You* would still treat that person.

JG: That must have a big effect on you?

M: I think it does. It is de-powering. Having to deal with the darker side of life for anybody is not a pleasant experience. Much the same as a concentration camp. You have to debrief, discuss it. And if it is too bad, you remove yourself from it. You don't want to be too exposed to those feelings.

JG: Do you think your gender has affected this?

M: Yes it has. . . . This environment can be *brutally honest sometimes,* but in some ways refreshing. If I had been younger, single and more attractive, I'm not sure. I think it would have been a very different ball game.

The disempowerment of Marta is symptomatic of a complex of disguising and using power. Marta as a trainer employed by the company to 'treat' language and literacy problems is asserting her 'professional distance' to protect her own dignity in the face of the 'darker side'. Exercise of covert power is functional, in part because Marta believes, as her medical analogy suggests, that through her professional role she can at least do some good: 'You would still treat that person'. For the construction workers, racism appears to be one way of asserting a form of power from what is the relatively powerless situation of requiring language and literacy assistance. There may well be some testing of Marta in this. She does not have the authority to damage their positions particularly, but she has the power to help them with problems that can (and do) carry social stigma. Maintaining a balance between allowing herself to be tested in order to 'help' is subtle and delicate. But as Marta says, she does not want to be 'too exposed to those [dark side] feelings'.

Recognition and feedback: what counts in Head Office?

The context of intersubjectivity means that every transaction is not simply a question of communicating information or intended meanings. Every communicative act is also a plea for recognition of the subject by the other, a plea which is routed through the Other (the unconscious). Speech itself can be seen as the means by which recognition is implicitly asked for, although not necessarily given, and according to Lacan can never be fully given. Even the most apparently straightforward act of communicating 'facts' has within it this implied plea and an implied positioning of the other in relation to the subject. The other's confirmation of or failure to confirm the ascribed position then 'returns to' and determines the subject's position and hence whether the plea for recognition has been heard and responded to (Usher and Edwards 1994: 71).

There are contested meanings about the HRD roles and purposes at the site – should training be profit-making? Who ought to pay for it? Should its primary purpose be to aid industrial relations harmony, or something else? How should 'competence' be defined, implemented and assessed? What formal recognition procedures (if any) should accompany training? How should HRD personnel fit in with the new team and partnering emphases? These questions are associated with recognition and feedback and have vital effects on informal learning.

Recognition and feedback come formally and informally.[2] As occupational boundaries increasingly dissolve, feedback can emanate from very diverse sources. Increasingly, but not conclusively, the new corporate culture's effort to establish team bonds and emotional commitments among team members is effective in this. As Lasch (1984) argues, 'the team-family culture bolsters a fragile corporate self formed under the influence of traditional hierarchies and weakened by the cultural narcissism of advanced industrial society' (cited in Casey 1995: 150). The point is that *belonging* to a corporate family, complying with its processes – including recognition and feedback systems – provides a compensatory effect to the 'acutely ambivalent and conflictual self' (Casey 1995: 150). That the employee feels valued and, in this instance, belongs to a major construction project, helps eliminate resistance. It helps maintain a corporatised self. It holds the promise of a future gratification. David's experience of the corporate recognition and reward system shows that a part of the gratification promise relates to one's *image*:

JG: Who notices *your* learning?

D: *Who notices?* Yes, good question. Mainly *me*, although with the performance appraisal system there is an opportunity to talk about [individual staff] development. But we usually don't focus on development we have gone through in the past year. It is usually about development we are going to go through in the next year. It rarely comes to fruition to be quite honest – because you can't really foresee the learning opportunities ahead. The game changes so rapidly. . . . Ideas are our business, but we work in a business environment where our performance is presented each month on a graph, for everyone in the team. The graph shows your target incomes and how much you actually achieved. This can be demoralising when, for example, you are developing a concept, an idea and not bringing in an immediate return. But you are being measured in dollars and cents terms. This *doesn't* reflect what we are really about. . . . The people who notice are only those who have a network with me – mostly people in Phaedrus and parts of Head Office.

JG: So, what counts to people in Phaedrus and Head Office? What counts in terms of what is noticed, recognised and rewarded for having developed your knowledge base?

D: *Rewarded!* That is stretching it. The way I know that people have noticed is through my continued involvement. For example, people who are looking at rewriting aspects of the company's training program, or even starting one, always call me. They didn't call me before – they would just do it. So the involvement is important.

Although a formal performance appraisal system is in place, David's experience of it is that it 'usually doesn't focus on [individual staff] development'. The official appraisal has little bearing on salary negotiations; to an extent it belies the powerful influence of informal feedback processes. The question of 'who notices' skills and abilities is directly linked to what he calls 'the political game', which David says he does not feel comfortable with. Although it is 'not in his priorities', there is an underlying anxiety about how his performance is recognised, expressed in his comment that 'being measured in dollars and cents terms does not reflect what we are really about'.

This anxiety serves Phaedrus well: on the one hand it weakens criticism, for instance of the marginalisation of some aspects of training relative to the primacy of production. On the other hand, it channels disagreement into the production process itself by encouraging team members to 'brainstorm' and 'think critically' to solve problems in the name of consensual interests: team interests. Team interests have an astonishing alignment with executive expectations about production deadlines, budget projections and keeping the client happy. But complying with this agenda does not eliminate the individual's anxiety about performing. Nor does it alleviate the tension which accompanies the displaying of the trainer's 'monthly graph' to other staff. The graph, as David mentions, shows how performance is measured 'in terms of target incomes and dollars and cents terms'. Its display generates considerable consternation about what happens next in workers' careers, and whether they are making the correct moves in the present:

JG: Where do you see your career heading now?
D: I can see the glass ceiling very clearly. There is a perception that people with trades backgrounds are limited in the kind of work they can really do. . . . There are also barriers in HRD. I do not have the political skills to get over or through. I'm chipping away, but to be quite honest I'm not really motivated to deal with that stuff [office politics]. I tend to focus on a project and attempt to do that to the best of my abilities. Where I fit into the pecking order doesn't really matter, generally – up until the point where I get really pissed off, whether by lack of recognition or by some-

thing else. . . . I think it has a lot to do with recognition. People often say status doesn't matter. *Status bloody well does matter!*

JG: What makes you say that so strongly?

D: For a long time I did not have *a title on my business card*. Others do. But I didn't. What is a bother sometimes is to see yourself referred to in relation to others, in a way you disagree with. . . . A linguist might say that words are chosen to represent a perceived reality. People are given titles which represent the way their roles are perceived. The company has always been meant to be a flat, non-hierarchical organisation. But it is not, of course. What we do with language represents power structures. The titles of positions, for example, signify a social and cultural structure. They're secretive about salaries. But we all know what each other gets. I can say that they do not regard me as senior project manager material – *I'm well below that* in terms of money.

Titles, money and status have been conventional reward systems in the modern workplace and remain powerful influences in Phaedrus. David keeps 'chipping away' but by his own admission is not really motivated to deal with office politics. 'Where I fit into the pecking order doesn't really matter, generally – up until the point where I get really pissed off'. His self-strategy when he gets 'pissed off' is of interest here. Confronting directly the politics which can make him angry is difficult, in part because this informal political territory is precisely the terrain of 'career gate keeping'. The inability to deal directly with this source of anxiety leads to the displacement of his anger, including into harder work and longer hours. The informal reward and recognition system functions to this end. The promise of future gratification; the promise of *being someone* in the hierarchy does count. As he says, 'People often say status doesn't matter. Status bloody well does matter!' I asked David to clarify how this matter of status affected him in his HRD role:

D: Having good presence and a profile with the chief executives is very important. Image and presentation are now very important features of the training landscape. . . . What I have learnt is that you can't separate learning from the politics and culture of the organisation. . . . I have a lot of responsibility and there is a title that goes with it. I'm now entitled 'National Skills Development Manager' within Phaedrus.

JG: Is that title now on your card?

D: No. But it is an identifiable thing; the title. I'm not a fringe-dweller any more. I still have the ability to walk between management and construction workers. I have affiliations with both. But I've got a name now. The company people actually had a nickname for me before. It was '*The Phantom*'.

David's nickname neatly captured part of his self-strategy for survival at the site. Indeed it became his own metaphor to describe his 'phantom-like' developmental role. His role, as mentioned earlier, tended to be made invisible. It was a role which 'must not get in the way of production'. These were his own words. Nonetheless, his corporate role was to assist workers to become better problem-solvers, better team members, even better thinkers. Such a role is presented by Phaedrus as unproblematic – almost 'civic-minded'. After all, it is intended to help workers develop transferable employment skills, and it has the support of the trade union movement.

From Foucault's work on discipline (1977) and technologies of the self (1988b), David's experience of recognition and feedback and his phantom-strategy can be read as a form of disciplined self-regulation. Foucault argues that the methods of discipline and punishment used in Western cultures have shifted dramatically over the past several hundred years, from ritual punishment delivered publicly by the sovereign, to an internalised, self-monitored technology of the self. Within this self-technology, individuals discipline themselves – in accordance with the norm. The norm at the Olympics site was for training opportunities to be available but 'out of the way', and the normalisation David experienced was thus not an overt form of repression. Rather, as Foucault explains, 'normalisation occurs through comparison, ranking, judging, measurement, differentiation and setting the limits in relation to the "Norm"' (1977: 183).

David said his 'performance' was 'measured in dollars and cents terms'. This was a part of his 'examination' which Foucault refers to as an instrument of discipline that combines the techniques of surveillance and normalisation. David's official examination took the form of a corporate 'ritualised ceremony of power which claims to establish an objective truth about the individual' (Foucault 1977: 183). This was an 'objective truth' David never felt comfortable with because he believed such instruments for assessing performance did not accurately reflect the elusive yet critical aspects of teaching and helping others to learn. Through David's performance review, the subject was made 'visible', while power was hidden. The subject, through this form of measurement, is both 'subject and subjected' (Foucault 1977: 184).

David said his early experiences with Phaedrus made him feel like 'a fringe-dweller'. He worked very hard to gain acceptance, however, and his performance was rewarded with a new title. Bestowing an important sounding title – 'National Skills Development Manager' – was corporate recognition. He did not get in the way of production, his graphs looked good and the title did not cost the company additional money. Within this story, the corporate image presented to the public – of the team-based, non-hierarchical, objective (and thus fair) management system – appears to be precisely that: *an image*. Contrasting with this 'good corporate citizen' image is another reality. Although David played along with, and was rewarded by the recognition and reward system – including its titles and financially-based performance reviews – read from a Foucauldian standpoint, his story highlights an individual's experience of the corporation's disciplinary regimes, panoptic 'group norms' and subtle 'technologies' for obtaining self-regulating professionals.

Situated ethics and 'adaptability'

Marta's experience of recognition and feedback was less tied to internal company reward systems, procedures and directions than David's. Marta, subcontracted to the site, was not as directly 'owned' by the company as David. Intrinsic/extrinsic motivations and rewards, gender factors, personal history, self-perceptions, values about what constitutes 'success' or 'failure' and career aspirations variously appear within the dialogue. But from site-based recognition and feedback, she sensed the potential at one level to be 'looked upon as a joke'. At another level, feedback confirmed to Marta her 'adaptability' – an adaptability Phaedrus ultimately approved of. Again, Marta's ways of dealing with situated ethics are of significance to her site-based learning, the development of her professional identity and her 'performativity'.

JG: Can you tell me whether you think you have been successful here, and how do you know?

M: *Feedback*. Informal and formal feedback on the fact that people perceive me as contributing in a positive rather than negative way. These are my indicators: feedback, people wanting to participate, wanting to relate and so on. I knew the potential was there for me to be looked upon as a joke; I knew that it would take time. I knew that my success was dependent upon factors outside of my control. The job has only served as a vehicle to clarify things for me (about my career) which were not directly related to this job. . . . I'm basically motivated by things which are tied to *the client service*. In playing the role that I've played, you represent the side of learning as distinct from the side of industry. As a teacher in the workplace, you carry a responsibility which is to take learning into industry, of providing a service which doesn't let down what is your primary agenda: that is, to take education into industry. So, I'm motivated by people saying, 'yes, this has worked', because enough common ground has been found between industry needs and educational desires. I am motivated by outcomes whereby the educational service satisfies people. I think both sides could do a lot of harm if you're only concerned about your own agenda. Again, it's the diversity which can lead to successful outcomes.

Marta viewed her primary agenda as 'taking education into industry', but finding enough 'common ground' was not so straightforward. The recognition of her work tended to be, as she put it, 'haphazard'. Feedback about the construction agenda was not. This one-sided clarity had the effect of acculturating Marta. The new corporate culture was demonstrating its willingness to accommodate a female trainer at the site. It was demonstrating, for instance to the client (the NSW Government), to trade unions – and even to sceptical university researchers – its abilities to integrate all its employees regardless of gender, age and race. But the success of this integration was set up as depending on *Marta's* adaptability. In relation to what learning was considered important (and who decides) she states it is 'an individual thing'.

As I have argued earlier, the corporation's deliberate location of a feminist in macho land rendered Marta simultaneously powerless and powerful. As an HRD practitioner located in the powerful discourses of 'improving performance', her own performance was subject to critical hooks into her desires to prove her worth as an educator in a high profile industrial context. The 'hooks' include her sense of responsibility for 'taking education into industry', her sense of guilt about whether she has compromised her principles related to fairness, equity, gender relations and so on, and her active acceptance of the messages of the learning organisation.

Her learning was not such 'an individual thing' as she may have suspected. It was part of the discursive practice of Phaedrus. The rewards associated with promoting measurable improvements and the subtle appeal to her desires, emotional investments and self-identifications with her 'educative' role were indeed seductive. She felt the potential was there for her to be looked upon 'as a joke', a proto-joke she was determined to refute. Her response was built upon a professional desire to succeed. She was working in relatively uncharted professional territory for a feminist whose training background was primarily with women. In her words, what she actually learnt from this was a notion of success 'dependent upon factors outside of my control'. Factors such as the 'delegation system' Marta referred to which was meant to devolve decision-making to the teams. This system generated a sense of pressure, of felt experience. The operatives who are meant to be making decisions (including herself) have to interpret 'haphazard' feedback filtered through the new Phaedrus culture. By simultaneously positioning Marta as powerless through exploiting her concern and guilt, and powerful through providing snippets of understanding, mastery and new ways forward for her learners/workers, she more readily accepts the messages of the corporation. This territory is teeming with situated ethical dilemmas that remain largely unaddressed in both theorising and researching the effects of workplace-based learning.

The acculturation of Marta into Phaedrus is significant because, more than ever, common grounds between 'industry needs' and 'educational desires' are being sought. HRD practitioners such as Marta and David are at the implementation point of those grounds. National governments throughout the post-industrial world are promoting the recognition of work-based learning and a competitive market place of education and training providers. New industry-led accreditation agencies are now with us. This strategy may well serve the era of performativity, but it provides no panacea for the complexities facing our education systems. It is a strategy riddled with conflicting discourses, ethical dilemmas and competing agendas about *what should really count* as 'learning'. Industry's insatiable demands for competitiveness provide a master discourse which, at the local level, is symbolised in aspects of Marta's learning from experience and her responses to the situated ethics of her HRD practices. Although in symbolic roles, Marta and David were active players contributing to the discursive shaping of Phaedrus's subcultures.

Conclusion

Drawing on Lyotard's notion of performativity, I have sought to examine how the HRD practices of Marta and David illustrate the powerful effects of corporate story-telling. But this is only part of the story. Marta and David are active participants in shaping the corporate matrix. They are relaying their particular versions of the corporate narratives. The discursive practices of the corporation do create new ways of being at work and there are powerful inducements for workers to actively accept (and challenge) the modes of operation and power at work. Discursive practices such as the promotion of a 'learning organisation' and competency-based standards are ways of representation. As Rose (1994) argues, such representation renders aspects of the world thinkable, and technologies, or ways of intervening, translatable into programmatic action. The discourses at play within Phaedrus are not uncommon in today's corporate environments. The discourses provide powerful meanings with effects on the players embedded in their everyday performance.

From this perspective informal learning can clearly be read as something radically other than contemporary HRD/human capital theorisations of it. A more radical interpretation implies challenges to conventional notions of learning in and for work, and of the connections between informal learning and formal education. It raises questions about the ways informal learning is constructed through the dominant discourses of particular work settings. Some intriguing questions for future HRD research thus include: 'How might discourse analysis be introduced into HRD practices?', 'As a new strategy how might discourse analysis affect the "transforming" of workplace cultures?', 'What new relationships and tensions will arise through such innovative HRD practices (and why)?', 'How will the professional goals of HRD practitioners be changed in specific work contexts as a consequence?', 'How are the ethical dilemmas that arise in daily practice "talked about" and resolved?' 'How does gender influence informal learning?' and 'What can HRD practitioners actually do with knowledge about the sheer complexity of informal learning?' From this study, these types of questions are directly relevant to constructing better understandings of informal learning and its relationship with practice. Chapter 7 examines such questions, re-thinking ways of viewing informal learning and what a retheorisation can mean for workplace learning practices.

Notes

1 The term 'mini-narrative' is used here in two senses: to contrast with the meta-narratives which have historically given modern science its epic purpose – the pursuit of a transcendent 'truth'; and, to 'recognise the meaningfulness of individual experiences by noting how they function as part of a whole' (Polkinghorne 1988: 173).
2 In this section I am not interested in distinguishing between recognition and feedback, though I acknowledge that they encompass a wide variety of practices. It is beyond the scope of this study to examine the details of this variety. The discussion and analysis here focus on corporate uses of recognition and feedback in shaping the informal learning of the trainers.

7 Retheorising informal workplace learning

> Professionals have the duty to profess. But professing in a postmodern age calls for the capacity to be open to multiple discourses and to engage, albeit critically, with them. It also calls for an integration of critical thinking in the three domains of knowledge, self and world. Proper engagement with multiple discourses demands no less.
>
> (Barnett 1997: 144)

Informal learning and training 'economic subjects'

I have argued in this book for a re-thinking of existing definitions of informal and incidental learning, emphasising the need to shift away from highly instrumental understandings that diminish informal learning to 'technique'. The hitherto narrow focus on informal learning is best abandoned in favour of acknowledging the subtle power of symbolic and communication patterns that shape it. In the sense of 'being shaped' I have argued that the ways we talk about informal learning influence what it becomes; informal learning is a discursive construction, configured by the multiple and intersecting discourses of particular work settings. But this is not the full story. In the design and re-engineering processes of contemporary corporations, worker/learners are not merely passive recipients of corporate injunctions. They are not automatons, but active subjects who, as Chapters 5 and 6 have shown, often *willingly comply* with the desired corporate ways. That compliance is often 'willing' is a key to the unmasking of learning at work. Compliance is obtained for a range of professional and personal rewards, but the rewards are not 'simply' monetary or in terms of enhancing status. They are also psychic – in the sense of being deeply personal. This view of informal learning implies that more critical and self-reflexive notions are in order if work is to be taken seriously as a 'learning environment' by higher education institutions seeking new work-based learning markets. It is also a view that indicated that the links between informal learning and formal education will need to build on richer notions of 'competence' or 'capability' than expressed in most contemporary workplaces.

Contemporary definitions tend to accept uncritically the contexts in which informal learning is given form. Workplaces are now considered 'authentic' settings for the development of 'really useful knowledge' and many educators are 'willingly' colluding with this. Marginson (1997) offers a compelling explanation of why this is occurring by showing how formal education is permeated by economy:

> Education is implicated in economic policy discourse; in strategies for population management; in the preparation of labour for work, and its retraining; and programs for unemployment. The management of education is shaped by economically defined objectives and methods, and increasingly driven by competitive economic pressures. The material resources available for education ('inputs') are defined in economic terms.
>
> (Marginson 1997: 13)

With the powerful economic and policy discourses shaping them, knowledge and skills are being redefined as competencies and capabilities. These conceptions are intended to serve well the strategy of 'flexible accumulation' of capital. Employer bodies and national training authorities intend informal learning to comply with observable competency-based standards which can make learning more manageable and the recognition of prior learning more precise. But as previous chapters have shown, such views of informal learning do not match the complexity of the phenomenon.

Such contemporary views of informal learning have been framed by human capital theory, which posits workers as 'economic subjects'. Human capital theory is itself a subject of the master discourses of free market thought à la Hayek and Friedman. Terms emerging from the free market perspective are aligned with the espoused needs of industries and businesses: to become more productive, more efficient and therefore competitive. Some re-configurations are in order if informal learning is to mean more than 'competence', its human capital version in corporate and academic worlds and discourse.[1] Otherwise the insatiable market place with its accompanying cultural/economic meta-narrative *will* determine what constitutes valid knowledge and learning.

In this study the stories of Marta and David illustrate the dilemmas and professional tensions experienced, in part, because of their relative powerlessness at particular sites. Paradoxically, HRD professionals are central to a powerful discourse in education/industry policy which obscures, even obliterates, other understandings of education in favour of economic ones. Rhetoric about human capital, resources, measurable outputs, productivity, best-practice, efficiency and bridging the gap between education and work characterise this discourse.[2] Hart relates this to current debates about work and education in which the balance between the two is based on a three-dimensional view of 'the economy', or of what drives the economy:

> all economic decisions are determined by a worldwide structure of economic competition; the need to compete on the world market requires a constant increase of productivity (measured in abstract indices of input/output); and this competition also requires an ongoing drive to reduce labour costs.
>
> (Hart 1993: 21)

Although this framework oversimplifies very complex issues, many businesses and many HRD practices do operate on the basis of striving for a competitive advantage in 'market' conditions. Within such a framework, the HRD project for industry appears clear: to 'train' human capital in the right kind of skills – 'the skills employers want' (Carnevale, Gainer and Villet 1990). The training reforms throughout the OECD nations, based on new 'partnerships' between education and industry, are meant to align with skills employers want. The needs of business and industry to become increasingly 'competitive' is the paramount concern.

Competency-based standards are being introduced for workers in most industries to facilitate business and industry needs to access flexible workers, developed with the 'right' skills. These provide guidelines and tools for learning at work, but leave little room for ambiguity about the functions, purposes or influences that shape the learning. The 'standards' are what Carnevale, Gainer and Villet argue are required 'to help American business to keep or regain its competitive edge on the world market' (in Hart 1993: 22). Hart points out that within this human capital perspective, the welfare or interests of the workers is seen as *entirely merging* with this purpose.

Expectations of the Sydney 2000 Olympics site management for the training function reflect economic and production imperatives. Worker interests were regarded as entirely merging with these. Such management expectations had deep effects on the informal learning of the HRD practitioners at the site. Their experiences of their performing roles, multiple HRD purposes, power relations, recognition and feedback, and the education/work-based training dichotomy exemplify this. That 'nothing must get in the way of production' (including competency-based standards) was an injunction David and Marta learned very early in their tenure at the site. Indeed, this was a significant source of professional tension that they had to 'deal with'.

Although Marsick and Watkins (1990a) chide those who focus extensively on the maximisation of profits, they have articulated a powerful conception of informal (and incidental) learning which owes its theoretical justification to human capital theory:

> human capital theorists present what may be the most compelling argument for a focus on informal learning in the workplace. Human capital theory refers to the productive capabilities of human beings that are acquired at some cost and that command a price in the labour market because they are useful in producing goods and services. Thinking in terms of value as a return on investment in a cost-to-benefit ratio, education is seen as a major means for organisations (and individuals) to increase the net worth of the worker's skills and abilities.
>
> (Marsick and Watkins 1990a: 205)

They argue that the 'human capital benefit' of employee training is enormous. But equally clear is the cost to a vast segment of the workforce who are denied access. 'For them, informal learning represents an alternative delivery system which may help them compete more successfully' (Marsick and Watkins 1990a: 205). This human capital framework for understanding informal learning, despite its apparent popular acceptance, has shortcomings.

Critical social theorists such as Anyon (1983), Hart (1993) and Welton (1995) point to inherent flaws in the capitalist economic structure, variously asserting that built-in class divisions are barriers to equal participation and ownership. A critical perspective interprets the 'mobilisation' of informal learning as a form of collusion between training and management to 'cool out the aspirations of the disenfranchised' (La Belle 1982, in Marsick and Watkins 1990a: 207), and ultimately to serve capital interests.

Marsick and Watkins reject this critique, however, on the grounds that the US needs to increase greatly the flexibility of its human capital base or face turbulent, even violent, upheaval in becoming more economically productive. Their theory has influenced much that has been written within HRD on informal learning. But its 'human capital' reasoning is based upon two major assumptions which require scrutiny.

The first assumption is that in contexts of rapid change, it is primarily workers who have to change to lift productivity by becoming more skilled and flexible – with informal learning offering 'an alternative delivery system' (Marsick and Watkins 1990a: 206). Human capital theory holds that individuals are essentially responsible for their own professional training, and in this way the workforce can become more productive and competitive. A basic problem with human capital theory here relates to its assumption that there is a relationship of cause/effect between vocational education and productivity. This problem should not go unchallenged. Integral linkages between informal learning, the purposes of work and the ways in which work is organised and conducted, are acknowledged by Watkins and Marsick, particularly in their subsequent work on 'building learning organisations' (1992, 1993). But the onus for flexibility in response to rapid change, currently conceived as workers performing more effectively and efficiently, cannot lie exclusively with individual workers. Nor can changes in approaches to work, rather than the worker, be assumed necessarily to enhance competitiveness. The current obsession with restructuring workplaces and making workers more empowered – to effect ever-greater efficiencies – rests on the fallacious cause/effect assumption of human capital theory. In turn, the notion of informal learning as a 'delivery system', although well intentioned, rests upon very unstable grounds.

An 'holistic' approach to learning at work, involving changes to work structures and patterns to include learning organisations, team approaches, quality circles, TQM and so on, may not result in 'improved informal learning'. The issue is the relationship of the individual to underlying questions such as the usefulness of the goods being produced or constructed, the treatment of employees, the uses (and abuses) of the natural environment and resources. Such questions underpin the professionals' adaptations to work requirements and seriously challenge conventional, taken-for-granted notions about work, its relationship to progress and development and the tensions between 'learning for work' and 'work for learning'.

In relation to taken-for-granted notions about work, Marsick and Watkins acknowledge that the *attitudes* of workers to workplace training constitute 'a kind of incidental learning that is highly tacit' (1990a: 207). In effect, this includes the internalisation of capitalism in practitioners and worker/learners and relates directly to the adoption of a processing orientation which, according to Barnett, implies that the *learning task* at the site is to 'interpret, assimilate and reproduce the sense data that comes their way' (Barnett 1994: 173).

Clearly, HRD personnel are not employed to question the way things are done. They are hired in the interests of capital and labour efficiency which, by definition, gives them an instrumental, input-output orientation. An unduly challenging mind can (and does – as found in Chapters 4 and 5) lead quickly to expulsion. Human capital representational methodology accepts this limited view of informal learning, in part because it embraces workplace 'givens' including demands for demonstrable outcomes of interactions, more efficient means to preconceived ends, and operational ways of knowing the world.

There is, however, a strong dialectical relationship between the individual's tacit or felt experience and production imperatives. The internalisation (and reproduction) of capital interests does not necessarily equate to acceptance of the underlying values and aspirations of capital. The 'self-regulation' and construction of professional identities described in Chapter 5, show that managerial attempts to re-engineer corporate culture create personal, professional and ethical tensions which deeply affect what is learnt from experience at work.

The second assumption of human capital theory is that conventional *notions of work* are also 'givens'. This premise directly relates to the core of the global economic system:

> that production is, above all, production for profit; that nature is dead, malleable matter entirely at our disposal; and that the immense social and environmental costs of our way of production can therefore be externalised, and [therefore] do not figure into our calculations of growth and development.

> (Hart 1993: 26)

Hart argues that normative assumptions about work need to be challenged. The practitioners at the Olympics site referred frequently to 'the primacy of production' and, with little time for reflection, this imperative was indeed a 'given'. As Chapters 5 and 6 argue, for professional survival both David and Marta had to adopt very low profiles to ensure that training was not perceived to be 'in the way of construction'. For David this meant a 'phantom-like' approach to the site. For Marta, who was highly visible at the site because of its dramatic gender imbalance, 'invisibility' took the form of a more marginalised, backroom training function. Although she says that she was never unhappy about that function, and that people were 'incredibly polite' to her, both she and David held doubts about what is 'truly' important and productive work. If it did not match dominant site conceptions about training and learning it was rendered dubious.

Their views were not measured exclusively against the profit interests of capital, or construction meeting its tight time frames. They related to the personal and professional values and beliefs about the purposes of their work and, in turn, to their life interests and the aspirations of participants in their training activities. Nevertheless, their resistance tended to be symbolic. Despite the subtle powers shaping informal learning, with much being predicated by 'the site', intrinsic matters and *life beyond* their immediate locations remained. The influence on informal learning of the Other is embedded in their language, as Marta's words illustrate:

> I know I've learned an enormous amount here. I've learned about the way people do things here. But I don't feel I've learned anything new. No, that's not quite right. It's more like the *layers of learning were re-experienced . . . in a new cultural context. It was like re-layered knowledge*. So, it was like 'here it is again', I've come across this before but in a different context. Like learning how to behave. You've learned it before, so it's not a new experience. It's a relearning of something you've actually known. It's not that the challenges were not great enough. Not at all. I've learned a lot about negotiation, about the company, about life on building sites. All that is new. But in the overall experience, I don't think there is anything about myself that it has faced me with. A lot of it has been relearning information about the way things work. It's re-applying strategies you already know, locating those strategies in a new culture.
>
> From my experience I would have to say that industry can harm education if it is only an industry/production agenda which is being pursued. Many in industry think educational goals are *too social*, and often educators think industry is too focused *on production* and business bottom lines. Finding the right balance is important, but not so easy.

These words do not reduce human actions and learning to the competent performance of skills at the prescribed levels of the industry standard. They represent a questioning that is a part of Marta's balancing of educational ideals with immediate industry demands – her professional self-regulation. A notion of informal learning that can encompass the processes involved in judging the merits of competing interests is different from the human capital notion. It is not solely about enhancing the interests of an abstract 'capital' which is simultaneously meant to benefit the individual, but also about dealing with situated ethics and difference. The professional is therefore *a discursive creator* through his or her critical thinking and actions.

Discursive creators

If understandings of informal learning are to move beyond the strait-jacket of pre-determined performance indicators and numerical measures, they will need to focus decisively on self-reflexivity and the disparate discourses that affect professional action. Where discourses collide, the issues of professional judgment and situated ethics are involved in one's informal learning. The art of handling multiple and conflicting discourses is one of the principal challenges facing the post-modern professional. And the question of how the informal shapes this art is of paramount interest. The idea of multiple and competing discourses opens the door to deconstruction as a strategy related to understanding and contesting workplace learning. A part of the challenge here is to articulate an epistemology of practice that questions absolute principles of reasoning and works through its own values, that is, an ethics of postmodern practice. One of the principal tools postmodern philosophers can use to accomplish this is deconstruction (Derrida 1978).

Deconstruction can be read as a form of ethical practice concerned with what happens to ethics as knowledge frameworks are increasingly challenged. It seeks to uncover contradictory and historically conditioned assumptions within a discourse, challenging the distinction between representation and 'real'. It assumes that discourse produces rather than simply represents. It is in this sense that all is discourse. Parker (1997: 68) elaborates four principles of deconstruction:

1   Deconstruction acts upon texts and regards everything – whether it be the laws of golf, a stance taken on the environment, a conversation, an argument or whatever – as text. It is texts that get deconstructed.
2   Deconstruction is a strategy for examining texts which works within the texts' own system of beliefs and values. The text itself provides the fuel for the process of deconstruction . . . devices are used from within the text to use upon or against the text.
3   Deconstruction is always concerned to show up or exploit weaknesses, often working to turn supposed strengths into weaknesses.

4   Because deconstruction is not a position but a strategy, it serves no
    particular mistress. There is no guarantee that the user will not in
    turn find themselves deconstructed.

Deconstruction is not ideology-free, however. Foucault points out that
discourses have a political nature – controlling what kind of talk
occurs and which talkers speak (1988c: 131). He makes a compelling
argument that links learning and 'the truth' as a function of the political construction of knowledge.

> In societies like ours, the 'political economy' of truth is charac-
> terised by the form of scientific discourse and the institutions
> which produce it; the object, under diverse forms, of immense
> diffusion and consumption; produced and transmitted under the
> control, dominant if not exclusive, of a few great political and
> economic apparatuses; the issue of a whole political debate and
> social confrontation (ideological struggles).
>
> (Foucault 1988c: 133)

Drawing on Foucault's criteria, deconstruction as a strategy can be
read as a discursive outcome of power relations. A concern here is that
the application of deconstruction to informal learning has the potential, ultimately, to represent political and economic interests in much
the same ways as human capital theory – preparing workers to meet the
labour requirements of a market economy – making subjects economically active but politically passive. But being an effective actor in this
world means being a discursive creator – one who contributes to and
challenges dominant discourses by establishing some powerful allegiances and speaking up, and not through passivity and compliance.

Deconstruction can offer a strategy to help produce discursive
creativity by making new types of contributions and challenges. This
contrasts with the application of human capital theory to workplace
learning practices as, unfortunately, what lies close to the surface in the
implementation of this theory is the performativity principle examined
in Chapter 6. This principle is not about challenging the underlying
purposes, effects and contradictions of work. It is about getting the job
done as efficiently as possible.

As I have argued throughout this book, 'getting the job done efficiently' has been presented as a 'given' in much of the writing on
informal learning to date. For instance, Tough, although not directly
concerned with 'performativity' as an underlying principle of informal
learning, implicitly endorses it by focusing solely on what he calls
'highly intentional' changes:

First the change must be deliberately chosen and intended. . . . Second, the person then takes one or more steps to achieve the change. . . . Choosing and striving are the two key elements: the person chooses a particular change and then takes action to achieve it.

(Tough 1982: 20)

Marsick and Watkins differentiate their version of informal learning from Tough's by playing down the extent of intentionality. They hold that 'informal learning can be planned, but includes learning that is not designed or expected' (1990a: 214), referring to unexpected outcomes of informal learning as 'incidental'. Both definitions are limited and thus limiting. Tough emphasises the voluntary, purposeful nature of self-directed learning. This conception privileges individual autonomy to a degree which does not sufficiently acknowledge the social conditions in which the self is embedded. By way of contrast, Marsick and Watkins emphasise the unintentional, unanticipated learning that is 'often influenced or triggered by a chance encounter with a person or event by a need *imposed* on the person by the organisation' (1990a: 215). They also include a 'collective dimension' to learning in organisations:

> people do pursue their own learning, but our research shows that the natural work groups, through which they learn, influence the learning process and outcomes. Thus we believe we should talk about two different kinds of self-directed learning, which are probably somewhat interdependent, when we talk about learning in group or organisational settings: learning directed at self-development, and learning by an individual in the pursuit of collective needs within a group or organisation.

(Marsick and Watkins 1990a: 215)

Their definition has much to commend it, but contains at least two significant flaws. First, it does not sufficiently acknowledge the representational effects of the human capital theory of learning, to which it owes its justification. This can be read as a serious deficiency as these authors are participants in a human capital discourse in which words are used whose previous uses carry meanings which go beyond our intentions. In this instance, the human capital version of informal learning is being used in instrumental ways that exceed the authors' intent. Human capital theory is not a representation of 'other' voices, such as more marginalised or disenfranchised people. These are, however, the very people informal learning is said by human capital theorists to aid.[3] Marsick and Watkins claim that human capital theory provides 'the most compelling arguments related to increasing the net worth of the worker's skills and abilities' (1990b: 20), and in this sense their argument is completely consistent. Their representational framework, however, has been harnessed within the 'field' of HRD with some unintended outcomes and uses made of their theory.

Chapters 5 and 6 provide examples of unintended *educational* outcomes derived from the human capital approach. At the Olympics 2000 sites, to facilitate Phaedrus's 'team' approach to work organisation, workers were encouraged to 'respect diversity'. Training was offered in support of the notion of 'respecting others'. In the process, and under the weighty influence of production pressures, 'respecting diversity' was reduced to one of the required competencies for the construction activity. Understanding and respect for difference became one of the needed skills – accomplished through informational training. This 'learning' may well represent an important educational advance in the context of the construction industry, but it is really about the acquisition of production-related skills. This skill-formation approach to learning contrasts with more critical approaches to education or, as Kegan put it, 'learning that reflects on itself, holding a "leading out" from an established habit of mind' (Kegan 1995: 232).

The second problem with Marsick and Watkins's (1990a) definition relates to the differentiation of informal from incidental learning. They define incidental learning as a 'by product' of some other activity such as sensing the organisational culture, or trial and error experimentation (1990a: 211). As such, incidental learning is never planned or intentional, as it may be with 'self-directed' learning, or where help is consciously sought. As incidental learning can occur as a result of involvement in intentional informal learning, they suggest it can be interpreted as a subset of informal learning. That is, in any informal learning there are taken-for-granted assumptions which underpin actions and influence the learner's intent, degree of motivation, commitment and emotional involvement. The key distinguishing feature for Marsick and Watkins is that informal learning is intentional, incidental learning is not. This distinction thus has the effect of separating 'planned' informal learning from beliefs and values which may surface within the 'incidental'. Such a distinction produces a false dichotomy. Indeed, attempts are being made to fashion 'corporate selves' through *felt experience* of the designer organisational cultures.

Informal learning, as Marsick and Watkins use it, contains a contradiction, it 'can be planned, but includes learning that is not designed or expected. Incidental by definition, includes the unexpected' (1990a:

215). With regard to both terms, they agree that learning is, at least in part, prompted 'by the needs of the organisation and sometimes by the direct command or request of others'. But the separation (albeit interwoven) of informal from incidental carries implicit assumptions about what is important, or 'what counts' as most important in workplace learning. It is not so much the unexpected, incidental side-effects which are prized. It is the planned, intentional learning, represented in mentoring and coaching schemes or self-directed approaches that contribute to the organisation's mission, which is prized. Putting this definition into practice therefore privileges 'the doing' within informal learning, rather than 'the questioning' which is implicit in learning from mistakes, involvement with others, experiencing hidden agendas, the politics and power relations of organisational life.

This definition of terms has an inherent contradiction: that self-direction is celebrated within it, but only in so far as it relates to the needs of the organisation or, as Marsick and Watkins say, 'the direct command or request of others'. In contemporary corporate life, it is not really 'self-directed' learning at all – as the mini-narratives presented in Chapters 5 and 6 clearly indicate.

Marsick and Watkins deal with this definitional conundrum by including 'the collective dimension of learning in organisations' (1990a: 214), in which individuals can pursue their own learning, but where work groups influence the learning process and outcomes. This leads to two different kinds of self-directed learning at work (which, they say, 'probably are somewhat interdependent'): 'learning directed at self development, and learning by an individual in the pursuit of collective needs within a group or organisation' (Marsick and Watkins 1990a: 215).

This framework, too, is underpinned by the notion of an autonomous self actively making decisions about 'self-development' and experiential learning needs. As I have argued earlier, this assumption should not be accepted as a given, as the dominant approaches to experiential learning are being challenged by new insights concerning the nature of human communication. The ambiguity of experience, and theory, is based on the uncertainty of human agency.

Kosmidou and Usher (1992) problematise this uncertainty as part of 'the dialectic of self and society'. Usher (1989) in particular has been critical of the dominant conceptions of experiential learning, especially the humanistic theorisations of autonomy and subjectivity which underpin Marsick and Watkins's definitional work. Usher points out that the idea of the 'subject' being conceived of as an entity or a 'self', which is 'real' and located in the natural world, is dubious:

the humanistic theorisation of subjectivity posits an essential inner core – a true self unique to each individual, which is permanent, coherent and known to the individual. . . . The conception of the autonomous subject is very powerful, because many of us share the assumption that because 'reflection' goes on in our heads it is unique to the knowing, rational self which is the source and the condition of legitimacy for both the process and product of reflection.

(Usher 1989: 27)

The trainers' informal learning in this study suggests that what is needed is an understanding of 'the subject' that is in the active sense of 'shaping' and the passive sense of 'being shaped': a dialectical approach to informal learning.

Learning the postmodern malaise

Power relations are rooted deep in the social nexus, not reconstituted 'above' society as a supplementary structure whose radical effacement one could perhaps dream of.

(Foucault 1982: 222)

Informal learning involves the complex interaction of self with the communication patterns or discursive practices of the workplace. As such it is more than a product or outcome of the material acts or tasks of work. 'What counts' as informal learning, and its linkages with formal education, can thus be viewed in relation to the nature of the workplace. As Chapter 4 shows, the planned training activities that take place at work, or for work, comprise what Casey (1995: 78) calls 'the manifest curriculum of work'. This is accompanied by the *hidden curriculum* of work that socialises adult workers. As this text has argued, much more is learned than the material and physical acts of *producing*. The construction of the facilities for the Olympics is not only of buildings and infrastructure. Chapters 5 and 6 conclude that there are other forms of construction taking place: learning constructions related to workers' selves. Workers learn to work *within* and *against* the corporate drive for 'acculturated' employees. Their accommodation and resistance entail powerful forms of informal learning that are rarely opened for discussion.

Accommodation to a dominant pre-text of learning at the site – instrumental competence – is manifested in a range of ways detailed in Chapters 5 and 6. The associated subtext – the assessment of competence to enable workers' on the job learning to be 'formally' accredited

– is a part of the reward system that complements this accommodation. Learning associated with resistance, however, appears to be more private, more internalised (such as David's adoption of the 'phantom' role), and outwardly largely symbolic (such as Marta's Nelson Mandela cake).

This shifts resistance in the new workplace away from a union-based opposition to dominant workplace expectations and management directives, and towards a simulated solidarity based on corporate teams. Workers are wary that resistance is more likely to be punished than rewarded unless it results in outcomes that contribute to the company's performance objectives. Rather than openly resisting, workers are learning to speak up 'appropriately' in the new 'empowered', self-directing corporate team context. Personal and professional identities have a range of 'investments' in the new work structures and processes with self-regulation a powerful technology of workplace governance. The self-regulation related to speaking up 'appropriately' has been shown to have problematic dimensions – exemplified in Michael's story in Chapter 4 where his expressed views on workplace reforms contributed to his own retrenchment.

In the pursuit by employers, unions and individual workers of recognition of informal learning, it is predominantly the visible and instrumental that is rewarded at the level of workplace implementation. Competence is most certainly one of the discourses shaping contemporary industrial training practices. Trainers, who invariably double as 'assessors', are expected by their employers to acknowledge 'competent performance' and not the learning associated with resistance or interruption. The latter has traditionally belonged to the critical distance allowed by formal education. But this critical distance is being eroded in the formal assessment of competence, which valorises a certain kind of doing – the observable.[4] Industry needs training and formal assessment. The notion of formal assessment of workplace skills is being pursued by universities, employers and unions in a mutually beneficial compact. Despite this 'compact' there remains a very fragile research base to inform the alignment of work-based learning and education, and what little research there is has largely been commissioned by the sources promoting the alignment.

A critical base from which to view this alignment is now urgently needed because training practices teach employees the competencies necessary to perform the job to the pre-set standards of the industry. This represents an impoverished notion of learning which, even so, has significant effects on the lifeworlds of worker/learners. This is manifest at the professional level, where managers and team leaders are being trained in how to practise the valuing of diversity, how to work in teams, how to communicate and negotiate more effectively. But sometimes this involves learning surface level inscriptions. For construction workers, beneath the surface is a culture once characterised by 'legends', smoke-filled rooms, sexist posters and calendars, shouting matches between unionists and bosses and between rival unions.[5] Following Head Office expectations and requirements, training practices are sanitising this culture; its practices are being adjusted and its image cleaned up. In this context, the unions are losing membership and power. It is now a lifeworld in which the corporation seeks from its members commitment to the new partnering and team arrangements; the new 'corporate family'. The HRD practices promoting 'learning organisations', TQM and so on, are expected to facilitate this corporate family which is, in turn, expected to lead to greater participation, energy and output. The new team-partnering approach is meant to be highly competitive and penetrate new markets such as those in Asia.[6]

Even with the competency-based approach to training and assessment, workers are learning more than the skills and competencies that are necessary to perform the job. They are experiencing the 'normal' stresses of the new corporate-partnering and team requirements and the 'self-regulation' that accompanies belonging to the 'corporate family'. Such belonging has an emotional effect on the lives of workers and on the broader community.

The informal learning experiences of corporate workers affect all aspects of their working and emotional lives. This was noted by all the participants in this study. Yet contemporary management and training and development literature continues an almost exclusive coverage of building learning organisations and 'family-style' participatory structures. This coverage glosses over deeper issues such as the *emotional toll* upon selves. The new partnerships, the family-style learning organisations, seek to absorb more and more of the worker's self into the organisation – the organisation which, above all else, must perform competitively – at peak efficiency.

The social structuring of work – the new designer work-culture – is significant for psychological functioning as it profoundly affects people's views of reality. Weber's (1958) classic *The Protestant Ethic and the Spirit of Capitalism* recognised such views as emanating from reciprocal relations among work, occupation, personality and religiosity. This reciprocity is exploited in contemporary corporate practices through 'real world' corporate and industrial practices and discourses, and results in individual tensions including conflicts between personal values and professional demands. What people do and learn in their work carries over into other spheres of their lives; their cognitive functions, values, priorities in life and conceptions of themselves are a part of the 'lessons' of work.

It is, therefore, extraordinarily unhealthy to remove uncritically the distance between contemporary workplace learning and formal education. In relation to universities, Barnett (1997) argues that higher education is indeed in a 'critical business', yet this shift underscores the training reforms throughout OECD nations. The reforms seek consistent nomenclature of occupations and occupational competence. Workers are expected to fit themselves into the technical logic of this discourse. Competence, after all, is rational and – say its proponents – can be fully explained. As such it is the embodiment of modern learning.

Traces of the instrumental rationality of Weber's iron cage of bureaucracy can still be glimpsed in the OECD movement on workplace learning. 'Iron cage' is, however, no longer a suitable metaphor. A more appropriate post-industrial metaphor is a 'virtual enclosure' – and a seductive one at that. The systematic fashioning of workers' learning is associated with science and technology which are viewed by multinational corporations (and national governments) as holding the key to ongoing competitive advantage over the tiger economies of Asia (currency crises notwithstanding) and, more generally, the developing world. Boje chillingly describes the implications of this scenario (for learning) as:

> embedded in a seamless web of instructional apparatus where we are taught to be 'politically correct' bureaucrats. The learning occurs in the minute-by-minute interactions and the spaces along the hallways, lunchrooms and e-mail networks. The iron cage of the bureaucratic teaching machine is so ubiquitous and [seemingly] benign that the prisoners of modern learning no longer see the bars, the gears, or question the learning agenda.
>
> (Boje 1994: 447)

Boje's 'bureaucratic teaching machine' can be readily linked with Foucault's ideas on the exercise of power, which is not 'a naked fact, an institutional right, nor is it a structure which holds out to be smashed: it is elaborated, transformed, organised: it endows itself with processes which are more or less adjusted to the situation' (Foucault 1982: 224). 'The situation' under scrutiny here is the merging of informal and formal learning which systematically produces instrumental outcomes in which learning no longer requires critical distance, dialogue and critique. This version of workplace learning cannot be accepted at face value. Critical distance, dialogue and critique cannot be expressed in the contemporary training jargon of 'observable competence' that tells only about surface detail – the surface that is noticed in the ever-onward spiralling competitive race. At the environmental level, evidence is mounting daily that this competitive race is ecologically unsustainable and evokes a modern 'madness' through the tension between work and emotion. Its symptoms range from 'mild distress, feelings of self-betrayal, stress and burnout to acute psychiatric disorders and irrationality' (Casey 1995: 81). This is the postmodern malaise.

Designer work-cultures promote a precise alignment of a person's values, attitudes and abilities with the needs of the organisation. Any traits that might impede work, or are unnecessary, are suppressed or eliminated. Corporate talk about a 'celebration of difference' is purely that: talk. Rather, attributes of toughness, aggressiveness, decisiveness and competence building are truly prized. These attributes relate well to the pursuit of grand construction and the exercise of power, and determine what is noticed within particular work sites – what counts – as learning.

What counts at specific local sites is expected to count as credit within formal education programmes. If it does not, the formal institution may be regarded with scorn: too academic, out of touch, and so forth. In some cases this may well be so, but the contemporary alignment of workplace learning with formal education is based upon some unhealthy premises. The postmodern malaise described above is being translated into formal education by processes of recognition of prior learning (RPL) that (at present) rely too heavily on relatively narrow competency-based assessments at work and that obscure power relations.

Against this backdrop, new links between informal learning and formal education (which entail, inter alia, assessment of competence, accreditation of work-based learning and mechanisms of RPL) are given new meaning. The hidden curriculum of work entails lifeworlds configured in favour of corporate interests, objectives and competencies. This operation can be exposed by 'discursive creators' – through the promotion of dialogue (with scepticism) about underlying assumptions related to work and development. Barnett (1997: 30) points out how Habermas's ideas about 'critical standards' can help promote such a dialogue: 'any speech act can be interrogated in any one of four ways. Is it true? Does the account hang together? Do you really believe that? And is its form appropriate to the context?'

Postmoderns are quick to point out problems with Habermas's 'rational' approach, indicating that such criteria are problematic in several ways as language and speech are distorted by power relations and historical meanings. The 'ideal speech situation' is no more than a noble sentiment, and besides, even if a speech is true it may be only partially true; and if an account 'hangs together', so what? Dialogue requires hearing the full spectrum of 'voices' affected by development. This means, therefore, not only access to dialogue, but sensitivity to the claims of minorities or people who have been marginalised – others and the Other. Dialogue will not work if simply a politically expedient or pragmatic act. Nonetheless, dialogue has the potential to occupy important space in workplace learning if it explores social, political and economic issues without privileging one particular perspective. This presupposes time for systematic reflection so that a deeper consideration of 'possibilities' for action, including transformative action, can be encouraged through learning at work *and* formal education programmes.

In relation to education and training, state policies increasingly 'designed' to increase productive capacity and market competitiveness do not foster or nurture individual development, critical beings, or a healthier 'lifeworld'. Underlying conceptions of *the person* and of work as a *learning environment* – in which values are oriented towards improving lifeworlds and conditions for human dignity – must account for the ever-present possibility of replacing one oppressive discourse with another. As Usher and Edwards put it, this means recognising that 'any reconfiguration is provisional and open to question' (1994: 213).

Rethinking the workplace as a 'learning environment'

The construction industry provides for several reasons an ideal vehicle for examining the concept of 'work as a learning environment'. The industry has intimate links between capital interests and labour relations, management and work organisation, industrial relations and workplace learning. Experience of such industry influences now constitute the grounds of 'valid' learning. But the 'validity' of work-based learning rests upon philosophical instabilities that are not often acknowledged. Pre-set competency standards exemplify this instability. At one level, they represent (in theory) measurable learning outcomes meant to enable career progression and clarify what employees need to 'master' for that progression. The desired worker-competencies are often embodied in extensive checklists of skills. At site level, the lists are deployed in the implementation of competency-based training. This approach to learning hinges on a positivistic behavioural psychology, and conventional positivism contains the discredited notion of a value-free social science. This is an objectivist illusion. The working framework of competency-based training is meant to resist sociological and ideological enquiry. But the real situation is that competency standards frameworks are saturated with the ideologies of technical-rationalism and free market economics. The trick is that by rules of inference, competencies are transformed into 'facts', social values into mere 'inputs' and irreducibles into 'givens'.

As this study has shown, doing the job is only a part of the story. Workplace *givens* are not necessarily the proper objects of investigation, which may include the presence of racism, sexism, or exploitation distinct from task performance. The so-called *facts* about learning, currently expressed in performance-based modes of knowing, cannot adequately represent the occupational influences on the processes involved. Nor can they capture the *character* of one's evaluations, beliefs, practical judgments, opinions and ethics – the phronesis – of one's knowledge. These features of human work and learning cannot readily be reduced to the measurable forms desired by industrial relations negotiators, managers and educators who remain faithful to cognitive psychology and positivism.

In most industrial contexts, like construction, the desired form of learning is based on measurable itemised elements that can be linked to remuneration, and excluded (or eliminated) if not conforming with the required nomenclature. The itemisation of adult workers' learning thus includes a socialising effect. It is a reductionist socialisation in which work produces not only material constructions, but 'acculturated employees' (Casey 1995: 78). It is the discursive practices of work, and not just what can be seen, that profoundly affect individual practitioners and, more generally, human relations.

It is thus symbolically appropriate that the principal site of study for this book was the Sydney 2000 Olympic Games site. The contemporary Olympic movement is itself a symbol of the contradictions and paradoxes of postmodern life: the notion of friendly sport between nations has become a commercially exploited product. Image-making possibilities are thoroughly exploited through global media coverage and strong and wealthy nations demonstrate their supposed 'superiority' over poorer nations. The rhetoric of 'going for gold' in this context remains, unfortunately, a subtext for jaded ideological 'games' or an outlet for the expression of intense nationalism. Although the official rhetoric claims that the Olympics is about participation and sharing between nations, *winning* has primacy.

At the construction site, Phaedrus executives used the expression 'going for gold' at inductions for construction workers. What this metaphor actually meant at site level was building a quality construction on time, under budget and without industrial disputation. This has been a bottom line operation with big dollars at stake. Economic considerations were never 'invisible' as were some aspects of the practitioners' learning.

Critical views/postmodern doubt

The current valuing of informal learning is partly influenced by a philosophy of experience that is quite instrumental. Priority is given to 'solving problems', 'competent performance' and 'assessment' based on observable outcomes. Learning needs to be directly aligned with the requirements of construction or else is considered dubious or even subversive. Learning in this context needs to be 'concrete'. Making sense of the world through asking and reformulating critical questions such as 'Why are we doing this project? How might it affect people? How will it impact on the natural environment, and indeed the eco-system? Do we really want this? Are team approaches to work organisation as desirable as the rhetoric suggests?', are completely out of bounds. These questions have traditionally characterised formal or 'academic' education. They are out of vogue in the drive for productive links between formal and work-based learning because they are inter-ruptive, and interruptions are 'bad news'. The 'productive links' between formal and informal learning are subtextual in the discourse of industries having to become more competitive in world markets.

This text has shown, however, that experiences of ambiguity, doubt, confusion, conflict, shifting priorities and allegiances characterise contemporary HRD professional practices. Informal learning is partly about *corporate survival* within the hierarchies of structural and implicit power. The trainers' accommodations tended to be in public. Their displays of loyalty to Phaedrus were 'visible'. Resistance tended to be a 'personal' affair characterised by an internal dialogue. Marta's 'Nelson Mandela cake', a symbolic gesture, was one of the few instances of public resistance to racist tendencies, both at the site and more generally within the construction industry. More typically the HRD practitioners referred to their need to become 'invisible'.

This metaphor of invisibility shows that the highly prized instru-mental learning available in the workplace forced critique and resistance underground (and dispersed). The new corporate approaches to work organisation and management appear to have an effect of suppressing critique and resistance. Yet this suppression is part of the experience of *belonging* to the corporation. This dialectic of suppression/belonging has the effect of privileging what is visible – competent, observable performance. Personal values and beliefs about difference, equity and ethics are 'processed' through self-regulation strategies which are required if one is to belong to the benefits and reward systems of the corporation. 'Developmentally educative workplaces constituted by a critically reflective learning environment' (Welton 1995: 4), are more ideals than realities in a contemporary corporate context.

Chapter 3 pointed out that humanistic notions of 'the learning organisation' have led to its popular adoption by corporations and enterprises. But it holds no overriding theoretical claims for an educative workplace. The learning organisation concept is intimately connected to the underlying capital ethos of productive growth, sharing the same overall framework of assumptions about what work is, what drives the economy and how 'progress' is defined. Hart, following two powerful currents of critical thought – Frankfurt critical theory and several varieties of feminism[7] – argues that what constitutes good or educative work 'cannot solely be based on an analysis of existing workplaces, thus relying on conventional notions of work' (Hart 1993: 20).

She argues that troublesome issues relating to social hierarchies, divisions, forms of exploitation and alienation are reflected in general social ideas such as 'what constitutes good or bad work, glamorous or dirty work, and highly skilled or lowly skilled work' (1993: 20):

> to perform a critique of the concept of work itself means to step outside the framework that defines the parameters of the current debate on work and education; to assume a broader more comprehensive perspective; and to call into question the values, assumptions and myths out of which this framework is constructed. Relocating one's point of departure has several advantages. First, it relieves the pressure of making a choice between a more 'pessimistic' and a more 'optimistic' interpretation of current changes and developments. For instance, in the current debate on the future of work, much energy is spent on deciding whether work is going to be more skilled or more de-skilled, with considerable evidence marshalled in favour of both positions. However, by examining the broader social context that gives rise to the division between skilled and unskilled in the first place, one can identify its underlying logic and its relationship to a myriad of

social divisions that not only determine the socially constructed meaning of skills, but also provide mechanisms for distributing opportunities for developing or practicing those skills.

(Hart 1993: 21)

Hart's argument, although compelling, is flawed because of its assumption that by adopting a more critical framework, one can avoid a new set of possible oppressive consequences. Her standpoint is that a broader, more comprehensive view allows for an analysis where questions concerning social divisions along lines of sex, race/ethnicity, or nationality can be fully integrated with class. In other words: 'questions raised by women, people of colour, or Third World people are not merely added to an otherwise gender-neutral, colour-blind, "general" analysis, but they provide its very foundation' (Hart 1993: 21).

These are issues with which many staff developers, HRD practitioners and adult educators (including myself) have deep sympathies. But it is the 'foundational' proposition which carries its main flaw. A foundational approach to any debate about workplace skills contains the elements of meta-narrative (Enlightenment) notions of freedom and empowerment. As such, this type of empowerment is co-implicated with liberal individualism. A consequence of this is that it still participates in the tradition of liberatory politics which privileges the individual as 'an agent of all social phenomena, signification and knowledge production' (Usher and Edwards 1994: 219). Hart is therefore investing in a paradigm of consciousness and agency. The philosophical justification of this paradigm rests on the notion of a rational 'knowing' (individual) subject who experiences 'false consciousness' caused by exploitative social structures. This justification is trapped in a discourse of 'true' or 'false' consciousness – a philosophically unstable binary logic.

The logic of false consciousness has been a theme in the modern tradition in which the 'self' is conceived as historically specific, and socially and culturally patterned. Marx, Durkheim and Freud each held, variously, the idea that the self is a social construction shaped by institutional processes, whereas Goffman (1959: 240) argues that the self is not a fixed entity but constituent upon 'technical, political, structural, cultural and "dramaturgical" perspectives'.[8] Charles Taylor's influential study further proposes that the self is ephemeral, contingent on 'connections between senses of the self and moral visions, between identity and the good' (Taylor 1989: x).

Postmodern ideas about 'the self' differ in that they focus on tensions between social production of identity – as subject to dynamic and multiple configurations, discourses of language, power, difference and plurality. Foucault's objective (in relation to the subject and power) was

> to create a history of the different modes by which, in our culture, human beings are made subjects. . . . [Including] the way a human being can turn him- or herself into a subject. . . . We have to know the historical conditions which motivate our conceptualisation.
>
> (Foucault 1982: 208–9)

Anyon refers to Derrida to make the point that:

> discourse does not (language does not) reflect either human consciousness *or* an external 'reality'. Poststructural and post-modern theorists define (helpfully) language in ways that attempt to free linguistic meaning from the determinism of structuralist definitions, in which meaning is fixed by pre-determined binary opposition.
>
> (Anyon 1994: 119)

Freud's [1915] (1966) psychoanalytic theorisation that subjectivity is not specifically constituted by consciousness is dramatically extended by Lacan (1977). Consciousness for Lacan *is* 'Other-determined', resting on the symbolic order of language and culture that decentres 'the ego'. His conception of self privileges signs, symbols and images. This is radically different from the subject of scientific and humanistic psychology – the very subject underlying Hart's critical-feminist position. Lacan's notion of consciousness differs in that meaning is not a function of an autonomous individual subject, but 'is a function of the connection or relationship between *signifiers*' (Lacan 1977: 150, cited in Usher and Edwards 1994: 65). Postmodern theories of language, discourse and power challenge the idea that meaning and intentions can have an existence separate from language and intersubjectivity, disrupting the philosophical tenets on which the 'consciousness paradigm' depends.

Hart's critical conception of work as a learning environment seeks to substitute 'the truth' of women's reality for modernity's patriarchal idea of truth. This position represents 'an aggressively radical assertion of women's truth as the foundation for feminist action' (Lemert 1995: 81). In Dorothy Smith's (1987) words, 'the critical force of these methods is contained in . . . enlarging women's powers and capacities to organise and struggle against the oppression of women' (in Lemert 1995: 81). This view of a women's 'truth', or 'truthful experience', foregrounds (emancipatory) politics by linking workplace practices at local levels with political action at the macro-level. This illustrates the importance of how one conceptualises *resistance* in relation to workplace learning.

As shown in Chapters 5 and 6, the space for resistance in contemporary corporate practices is circumscribed by the intricate web of communication patterns and enveloping work organisational structures and systems. Overt resistance will, in many instances, be viewed as 'subversive' and quickly eliminated. Hence Foucault's assertion that critical analysis must work from forms of resistance to modernity:

> rather than analysing power from the point of view of its internal rationality, [my method] consists of analysing power relations through the antagonisms of strategies. . . . [For example] there are two meanings of the word *subject*: subject to someone else by control and dependence, and tied to his own identity by a conscience or self-knowledge. Both meanings suggest a form of power which subjugates and makes subject to.
>
> (Foucault 1982: 211–12)

Resistance and transgression for Foucault, therefore, begin with oppositions, strains, differences *within and against* the dominant ideologies of modernity. It follows that a postmodern perspective on resistance and interruption does not automatically exclude or marginalise instrumental learning. Rather, it seeks alternative approaches to what might constitute 'valid learning' whereby differences (within and against) are more highly valued. Ironically, there is common ground between this postmodern position[9] and Hart's radical modernist position, although Hart's strategy, based on its existing philosophical justification, can lead to the replacement of one dominant discourse with another.

Most certainly, the HRD personnel in this study found their questioning of and resistance to workplace imperatives modified by the discursive practices of the corporation. This circumscription has been affected by corporate strategies that encourage 'participatory' decision-making structures, partnering arrangements and team structures. These strategies are supposed to 'enable' employees' ideas to be valued and utilised by management. But instead of opening communication patterns, the designer corporate language and culture can bind employees more firmly to the company's goals and production targets. The players are actively and willingly complying with the construction of such targets. Within these binding processes, a form of workplace learning is constituted that leaves little space for critical reflection and even less for resistance, although these are never totally eliminated.

A consequence for the 'transformational' dimension of learning is that one of its central tenets: *praxis* – which entails action-reflection-action as a workplace learning method – is re-encoded to performativity.

Against these findings, Hart's (1995: 124) suggestions for radical social transformations including – 'the overall humanisation of the workplace' – appear noble, but wishful thinking. Indeed, 'given existing power inequalities, and the state's role in mediating, supporting, engendering and reproducing them' (Usher and Edwards 1994: 220), it appears over-optimistic to expect that informal learning alone might hold seeds for a qualitatively better future for employees within contemporary workplaces. It is clear that current conceptions of both informal learning and of workplaces as learning environments are 'framed' by their location within discourses of market economics and human capital theory. These discourses narrow what it means to 'be critical' and this narrowing represents a major challenge for universities chasing new markets in work-based learning degrees.

Existing definitions do not adequately problematise what informal learning actually is. There is a silence about the power of discourse to delineate the sayable and to highlight those features of informal learning that are 'made' more or less important. Informal learning does not simply fit the neat, measurable units and elements of competence that many in government agencies, industry bodies and trade unions might be hoping for. There is much going on with informal learning beyond its articulation through human capital and experiential learning discourses. The narrative stories in this book have revealed that by adopting a broad view of informal learning it becomes less amenable to objectification and more problematic for 'measurement'. Yet a broad view may become very important to people's working lives and beyond. The contemporary attempts to 'informalise' training, and workplace learning more generally, so that the informal can be 'mobilised' to comply with the latest classification framework, TQM requirements, or production schedules, evoke Foucault's point that opportunities for resistance are offered in the contradictions and ambiguities of modern discipline: 'discourse can be both an instrument and an effect of power, but also a hindrance, a stumbling block, a point of resistance and a starting point for an opposing strategy' (Foucault 1982: 101).

Whether a postmodern interpretation of informal learning offers sufficient leverage to be a 'stumbling block' to contemporary power/knowledge formations is examined in Chapter 8. Written as a postscript, it contemplates whether postmodern doubt, although offering valuable critical perspectives on workplace learning, offers enough to challenge the construction of 'what counts' through the dominant discourses of technical-rationality. Indeed, when considering what is to be done, the theory one holds becomes central – and no single theory or perspective tells an adequate story about such sheer complexity.

Notes

1   Barnett points out that operational (or corporate) competence is linked with 'know-how, outcomes, economic strategies, experience, organisational norms and better practical effectiveness' (1994: 160). Academic competence on the other hand is characterised by 'know-that, intellectual fields, propositions, metacognition, disciplinary knowledge, truthfulness and a search for better cognitive understanding'. Barnett argues that both are flawed.

2   Philosophy and sociology are two disciplines currently targeted for cutbacks and even departmental closures in a number of universities which cite, as principal rationales, the 'funding crisis' and the need for 'interdisciplinary approaches' to match changes in industry.

3   While I do not bring the voices of marginalised or disenfranchised groups into my own text, I have not claimed that I am doing so, nor do I claim informal learning in the workplace (as currently conceived within HRD) will necessarily benefit disadvantaged groups.

4   This 'valorisation of the observable' can have the effect of separating professional judgment from practical knowledge. Aristotle helps us understand this separation by distinguishing *phronesis* (which contributes to ethical virtue), and *techne* (which implies a skilful means of 'getting there') (Beckett 1993: 8).

5   I am not wishing to convey a romantic picture of the 'old' culture here. It involved embedded corruption, racism and sexism. The new 'sanitised' sites are attempting to redress some of these problems.

6   The *New York Times* (27 October 1995) reported that the largest single construction project in the world at that moment revolved around the new Hong Kong airport and its infrastructure. The report noted that no serious environmental impact studies were required for development, and construction occurs 'around the clock'. The report was attempting to explain why US construction firms had failed to win any significant building contracts there, and concluded that such [Western] firms would, in future, need to 'tune into the cut and thrust of Asian ways of doing business'. Training of Western construction experts to 'cut-it' in this context will need to be very flexible indeed, with ecological and ethical bases for development thoroughly tested.

7   Hart's work has been associated with a 'womanist' stream of feminist thought which, inter alia, examines how power distorts relations between men and women (Welton 1995: 8).

8   Goffman adopts a symbolic interactionist approach to demonstrate the importance of the 'dramatic' way people represent themselves to one another – hence the dramaturgical or 'staging the self' perspective. This perspective highlights techniques of 'impression management' as a way of

'ordering facts . . . and the identity and interrelationships of the several performance teams which operate in the establishment' (Goffman 1959: 240).

9   Lemert points out that there are currently three broad positions in a complex debate in the theoretical space where once ideology [unopposed] stood. Each position acknowledges that 'truth' might no longer serve as a normative standard for thought or action. These positions are, broadly:

1 Radical postmodernism which abandons the very idea of truth; accordingly, the problem of ideology is relieved.

2 Radical modernism which seeks by several means to retain the idea of truth and thus retain ideology as at least a rhetorical cover for more complex riddles.

3 'Strategic' postmodernism which attempts the trick of destroying modernity's foundational quest for truth by revising without completely rejecting modernity's categories.

(Lemert 1995: 78)

8 Doubts about postmodern doubt
Postscript

Are we free, truly free, to choose what we see? Clearly not. On the other hand, are we obliged, absolutely forced against our will to perceive what is first merely suggested then imposed on everyone's gaze? Not at all!

(Paul Virilio 1997: 95)

In this text I have tried to create new understandings of what informal learning can be 'read as'. In particular my story has unfolded a more dialectical approach to understanding informal learning. What has emerged is neither a set of recommendations nor an alternative model for practice. Nor does this postscript summarise key findings. Rather, what has emerged for me is the significance of discourse as a primary shaper of informal learning. How one talks about and theorises informal learning influences what it becomes and thus what it excludes. I have drawn on the post-structuralist ideas of Foucault and Lyotard in particular to examine how the discourses of HRD constitute particular forms of subjectivity associated with the exercise of power and how the 'educative' interventions of daily practice socially construct professional behaviour. I have argued that it is not so much a question of finding natural traits, abilities and competencies that match work requirements, but rather it is uncovering the educative effects, the informal 'meaning-making' that accompanies everyday practice, that offers a key for a better theory–practice relationship.

Practices are not only given meaning by their location in discourses, but discourses are also practices. Discourses are ways of thinking and ways of doing – knowledge and power. Meanings are organised and constituted through discourses. For HRD practitioners, capability may be increased in so far as one can translate meaning between and across the different discourses that are found within and around HRD practices – including the master discourses of the moment. In this 'discursive' approach, scientific disciplinary knowledge as the foundation of professional expertise is displaced to include a wide variety of interpretive practices, and 'naturally' such an approach will not be to everyone's liking. As a strategy, it is clearly not without problems. These will need to be worked through and subjected to the same scrutiny I am calling for in practice – and this process is never ending.

Contemporary HRD knowledge frameworks are unashamedly linked to market economics. It is the master discourse of market economics which gives the cues to the sub-discourses of HRD practices; consultancies, re-engineering, downsizing, outsourcing, negotiating and image-making on one hand, and discourses of quality performance on the other – capability, competence, TQM, empowerment, self-direction, learning organisations and so on. Economic and instrumental rationality are at the heart of the knowledge frameworks associated with each of these discourses as they are applied in Western societies. Knowledge is prized in so far as it can generate a market advantage (or service an operational area that has the capabilities of bringing the organisation a market advantage). This book has shown how it is the generation of efficiencies, profit, and institutional or organisational prestige that is primarily valued. This, of course, is not a bad thing per se. But in such a regime, knowledge becomes characterised by what people actually do and are seen to be doing – their 'visible' performance. Financial and numerical performance indicators become valorised.

HRD practices are set against a backdrop of postmodern conditions – globalisation, discourses of 'market penetration', de-regulation, privatisation, marketisation, dispersal of authorities (and of subsequent knowledge formation) and the feverish search for new 'self' definition – or as Bauman (1997: 14) puts it 'a polyphony of value-messages and the ensuing fragmentariness of life which characterises the world we live in'. Power structures are changing, decision-making centres are shifting and traditional notions of knowledge construction, such as through universities and their research, are being radically challenged. Postmodern ideas bring a set of epistemological challenges – a questioning of anything that suggests absolute principles of reasoning. Yet ironically, even with postmodern doubt, faith in market economics at political and national policy-making levels appears to have reached a virtually unchallenged position in relation to framing thought and action. What is constituting 'valid' knowledge is the direct and measurable link between thought and action; the idea and the market power of the product. Such a link, by definition, permeates the processes of self-identity formation including the attempt to locate where one 'belongs' in the work maze.

Managerial requirements of HRD practices are not to promote doubt or to problematise issues. HRD practitioners are meant to be problem-solvers. Ultimately, in a market-forces ideology, it is assumed, as I argued in Chapter 1, that issues to do with social justice, fairness, ethics, equity and so on, will be resolved via 'the market' by the 'natural order'. When the notion of a 'market-forces' determination of valid knowledge is read in conjunction with Foucault's proposition that scientific discourse is linked to the tightening of surveillance and control, this notion becomes deeply troubling. Using Foucault's theory, I have shown how HRD knowledges and performative practices can be read as technologies of compliance and control that refine self-regulation and dependency. But the technologies work in complex ways and take many different forms. Some of them are actually meant to decrease dependency and enable resistance to the determining criteria of market economics. Indeed, as argued in Chapter 7, 'discourse can be both an instrument and an effect of power . . . a point of resistance and a starting point for an opposing strategy' (Foucault 1982: 101). Foucault's theoretical proposition is that it is through continually exploiting the contradiction and ambiguities of modern discipline that resistance to dominant practices is always possible. The effects of power–knowledge formations are never complete. But does this theory give adequate purchase to resistance strategies? How can one resist the overwhelming power of market economics and its profound effects, including fragmentation and plurality, on human relations? To where might HRD practitioners look for richer sources of knowledge to inform their practices? How can the notion of 'discourse' be deployed to examine new possibilities for action? What are some of the futures for HRD practices? Indeed, what is to be done?

Possible futures for HRD practices

In the postmodern sense, there is always scope for HRD practitioners to create space and challenge organisational practices that are perceived by them to be worth challenging. HRD practices in both private and public institutions are frequently subject to the governing rules of market economics – rules which apply, at this historic moment, almost absolutely. Donald Schön's (1983) landmark study of the ways professionals think in action indicates that the knowledge processes of expert practitioners are adjusted in the light of everyday professional experience and reflective thought. Schön described the ways professionals construct and revise their practices through trial and error, coining the phrase 'reflection-in-action'. In short, through the idea of reflection in action, he helped popularise a theory of experience-based learning in which knowledge is derived in part from direct experience of *doing the job*. He argued that theoretical knowledge should not be privileged over practical knowledge but this happens through the power of the 'technical-rationality model' of practice.[1]

Everyday choices of which actions to pursue in order to reach the desired effects are most often informed by previous experience. Theorised prior experience as distinct from theoretical prediction is central to Schön's perspective. Prior experience is a critical basis of pragmatic knowing, and the test for pragmatic knowledge is not whether it corresponds with an objective reality but, in the postmodern view, whether it functions successfully: does it work? From a postmodern perspective, some possible futures for HRD practices can be discerned in this theory–practice relationship. This relationship is shaped increasingly by a 'pragmatic knowledge' that is being constructed by a collection of examples of experience and action that have delivered desired results. Thus an influential discourse that underpins contemporary HRD theory and practice is that of experience-based learning.

Learning from experience, now valorised by many HRD academics and practitioners, has been taken up by many staff developers and trainers as 'the' most meaningful way to promote individual and organisational learning. One runs the risk of marginalisation if one is too critical of this popular discourse, as the use of the individual's experience as a valid commencement point in the learning process is now mainstream. It is economically useful and intimately tied to trends toward, and investment in, flexible delivery systems. It is precisely the use of personal experience as the starting point for planned learning processes that is being questioned by postmodern ideas about the influences of language, discourse and power/knowledge formations. The professional experience of today's HRD manager is significantly influenced by the circulating discourses of HRD and their tie-in to the master discourse of market economics. Professional survival now depends on negotiating one's way successfully through the maze of organisational structures, management styles, group dynamics, industrial relations problematics and training. The capable modern professional is also required to respond rapidly and flexibly to the imperatives of the external environment. No-one can stand outside the circulating discourses that shape one's personal day-to-day experiences. It follows that personal experience as a commencement point for learning can be deepened when considered in conjunction with the effects on experience of the circulating discourses.

Logically this theorisation would mean taking deconstruction more seriously than it has been taken in HRD professional practice and academic teaching to date. In practice, this means understanding one's professional practices as socially constructed and historically framed by the dominant discourses within which they are located. Understanding one's role as an HRD practitioner (or manager) working within a set of practices would also be viewed as tied to collections of individual and collective behaviour, both contextually informed and localised. From this standpoint the HRD profession would be informed increasingly by particularised knowledge, for instance, of case studies of successful practice, of the 'know-how' generated from engagement in the day-to-day maze of the job. Such 'know-how' is very distinct from general models or off-the-shelf pre-packaged modules. It is not predictive, disciplinary-based nor universally 'true' in the sense of having a 'methodologically validated' correspondence with an independent reality. The body of knowledge that would be most likely to inform HRD practices in the postmodern moment is more likely to rest on trans-disciplinary knowledge, a collection of experience-based case studies of 'successful' practices, and micro-generalisations that serve as sense-making guides for local situations and for helping to address the needs of particular clients.

One of the principal concerns of this book has been that the influences of market economics on thought and action can 'reduce' developmental opportunities to projected statistics on corporate balance sheets. Such thinking can and does lead to 'law of the jungle' behaviour where the choices of action are circumscribed by financial accounting, obsessive measurement and associated political imperatives. Survival of the fittest is a desired outcome of free market economic philosophy and again, this is assumed as 'natural' and thus 'good' without this philosophy being attenuated and overlaid by life-world discourses and everyday interactions.

There is, however, an emerging counter-movement in the business world which is challenging the current (over) reliance on financially based instruments for assessing the merits of training and development. Karl-Erik Sveiby (Sveiby and Lloyd 1987), who set up the Swedish community of practice involving forty firms sharing with each other new ways to express what he calls 'intangibles', is advocating the idea that corporations must develop new ways of valuing which go beyond corporate balance sheets. Following Sveiby, some American companies are beginning to question whether training and development should be treated as capital expenditure or as corporate overheads. Drucker argues in the *Harvard Business Review* (Drucker 1995: 37) that many American businesses have (sensibly) already shifted from traditional cost accounting to 'activity-based costing' which integrates value analysis, process analysis, quality management and costing. This represents a change containing the potential to combine management theory, organisational development and statistical thinking with richer notions of lifelong learning. But it must be acknowledged that this 'integration' is discursively constructed, shaped by market economics. For 'richer notions' of lifelong learning to be translated into HRD futures in ways that do not become new and more subtle forms of oppression, they will need to address the dark side of performativity, the contrariness of postmodern times, the interconnectedness of experience and situated ethics and not merely the high-gloss.

Some conclusions? The deconstructability of deconstruction

One suggestion here is to use deconstruction as a HRD strategy. This suggestion rests on Derrida's philosophical notion that texts contain 'conceptual hierarchies' (in Parker 1997: 72). Hierarchical ordering is a symptom of the way in which a text (or a person's story) assumes 'normative' standpoints. From the assumed norms perspective, other perspectives (not normative) can be presented as simply negatives, distortions or perversions of the text's (story teller's) concept. Derrida claims that this presentation entails philosophical oppositions in which some terms (the normative) dominate the others. There may well be some reasonable explanations for this domination, but the idea of deconstruction is to contest the oppositional hierarchy and unsettle it. Deconstruction, in this unsettling sense, is a particular strategy that can help address the prevalent HRD theory–practice binary, and the ways the binary is fuelled by the discourses of economic rationalism. In HRD this 'fuelling' entails the valorising of practice knowledge 'over' formal or disciplinary-based theory which, in turn, is an effect of the valorising of experience as 'natural' or 'given'. It is precisely this alignment of experience-based learning theory with the 'natural order' which allows it to be easily re-inscribed by the powerful influences of the so-called 'market place'. A key question that needs to be asked here is how the discourse of theory can intervene in practice without contributing to oppression.

Reflexive difficulties exist with deconstruction as an HRD

approach. Deconstruction is provisional in nature. As a strategy, it can be subject to its own devices. In this sense professional development and pragmatic knowledge is always in process and can never be complete. Professional developers are thus working with tools that make no promises for solving problems or producing rational complete solutions. It is a problematising approach which involves an examination of the exercises of power at work – in the micro-practices of daily life. As practitioners (and I am including myself in this) we are situated in power relations that are often virtual 'givens'. Examining power relations and their effects on professional practice will never be simple or even desirable. Nonetheless the effects of local power relations will be present in some form at all times.

It is in the sense of my 'afterthoughts' that some suggestions are made as to how informal learning might be addressed in future research and work-based learning practices. In the workplaces using competency-based standards to measure performance, this study has found that the pre-defined nature of competencies can remove elements of professional judgment. They can be prescriptive, emphasising technical requirements. Skilled workers can thus be denied aspects of professional judgment. What 'counts' as 'valid' informal learning has been shown to be tied to discursive communication patterns, power relations and particular types of workplace imperatives. Analyses of informal learning in contemporary corporate conditions thus require openness to knowing and demystification of management and HRD practices. Indeed, Foucault questions the way in which knowledge circulates and functions – its relations to power – focusing on problems of the present and of where we are at this very moment:

> the political, ethical, social, philosophical problem of our days is not to try to liberate the individual from the state, and from the state's institutions, but to liberate us from the state and from the type of individualisation which is linked to the state. We have to promote new forms of subjectivity through the refusal of the kind of individuality which has been imposed on us for several centuries.
>
> (Foucault 1982: 216)

Foucault reminds us that dialogue and argument have been historically shaped. They may well be central to progress in the lifeworld but can easily slide into the exercise of power through an emphasis on operational competence. How, for instance, can workplaces with a precarious harmony of union and management relations hope to engage in practices of dialogue and argument without slipping back to well-worn paths of conflict and contestation?

For Foucault, hope remains in so far as there is an inseparable relationship between power and freedom's refusal to submit:

> At the very heart of the power relationship, and constantly provoking it, are the recalcitrance of the will and the intransigence of freedom. . . . Rather than speaking of an essential freedom, it would be better to speak of . . . a state of permanent provocation.
>
> (Foucault 1982: 222)

Within the state of 'permanent provocation', Barnett points out, *'nothing can be taken on trust* . . . ideas, statements, symbols, ethical stances, institutions and ideological stances – the totality of one's experiences, both immediate and mediated – must come under continuous scrutiny' (Barnett 1994: 181). By definition, this is a process which can have no end. We learn from our mistakes, from trial and error, but what is ultimately at stake here is some conception of a common good and this cannot be defined a priori, but has to emerge out of, and be challenged by, open dialogue and critique.

Such a theory implies ethical, environmental and political considerations that contrast to the lip-service given them at the moment. This is a pathway that seriously challenges conventional notions of work, progress and development and of work's implications for learning and education. It is a pathway that helps interrogate the cult of 'modernist efficiency'. The so-called superstructure is now an elusive global electronic complex in which production is not necessarily material. Image, symbol production, consumption and decentred work practices are now a part of our postmodern world – aptly illustrated by the hyperreal Olympic Games site (which was formerly the NSW State Brickworks, an abattoir and a garbage dump). For such reasons, theoretical development related to workplace learning needs to include the notion of multiple, fragmented and competing discourses, even though such inclusions will present new and unpredictable mental demands.

Furthermore, contemporary HRD functions are shifting from specialist practitioners to the flexible new multi-skilled others who now have to pick up 'training skills'. The roles of specialist trainers and staff developers are also changing. In the corporations studied here, these changing roles embrace strategic planning, facilitation and corporate development – with correspondingly fewer specialist training jobs. These movements are directly related to the principles of operational efficiency. They are outcomes of the application of human capital theory to workplace learning, now expected by corporations to happen continuously – at the location workers are actually *doing* the job.

Present HRD orientations focus on 'the doing', the *techne*, and on driving up efficiencies. To counterpoint this drive and its potential to move us further into a world where everything is regulated in advance – the totally managed, technological world economy with a competent workforce – a more reflexive approach in developing ethical practices is suggested. Horkheimer and Adorno warn that this 'regulated' world is upon us:

> the fallen nature of modern man [sic] cannot be separated from social progress. On the one hand the growth of economic productivity furnishes the conditions for a world of greater justice; on the other hand it allows the technical apparatus and the social groups which administer it a disproportionate 'superiority' to the rest of the population. The individual is wholly devalued in relation to economic powers, which at the same time press the control of society over nature to hitherto unsuspected heights. Even though the individual disappears before the apparatus which he serves, that apparatus provides for him as never before. In an unjust state of life, the impotence and pliability of the masses grow with the quantitative increase in the commodities allowed them.
>
> (Horkheimer and Adorno [1944] 1993: xiv)

Horkheimer and Adorno argue convincingly that under existing conditions, all cultural values are 'purchased and re-sold in a sell-out of culture; they are doled out to satisfy consumer needs' (1993: xv). Under existing postmodern conditions, professional practice, and more generally the links between informal learning and formal education, face a massive challenge. This challenge could be assisted, as this text has argued, by unmasking taken-for-granted assumptions about workplace learning, how it is constituted, recognised and assessed. This unmasking includes developing more critical approaches to workplaces as learning environments and generating a greater awareness of the importance of situated ethics to informal learning. Such measures, I suggest, will be welcomed by business, industrial and academic institutions – but at this moment, are not reflected in the ensemble of government rules, policies and procedures inserting 'the market form' into higher education.

Note

1   The technical-rationality model assumes that theoretical knowledge must be a foundation of practice because it is research generated, systematic and 'scientific' knowledge. In the technical-rationality model, theory is

conceived as revealing the nature of the world. This knowledge takes the form of generalised propositions, the only knowledge considered worthwhile and secure (Usher, Bryant and Johnston 1997: 125). These writers argue that this privileging is taken to the point where every other kind of knowledge is 'demonised as mere belief, opinion and prejudice'.

Appendix
The research methods

Theoretically, this research is indebted to the post-structural notion that identities are constructed within, not outside, discourse. It thus follows that one's informal learning needs to be understood from the point of view of its production in certain historical and institutional sites – 'within specific discursive formations and practices, by specific enunciative strategies' (Hall 1996: 4). Informal learning in this text is viewed as emerging within (and against) specific modalities of power. It thus has a significant relationship to the marking of difference and exclusion, 'visibility' and 'invisibility'. The mini-narratives gathered for this analysis therefore represent, on the one hand, the discourses and practices of specific sites. The narrators speak to us as social subjects of particular discourses. On the other hand, the narratives represent processes which produce subjectivities; they indicate points of 'temporary attachment to the subject positions which discursive practices construct for us' (Hall 1996: 6).

Although this theorisation offers a compelling formal account of the construction of subject positions, it does not adequately address questions related to why it is that certain individuals occupy some subject positions and not others. It was my specific intention therefore to analyse how the social positions of individuals interact with discursively constructed subject positions. This approach reflects commitments held by the researcher which emphasise the individual's subjectivity as constructed through interaction with their contexts. My own concerns, which have been illustrated throughout the text, relate to a desire to unmask 'popular' notions of informal learning that are increasingly used to justify a new (conservative) political economy of education. In adopting this theoretical orientation, the enquiry presupposes a form of dialogue between the researcher and the practitioners whereby its methods interactively generate narrative accounts about their day-to-day work, how they know their job, what their own concerns, perceptions and understandings are, in addition to how these are shaped. My interests are reflected in the research methods which ask professional HRD practitioners to surface their taken-for-granted lifeworld.

The research procedures

This research attempts to make sense of the complexity of informal learning *in context*. The context includes the social reasoning embedded in everyday work. Rather than beginning with a reified view of the organisation as a structure – separate from those who make it up (à la systems theory) – I approach the practitioners involved as active constituents of their organisations. The initial interviews with the six HRD practitioners highlighted in Chapter 4 were to enable a constant comparison of emergent ideas and theoretical concepts, and to inform a second, more in-depth phase of the research. The two phases involved:

- Two rounds of in-depth interviews with the above mentioned six HRD practitioners. Each came from a different industry and was asked about their roles, responsibilities, principal concerns and learning in the workplace. This phase provided stories about the circulating discourses at work and individual experiences within them, including their own informal learning. The purpose of this phase was largely to inform phase two.
- An in-depth case study based upon numerous field visits, interviews and observations at one specific site – the Sydney 2000 Olympic Games construction project. This phase examined, over twelve months (1994–5), the informal learning of HRD practitioners at a large complex construction site. The site was selected, after completion of phase one, and explored local influences, including the links between work-based learning and work organisation, skill formation practices, the site culture and the activities meaningful to the trainers themselves.

Each participant was asked to think about how they went about doing their job – what they needed to know, who (or what) in the organisation helped them, and what they considered to be significant workplace learning for themselves. In addition, a critical incident technique was included, in which the participants were asked to describe a complex or problematic work situation that made them feel they had lacked the necessary skills or knowledge. Each interview was conducted at the participant's own workplace and 'in private'. Each interview was approximately two hours long. I began by explaining the broad aims of the research and encouraged the trainers to ask any questions to ensure they had the information to feel comfortable about participating (or indeed withdrawing). Although the interviews were not formally structured questionnaire-style, they were guided by opening questions located in particular discourses pertinent to HRD and which sought to enable the practitioners to tell their stories.

I taped the interviews (with permission) and later transcribed them. After each interview, the tapes were transcribed and sent to the partici- pants for comment. This allowed for clarification of any points which they felt they had not made clear or that they did not want included. In a few instances they made minor changes clarifying their meanings. Mac an Ghaill (1991: 114) points out some procedural and ethical dilemmas of this kind of research, arguing 'that a more damning criti- cism could be subsumed under the heading "paternalism" . . . and the arrogance of the researcher invading another group's world in order to get information to relay it to the outside world'. The African-American author bell hooks is even more scathing on this issue, particularly where it applies to marginalised others:

> often, speech about the 'Other' annihilates, erases: No need to hear your voice. Only tell me about your pain. I want to know your story. And then I will tell it back to you in a new way. Tell it back to you in such a way that it has become mine, my own. Re-writing you, I write myself anew. I am still author, authority. I am still the colo- nizer, the speaking subject, and you are now at the centre of my talk.
>
> (hooks 1990: 151)

Using the stories of others clearly raises important political questions. Whose side is the researcher really on? What is the researcher's agenda? What purposes and interests will the outcomes ultimately serve?

The 'political' questions raised by Mac an Ghaill (1991) and by hooks (1990), cannot be taken lightly. They are magnified when the research concerns a group labelled as 'disadvantaged'. In this research, the HRD practitioners were aware that a study of this nature could be highly critical of workplace practices. Nonetheless, they were keen to participate and derive any insights about their own learning at work. At no stage have I suggested that they represent a disadvantaged group in the community (even though some of their work has the potential to be exploited through productivity and managerial discourses). My experience throughout the study was that they actively wanted to participate in the research and were far from naive about potential consequences of the findings.

The Olympic Games site and the subjects

The Olympics site presented many advantages for the research. My personal interest was high due to the local excitement and scepticism generated by Sydney's hosting of the Olympic Games for the year 2000. A part of this local 'excitement' translated to extensive media coverage, some related to training. For example, the *Daily Telegraph* reported 'building workers are on a collision course with the State Government after vowing to use their bargaining power on major projects in the lead up to the 2000 Olympics to push for improved industry training' (*Daily Telegraph* 11 July 1995).

Such features made the project attractive for in-depth analysis. An aim of this phase was to build on existing ideas, networks and my ongoing re-thinking of the political processes which influence informal learning. I had already met a number of the construction workers through an earlier research project. This proved to be a huge advantage when I arrived at the Olympics site, as I was known to several workers there and had established relations I could build upon. These contacts quickly introduced me to local power-brokers from unions and management. They were also more willing to speak openly about their personal experiences at the new site, comparing it to the previous site. After having gathered extensive information on the context and the discursive or communicational features of the Olympics site, its two principal HRD personnel – David and Marta – were interviewed extensively and in a various ways, including formal and conversational approaches.

Entering this site required a number of approvals – the university, the Corporation Head Office (the developer), Phaedrus (the principal contractor at the site), the NSW State Department of Public Works (the client) and key unions. This process took time and patience. Although I had a letter of introduction to the site general manager from Head Office, possession of a developed research protocol and the necessary approvals, these provided no guarantee of acceptance at the site. Whatever documents were possessed, whatever might be said about my research interests, or perspectives likely to be represented, these would remain unclear to the workers themselves for some time, and trust in this industry does not come lightly.

At the construction site, I was allocated a shed for conducting interviews and was required to attend, initially as a participant (later as an observer), an induction training programme for new construction workers at the site. Attendance was also mandatory at an occupational health and safety meeting for familiarisation with the site's safety requirements. At this meeting, I discovered that I needed to wear a hard-hat and heavy boots for site visits. This was my first indication that safety was viewed by unions and management as a serious industrial issue. The hat and boots were also symbols of hierarchy which accompanied my foregrounding to the site-text!

The research plan was to interview initially a cross-section of workers from the site. This was not to be a random sample or even a stratified sample. Positivistic sampling was not the intention. Rather, an initial set of names of workers who might be prepared to be interviewed was provided by one of the trainers. Further names were added by the various stakeholders (unions, managers, foremen, subcontractors and labourers) who wanted to discuss their particular points of view. This pyramid-type process allowed me to gather data about the context from as wide a range as possible. Unfortunately, not everyone could be interviewed and, anyway, a census-style procedure was too cumbersome.

No interviewees are identified for reasons of confidentiality. Wherever quotes are used, the respondent was shown how the written material was to be used. In some cases, respondents did not want their comments recorded because they feared they might be identified even though names and positions were disguised. In such instances their comments were excluded.

In fulfilling ethical and consultative requirements, it was clear that site managers and union delegates were very important to interview access. This was made 'crystal clear' to me, in the vernacular of the site. An essential agreement was reached that a union representative, a trainer and a project manager would form an informal 'advisory' committee to assist the research. The assistance took two principal forms: approvals for workers' release from construction activities to be interviewed; and, critically, 'symbolic endorsement' of my presence at the site.

A possible third reading of this 'committee' is that it could have been a surveillance/control mechanism. I have not taken this reading seriously because it did not really attempt to censor my movements, nor my ideas. By their own admission committee members had not been exposed to this type of research before and were intrigued about its method. The committee also helped clarify some of the communication features of Phaedrus. That I was perceived at the site as 'not owned' by management or the union was fundamental to obtaining some of the startling disclosures from the workers which ensued.

The field study at the Olympics site took twelve months. I was based full time at the site for January, February and March 1994 and then at least one day per week until the end of June 1994. The six months from July to December 1994 involved obtaining feedback, meeting participants to discuss draft material, seeking clarification on the many issues raised and ensuring accuracy. (This process continued with David and Marta throughout the entire project.) As a higher degree of trust was built with the workers at the site, questions related more to their personal experience and learning.

Most of these interviews with David and Marta were taped. As we began to know each other better, we often met to discuss possible meanings embedded within transcripts. We did not always agree upon interpretations. The system for the transcriptions was not based on a formal convention or coding method that might, for instance, characterise language research (see Gumpez and Berenz's (1990) suggestions for transcribing and reporting conversational exchanges). For consistency and clarity, however, *italics* were used whenever the speaker was emphasising a point (i.e. italics in the transcripts equals the speaker's own emphasis).

On occasion, informal discussions and observations required immediate note-taking into my 'field-book'. The use of note-taking and the observation book obviously has limitations, but I found it a most efficient method in the context. Thoughts about taping all interviews were dropped soon after entering the site, for various reasons. For example, the research followed soon after a Royal Commission into corruption and mismanagement in the industry. This alone made tape-recording conversations 'suspect'. Taping is not a part of the culture. Taping interviews with David and Marta was the exception.

For reasons of confidentiality, ethics and economy, some of the data gathered with David and Marta has not been included in the body of the text. Excerpts of the transcripts, however, are included in Chapters 5 and 6. These show examples of the questions asked, the nature of the responses and analytic interpretations.

Interviewing on site raises several contextual considerations and representational issues. At the practical level, creative approaches and procedures were required to suit the work context. I sometimes asked questions about activities while workers were in the actual process of 'doing it'. This presupposes an intelligibility about the experience being studied which is not always fair. Marta's experience of conducting a literacy course exemplifies this. Her personal experience would have had certain unique qualities which the research sought to identify and understand. If the 'personal qualities' related to, say, a power dynamic, a key issue for the methodology is to explore this dynamic. It may involve asking: What is her experience of this? What is involved in this power relationship? How can we better understand the nature of this power dynamic? What is its relation to Marta's informal learning? These questions are not necessarily best approached directly with, in this instance, Marta. They require, in addition to her voice, careful observation of the context within which her activity was set, and a deconstruction of her narrative account. In turn, the researcher's own observations require scrutiny, as does the issue of research subjects/researcher interaction.

Representationally the research activity needed to be closely intertwined with daily activities. The writing was a construction of the interaction with David and Marta and indeed was inseparable from my experience and theorisation of site practices. The structure of the text, in its decisive form, emerged after initial dialogue with the participants and the whole research process constructed the text in its final form. This process included meetings with David and Marta in which we sometimes disagreed about interpretations. This issue has very important ethical and epistemological dimensions. The site had a powerful tacit intensity about it and we sometimes shared intense conversational interviews. These led each of us to new levels of self-awareness with accompanying possibilities for changes in lifestyle, work-practices and shifting personal priorities. There is, of course, no blueprint to follow to resolve this conundrum, although my approach was to keep a sense of the overall project and address broad themes rather than a particular point or contested notion. The research itself became part of the informal learning of Marta, David and myself. Where we remained in disagreement about an interpretation, this is acknowledged in the text.

'Working' with the data

As the genre of this study is post-structural, I need to acknowledge the risk taken in researching and retheorising informal learning. But the contingency and plurality of knowledge does not preclude such use of theory. In doing the research I spent a great deal of time with individuals, interviewing them and observing them in their work roles. At the Olympics site I got to know a range of workers, had lunch with them, and visited some at their own homes after hours. I met with a range of industry leaders from trade unions, corporate head offices and government. In many respects I entered the lifeworlds of these workers – a particularly privileged position, and a position that carries an important duty to understand their narratives in a way that justifiably makes sense of their lives within their industry contexts. This has left me with niggling doubts about whether I could have 'worked the data' a little harder or pursued further specific insights in greater depth. Indeed, the status of the mini-narratives of David and Marta is, as Usher and Bryant (1989) point out in their analysis of theory development, limited: 'experience without critical analysis can be little more than anecdotal reminiscence; interesting, but unconnected, experiential travellers' tales from the front lines of practice' (in Brookfield 1993: 30).

After extensive time involved with people – in which my views were actively sought, where workers divulged to me sensitive personal and professional information, and where I made new friends and colleagues – it would be wrong to assert the authoritative voice of the calculating scientist. The narrative presented here is my construction. Although it is based on a systematic methodology, there is no illusion that the selection of data, the choice of quotations for inclusion, the theorising, is definitive and objective knowledge. It is not. It is a construction that strategically represents my observations and insights following several years of research with the 'subjects' of the study. As such, the discussion and analyses are not attempts to give voice to the participants. The results here achieve credibility, I would argue, from methodically gathered data *and* their theoretical representation.

The theoretical representation is itself a narrative portraying one story. By definition this rejects any closure on the topic of informal learning. I have drawn on postmodern insights to work towards a better theory of workplace learning, a theory that challenges conventional 'humanistic' and 'economistic' views of adult education and HRD practices. But it does not and cannot represent an all-encompassing narrative.

Glossary

The purpose of this glossary is to clarify the ways technical terms and philosophical phrases are used in this text, highlighting research and postmodern concepts. Often the terms have complex and multi-faceted dimensions and have been simplified here for the purposes of accessibility and economy.

Adult learning   Brookfield (1986) espouses six basic principles of effective practice in facilitating adult learning:

- Participation in learning is voluntary; adults engage in learning as a result of their own volition. Circumstances prompting learning may be external to the learner (e.g. job loss, change) but the decision to learn is the learner's. Hence, excluded are settings in which adults are coerced or intimidated into learning.
- Respect among participants for each other's self-worth underlies all facilitation efforts. This does not exclude criticism, but statements on behaviour which belittle others should be absent.
- Facilitation is collaborative.
- Facilitation aims to foster in adults a spirit of critical reflection.
- Self-direction and improvement is fostered.
- Learners and facilitators are involved in a continual process of activity, reflection, new activity and collaborative analysis.

In this text, these principles are examined critically, as they can be misleading. In the context of 'work-based' learning for instance, subtle and discursive corporate influences and political coercion often apply. The underlying assumptions about 'self-direction' and learner 'autonomy' are shown to be flawed. Even so, the above principles are often taken for granted within liberal/humanist adult education practices, and exemplified in much of the work-based learning (human resources development) literature. In HRD, a broad range of people make decisions about learning programmes and their design. Learning in the applied or instrumental sense is often about the acquisition of competencies that can be applied to one's work. Nadler (1992: 104) applies a taxonomy to the HRD field to distinguish major types of work-based learning programmes, viz:

• Training – learning related to the present job of the individual.
• Education – learning related to a future, but defined job for which the individual is being prepared.
• Development – learning for the general growth of the individual and/or the organisation.

Such distinctions represent false dichotomies as they are interrelated, but Nadler (1992: 106) argues that there are different models for learning appropriate to each category. For example, that the 'training model' must be related to the job as it is actually being done by the individual. Present performance on the job and 'observable' outcomes are essential parts of such a model for adult learning.

Being   'Being' is the most central concept of Heidegger's hermeneutic phenomenology. Being does not describe an entity or ultimate ground but rather it is a term that represents Heidegger's ontology: 'Being is always the Being of an entity, and so to ask for the Being of something is to inquire into the nature or meaning of that phenomenon' (1962: 29).

Heidegger's professed aim is to let the things of the world speak for themselves. He asks: What is the nature (Being) of this being? What lets this being be what it is? 'Being', in the Heideggerian sense, is a fundamental term of the interpretive research process.

'Being-in-the-world' is a Heideggerian phrase that refers to the way human beings exist, act, or are involved in the world, for example, as parent, as teacher, as man, as woman, as child, as trainer and so on.[1]

Critical theory   has identified itself with the Marxist legacy of attempting to forge a dialectical synthesis of philosophy and a scientific understanding of society based on:

1   an appeal to a widened notion of rationality
2   a resistance to all forms of domination
3   an orientation to praxis
4   the centrality of the concept of emancipation.

Critical theory is now usually identified with the past work of representatives of the Frankfurt School, and with the work of Jürgen Habermas (Barnett 1997: 30). In *Knowledge and Human Interests*

Habermas (1978) distinguishes three forms of knowledge and associated cognitive interests: the technical, the practical and the emancipatory. Each of these 'knowledge interests' is seen to be rooted in primordial human activities: work, symbolic interaction and power.

It is the empirical-analytic sciences which Habermas identifies as expressing the technical interest; the practical interest is seen to be incorporated in hermeneutics of the human sciences; and the emancipatory interest is served by the critically-oriented sciences. Habermas's critique of modern society is based on a critique of instrumental reason, which is seen as governing dominant social science – through which society understands itself – and by way of which society legitimates its oppressive economic, political and social practices.[2]

In education, research based on critical theory aims at promoting 'critical consciousness', breaking down institutional structures and arrangements which reproduce oppressive ideologies, and removing social inequalities that are sustained and produced by social structures and ideologies.

Deconstruction is the term most familiarly appropriated from Derrida's texts. It gains its rationale and purpose from the characteristic of language and texts. Deconstruction, although oversimplified here, can be described as:

> The name given simultaneously to the stress created in texts (between what they want to say and what they do say) and to the detection of such gaps. A deconstructive reading attends to the deconstructive processes *always* occurring in texts and *already* there waiting to be read.
>
> (Payne 1993: 121)

Deconstruction is conventionally understood as a strategy for reading texts. On the other hand, as is clear in Payne's quote, there is more to it than this since deconstruction or a 'deconstructive process' is already present in texts. It is because of the existence of this process that a deconstructive reading can take place.

Payne argues that Derrida's account of language, rather than controlling meaning, defining it, making it present, 'is inundated by signification' (1993: 121). Thus, closure and openness, dissemination and the fixing of meaning, contingent and certain knowledge, limiting the unlimitable, are all dual aspects of the process of marking off, of boundary setting.

Enlightenment   In the Enlightenment's interpretation, 'thinking is the creation of unified, scientific order and the derivation of factual knowledge from principles, whether the latter are elucidated as arbitrarily postulated axioms, innate ideas, or higher abstractions' (Horkheimer and Adorno [1944] 1993: 82). In the Enlightenment it is logical laws that provide the pathway towards freedom from oppression. Reason contributes the idea of systematic unity – and unity resides in agreement. In their seminal work on the Enlightenment Horkheimer and Adorno ([1944] 1993: 83) say that the resolution of contradiction occurs through a system based on the form of knowledge which 'copes most proficiently with the facts and supports the individual in the mastery of nature i.e. scientific knowledge'. In relation to informal learning, Usher, Bryant and Johnston (1997: 120) point out that with its Enlightenment inheritance 'learning is impelled to be constructed as something purposeful, goal-directed and empowering'. Of the story adult education tells itself, they assert:

> the story which provides the narrative structure of its identity and thus gives meaning to what is done in its name, is still very much the Enlightenment story of progress, objective knowledge and certain truth – all underpinned by the humanism of the pre-given self 'liberated' through structured curriculum-shaped learning.
>
> (1997: 120)

Hermeneutics   is the theory and practice of interpretation. The word derives from the Greek god, Hermes, whose task it was to communicate messages from Zeus and other gods to the ordinary mortals. 'Hermeneutics is necessary when there is possibility for misunderstanding' (Van Manen 1990: 179). Schleiermacher opened up the idea of hermeneutics as a theory of 'technology' of interpretation, especially with respect to the study of sacred (biblical) and classical texts. Schleiermacher's programme was critical (as the struggle against misunderstanding) and romantic (in desire to recover the particularity, or animating genius of the notions of authors' thoughts) – 'his aim was to understand an author as well or even better than he or she understands himself or herself' (Schleiermacher, in Van Manen 1990: 179).

The emphasis for Dilthey (1985) was not the fundamental thought of the other person but the world itself, the 'lived experience', which is expressed by the author's text. Dilthey's hermeneutic formula is:

- *lived experience*: the starting point and focus of human science
- *expression*: the text or artefact as objectification of lived experience
- *understanding*: not a cognitive act but the moment when life understands itself.

Heidegger (1962) more radically 'de-psychologised' the notion of understanding. The notion of hermeneutic understanding for Heidegger was not aimed at re-experiencing another's experience but rather the power to grasp one's own possibilities for being in the work in certain ways. To interpret a text is to come to understand the possibilities of being revealed by the text. Heidegger's hermeneutics is described as an 'interpretive phenomenology' (Van Manen 1990: 179).

Gadamer (1975) asserts that in interpreting a text we cannot separate ourselves from the meaning of a text. The reader belongs to the text that he or she is reading. Understanding is always an interpretation, and an interpretation is always specific – an application. For Gadamer, the problem of understanding involves interpretive dialogue, which includes taking up the tradition in which one finds oneself. Texts that come to us from different traditions or conversational relations may be read as possible answers to questions. To conduct a conversation, says Gadamer, means to allow oneself to be animated by the question or notion to which the partners in the conversational relation are directed.

Hermeneutic phenomenology   tries to be attentive to both terms of its methodology: it is a *descriptive* (phenomenological) methodology because it wants to be attentive to how things appear, it wants to let things speak for themselves; it is an *interpretive* (hermeneutic) methodology because it claims that there are no such things as uninterpreted phenomena. The implied contradiction may be resolved if one acknowledges that the (phenomenological) 'facts' of lived experience are always already meaningfully (hermeneutically) experienced. Moreover, even the 'facts' of lived experience need to be captured in language (the human science' text) and this is inevitably an interpretive process.

Human science   The term 'human science' is derived from Wilhelm Dilthey's (1987) notion of *Geisteswissenschaften*, in which human (mental, social, historical) phenomena require interpretation and understanding whereas natural science involves external observation and explanation. 'We explain nature; humans we must understand', said Dilthey, who sought to develop in hermeneutics a methodological basis for human sciences. According to Dilthey we can grasp the fullness of lived experience by reconstructing or reproducing the meanings of life's expressions found in the products of human effort, work and creativity.

Hermeneutics and phenomenology are involved in all the disciplines of the humanities and social sciences that interpret the active inner, cognitive, or spiritual life of human beings in social, historical or political contexts. That is, human science is the study of meaning: descriptive-interpretive studies of patterns, structures and levels of experiential and/or textual meanings.

Human science research is the activity of explicating meaning. The orientation of all human science research is more closely aligned with the critical-hermeneutic rationality of the humanities and philosophy than with the positivist rationality of empirical-analytic or behavioural cognitive science.

Intentionality The term 'intentionality' indicates the inseparable connectedness of the human being to the world. Brentano, and later Husserl, argued that the fundamental structure of consciousness is intentional, and every conscious experience is bi-polar: there is an object that presents itself to a subject or ego. This means that all thinking (including imagining, perceiving, remembering) is always thinking about something. The same is true for actions: grasping is grasping for something, hearing is hearing something, pointing is pointing at something. 'All human activity is always *oriented* activity, directed by that which orients it. In this way we discover a person's world or landscape' (Van Manen 1990: 181).

We are not reflexively conscious of our intentional relation to the world. Intentionality is only retrospectively available to consciousness. Or as Merleau-Ponty said, 'the world is revealed to us as ready-made and already there' (1964: 43). It is not possible to experience something *while* reflecting on the experience: for example, our experience of anger may dissipate when we try to analyse or reflect on it.

'Specific intentionality' refers to the directedness of thinking and acting here and now. 'General intentionality' is when we are being directed to the world in a certain way, for example, as man, woman, child, mother, father, teacher, author, and so forth.

Lifeworld The idea of the lifeworld (*Lebenswelt*) – the world of lived experience – derives from Husserl's (1970) posthumously published *The Crisis of European Sciences and Transcendental Phenomenology*: [the lifeworld is] 'the world of immediate experience, the world as already there, pre-given, the world as experienced in the natural, primordial attitude, that of original natural life' (1970: 103–86). Husserl makes an historical and phenomenological distinction between our theoretical attitude to life, borrowed from the Greeks, and our natural pretheoretical attitude to life on which all theorising is based, and from which all theorising is ultimately derived. Husserl uses the term 'natural' for what is original and naive, prior to critical or theoretical reflection.

The theoretical attitude that Western intellectual and scientific culture borrowed from the Greeks must be recognised as a new (historically speaking) and distinct style of life. In contrast, the natural attitude of the lifeworld is always 'pragmatic', always directed at the world 'toward this or that, being directed toward it as an end or as a means, as relevant or irrelevant, toward the private or public, toward what is daily required or obtrusively new' (Husserl 1970: 281).

Plato and Aristotle attributed the origin of the desire to know (philosophy) to simple wonder at things being the way they are. While wonder is a natural occurrence in everyday life, modern theoretical attitudes can turn us into non-participating spectators, surveyors of the world. Paradoxically, the theoretical attitude of modern science often silences our sense of wonder, which Merleau-Ponty relates to 'the demand for a certain awareness, a certain kind of attentiveness and will to seize the meaning of the world' (1962: vii–xxi).

According to Husserl, each lifeworld shows certain pervading structures of styles which need to be studied. Heidegger (1962) gave the idea of lifeworld structures an existential thrust by speaking of phenomenology as the study of Being – the study of our modes-of-being or ways-of-being-in-the-world. Wittgenstein's (1982) notions of 'form of life' and 'language games' can be understood as a linguistic approach to the idea of lifeworld. Van Manen points out that more recent formulations associated with 'the project of phenomenology also seem to have turned toward more semiotic directions' (1990: 181).

Phenomenology   Immanuel Kant (1964) used the term to distinguish the study of objects and events as they appear in our experience (phenomena) – from objects and events as they are in themselves (noumena). Phenomenology can be referred to as the study of phenomena.

In *The Phenomenology of Mind*, Hegel (1977) formulated phenomenology as the science in which we come to know *mind* as it is 'in itself', through the study of the ways in which it appears to us. With Husserl, phenomenology became a descriptive method, as well as a human science movement, based on modes of reflection at the heart of philosophic and human science thought. For Husserl, phenomenology is a discipline that endeavours to describe how the world is constituted and experienced through conscious acts.

Phenomenology must describe what is given to us – in immediate experience – without being obstructed by pre-conceptions and theoretical notions. Husserl, in his last major work – *Crisis of European Sciences and Transcendental Phenomenology* – formulated the notion of 'the lifeworld' as the everyday world in which we live in the natural, taken-for-granted attitude. This notion of the lifeworld aims at describing how phenomena present themselves in lived experience. For Heidegger (1962), phenomenology is a study of the modes of 'being in the world' of human being.

Postmodernism Postmodernism views as 'incredulous' (Lyotard 1984) Husserl's notion (derived from Kant) of the 'transcendental', and Heidegger's aim to 'let things of the world speak for themselves' – on the grounds that we do not, and cannot, speak for 'ourselves'. Humans are historically and culturally 'inscribed' – our voices are not 'of ourselves', but represent our historical situatedness and our inscriptions. Postmodernism, as a philosophy, thus represents a profound counterpoint to the ontological assumptions of hermeneutics and phenomenology. Paradoxically, much within postmodern philosophy has evolved out of phenomenology.

Norris (1993) claims that postmodernists are erroneous in rejecting the 'transcendent' on the grounds that much of this rejection derives from Foucault's 'misreading' of Kant. Norris argues that Foucault:

> demotes the claims of 'transcendental' reason (or critique) to the status of a merely localised episode in the recent history of thought. [Foucault also] identifies truth – for all practical purposes – with that level of contingent events or shifts in the order of power/knowledge relations which can best be revealed through a jointly 'archaeological' and 'genealogical' approach. Insofar as the Enlightenment project survives, it does so in a sharply delimited or relativised form, as an impetus to the kind of investigative thinking – the inquiring-back into its own genesis and historical conditions of emergence – which can offer no hold for the truth-telling claims of old-style 'universal' reason.

> (Norris 1993: 37)

Burbules, however, points out that:

> postmodernism is not a specific theoretical position itself, but an intellectual trend that comprises several quite different philosophical theories. Some of the characteristics of postmodernism are 'the rejection of the Enlightenment: it is about the infusion of power into our theories of knowledge, language and ethics; it is

rationalistic; it offers a radical social constructiveness; it privileges difference over commonality; it is about the discursive constitution of social (and natural) reality; it stresses a de-central view of the subject and the fungibility of identity.

(Burbules 1995: 2)

Many writers, including Bauman (1993), Couzens Hoy (1989), Featherstone (1991) and Usher and Edwards (1994), argue that it is not particularly useful to construct an all-encompassing definition of 'postmodernism' – suggesting it is more useful to look at the family of terms such as 'postmodernity', 'postmodernisation', 'post-structural' and 'the postmodern'.

Bauman (1993) argues that in contrast to 'modernity': 'postmodernity is marked by a view of the human world as irreducibly and irrevocably pluralistic, split into a multitude of sovereign units and sites of authority, with no horizontal or vertical order either in actuality or in potency' (cited in Usher and Edwards 1994: 12).[3]

Reflection (and critical reflection) Mezirow (1990) says reflection is 'an examination of the justification for one's beliefs, primarily to guide action and to reassess the strategies and procedures used in problem solving'. Critical reflection is distinctive in its focus on the validity of the presuppositions which underpin those belief structures.

Critical reflection, say Boud and Walker (1992), is 'reflecting on the presuppositions which we hold about ourselves and the world and which limit our freedom and constrain our actions'. It thus involves coming to recognise the assumptions that give rise to these 'constraints' and developing an understanding of the ways they were acquired. As such, critical reflection is connected with emancipatory education. Mezirow's (1990) idea is that critical reflection includes an organised effort to precipitate or facilitate the reformulation of the meaning of one's experience – which he refers to as 'transformative learning'.

Boud and Walker's (1992) presuppositions of critical reflection distinguishing it from reflection are as follows (my notations are included):

1   We do not simply see what is there but perceive each situation according to our own prior experience. Here perception is not conceptually neutral but is structured by our personal foundation of experience.
2   Society and cultures create norms, values, beliefs, structures, language patterns and categories within which experience is

understood. Kemmis saw reflection as not a purely internal psychological process, but action-oriented and historically embedded 'like language it is a social process and as such is political and shaped by ideology' (1985: 143).

3   Historical and cultural influences are internalised as part of our personal foundation of experience. Not only are socially constructed events interpreted as natural realities, we internalise these influences. By accepting their legitimacy we give these social influences power over ourselves. Mere recognition of this process in itself may not be powerful enough to bring about change. The power it wields over us will not necessarily be removed because the process is recognised, but it can remove the conviction that this is the only way to look at things.

4   The effect of internalising the influences of society is that we may be in a state of false consciousness, wherein we accept as true things which may not be true; we may accept that what is in the interests of one group in society is normative for the whole society; we may accept beliefs that seem to be in our interests but are not; we may accept social descriptions as 'facts'; we may accept things which, with better information or insight, we may see as false. Boud and Walker (1992) point out that the concept of false consciousness is problematic as it implies a greater or 'knowable truth', or at least a different truth more in line with one's social and economic interests. There can be no external arbiter of what is false, and an individual will only be able to give limited direction to critical reflection.

5   Our freedom is inhibited by the limits set by the assumptions we internalise.

6   There are ways of criticising and evaluating our beliefs so that we can become more aware of the constraints imposed on us, for example, by examining the assumptions underlying the constraints and their origins. Brookfield (1991) reminds us that the awareness that assumptions and constraints are socially created does not mean they are easily removed.

7   Critical reflection explores the personal and social framework within which one works, rather than just working within it. Critical reflection is not an empirical observation as one might find in the natural sciences.

8   Personal interests can emerge from critical reflection if one obtains a clearer vision of the issues involved.

9 The process of exposing false assumptions can lead to restructuring the social situation. Critical reflection thus has an action orientation.

Boud and Walker (1992) argue that within our historical and cultural situation, certain attitudes and presuppositions have been internalised which help individuals deal with obstacles in 'positive' ways. This is at odds with much that has been written about alienation (in the traditions of critical social theory) and with postmodern doubt about identity formation in post-industrial conditions. (See Chapter 3.)

Reflexivity   What is going on in this research? What kind of world or 'reality' is being constructed by the questions asked and the methods used? What epistemologies are carried within the research? These are important questions to reflexivity. Usher and Edwards (1994: 149) refer to it as the '*sub-text* of research'. At its simplest, reflexivity claims that since the activity of the knower always influences what is known, nothing can be known except through those activities. This leads to a key question – what kind of problem is reflexivity, indeed is it a problem at all? By foregrounding how we construct what we research, reflexivity is no longer a problem but a resource:

> It helps us to recognise that we are a part of rather than apart from the world constructed through research. More than this, however, by becoming aware of the operation of reflexivity in the practice of research, the place of power, discourse and text, that which goes 'beyond' the purely personal is revealed.
>
> (Usher and Edwards 1994: 149)

Going beyond the personal means more than being up-front about one's values and beliefs however. Ashmore (1989), Lather (1991) and Usher and Edwards (1994) argue that the notion of reflexivity relates to an author's autobiography – marked by the significations of gender, sexuality, ethnicity, class, race and so on. Usher and Edwards argue that these significations are 'socio-cultural products that are part of a practice of writing with effects upon both the form and outcomes of research' (1994: 149). They refer to this as the *con-text* of research.

A reflexive approach to research does not automatically imply a subjectivist position. Rather, it foregrounds the implications of the personal within the practice of the research. From a postmodern perspective, Usher and Edwards argue forcefully a case for the use of reflexivity in educational research:

Even when we have some confidence that our research is useful or even emancipatory, we are still 'objectifying', still speaking *for* others in the name of doing good by them. We are still attempting to mould subjectivities in a modernist way, still attempting to bring about changes in the name of 'progress'. Thus an awareness of reflexivity enables us to interrogate our own practices of research, in terms of how they can become part of dominant and oppressive discourses through a 'reflexive' acceptance of neutrality of research, and in terms of how we, as researchers, are implicated in such discourses despite our best intentions.

(Usher and Edwards 1994: 152)

To understand reflexivity is therefore to acknowledge that research is always more than understanding, interpreting or finding out about any 'pre-existing' world.

Semiotics Texts or signs, and their structural relationships, are the subject of study for semiotics. In semiotics, there is no innocent, pure or pristine experience of a real external world. We 'encode' our experience of the world in order that we may experience it – there is no neutral text. This encoding produces certain styles. Barthes concludes that writing is all style, a highly conventionalised activity. Barthes' deconstructive writings represent moves to expose how modern society 'codifies reality' in its own image (usually through mass media). Once this reality is produced, one proceeds to believe that it is the only reality possible.

From a semiotic viewpoint, any social behaviour or practice signifies and may be read as a text, as a language. For example, nobody merely talks; every speech-act displays a complex of messages through the 'language' of gesture, accent, clothing, posture, perfume, hair-style, facial manner, social context, etc. above, behind, beneath, beside and even at odds with what words actually say. Similarly, everything around us systematically communicates something meaningful to us, and one can thus speak of 'the world as a text'.

Derrida (1978) provides an influential approach to the semiotics of writing. In his 'grammatology' (science of writing) he argues that our logo-centrism and our tendency to treat oral language as primary over written language commits us to a falsifying 'metaphysics of presence'. It is based on an illusion that we are able, ultimately, to come face to face with each other and with things. According to Derrida, this belief in 'presence' expresses a yearning hope that, in spite of our always fragmentary and incomplete experience, there is reason to insist on the existence of a redeeming and justifying wholeness, an ultimate notion of one-ness, essence, ground, or a faith in objective reality. As reader-interpreter, Derrida practises a deconstructive analysis of the text: a double reading which has the effect of showing the ways in which the argument of a text calls its own premises into question.

Symbolic interactionism Symbolic interactionism is a theoretical perspective in social psychology, originally connected with Mead (1967) and the Chicago School. Its foremost proponent has been Blumer (1969), who understands social reality as a complex network of interacting persons, who symbolically interpret their 'acting' in the social world. The methodological rule is that social reality and society should be understood from the perspective of the actors who interpret their world through and in social interaction. Its application is generally in studies of role behaviour and perception.

From a symbolic interactionist perspective, human beings tend to act on the basis of how they believe other people behave towards them. Their self-perceptions and feelings tend to be mediated by how they think others see and feel about them. In education this principle has been illustrated by studies showing the so-called 'Pygmalion effect' of teachers' perceptions of children and the effect of those perceptions on the children's sense of self and academic ability. In short, symbolic interactionists study the functional relationships between how we see ourselves (self-definition), how we see others (inter-personal perceptions) and how we think others see us.

Notes

1 Also see Emmanuel Levinas's *Time and the Other* (particularly pp. 39–57) for a repudiation of aspects of Heidegger's ontology of 'being'.
2 Also see Foucault's (1982: 218) critique of Habermas's 'transcendental' tendency.
3 Implications of various postmodern ideas for adult education practice are elaborated in *Postmodernism and Education* by Usher and Edwards (1994).

Bibliography

Acker, J. (1989) *Doing Comparable Work: Gender, Class and Pay Equity*, Philadelphia: Temple University Press.

Acker, J., Barry, K. and Esseveld, J. (1983) 'Objectivity and truth: Problems in doing feminist research', *Women's Studies International Forum*, 6(4): 423–35.

Andresen, L., Boud, D. and Cohen, R. (1995) 'Experience-based learning' in G. Foley (ed.) *Understanding Adult Education*, Sydney: Allen and Unwin: 207–19.

Anyon, J. (1983) 'Intersections of gender and class: Accommodation and resistance by working class and affluent females to contradictory sex-role ideologies' in S. Walker and L. Barton (eds) *Gender, Class and Education*, New York: Falmer: 18–36.

—— (1994) 'The retreat of Marxism and socialist feminism: Postmodern and poststructural theories in education', *Curriculum Inquiry*, 24: 115–33.

Argyris, C. and Schön, D. A. (1974) *Theory and Practice: Increasing Professional Effectiveness*, San Francisco: Jossey Bass.

Aronowitz, S. (1981) *The Crisis in Historical Materialism*, Massachusetts: Bergin and Garvey Publishers.

—— (1992) *The Politics of Identity*, London and New York: Routledge.

Aronowitz, S. and Giroux, H. A. (1985) *Education Under Siege*, Massachusetts: Bergin and Garvey Publishers.

—— (1991) *Postmodern Education: Politics, Culture and Social Criticism*, Minneapolis: University of Minnesota Press.

Ashmore, M. (1989) *The Reflexive Thesis: Wrighting Sociology of Scientific Knowledge*, Chicago: University of Chicago Press.

Ashworth, P. D. and Saxton, J. (1990) 'On competence', *Journal of Further and Higher Education*, 14: 3–25.

Bagnall, R. (1990) 'Lifelong education: The institutionalisation of an illiberal and regressive ideology?' *Educational Philosophy and Theory*, 22(1): 1–7.

Bailey, T. (1989) *Changes in the Nature and Structure of Work: Implications for Skill Requirements and Skill Formation*, Technical Paper No 9, New

York: Institute on Education and the Economy, Teachers College, Columbia University.

Ball, S. J. (1987) *The Micro-politics of the School: Towards a Theory of School Organisation*, London: Methuen.

—— (1991) 'Power, conflict, micro-politics and all that!' in G. Walford (ed.) *Doing Educational Research*, London: Routledge: 166–92.

Barnett, R. (1994) *The Limits of Competence: Knowledge, Higher Education and Society*, Buckingham: The Society for Research into Higher Education and Open University Press.

—— (1997) *Higher Education: A Critical Business*, Buckingham: The Society for Research into Higher Education and Open University Press.

Baudrillard, J. (1988) 'For a critique of the political economy of the sign' in Mark Poster (ed.) *Jean Baudrillard: Selected Writings*, Stanford: Stanford University Press.

—— (1993) *The Transparency of Evil: Essays on Extreme Phenomena* (trans. by J. Benedict), London: Verso.

Bauman, Z. (1978) *Hermeneutics and Social Science: Approaches to Understanding*, London: Hutchinson University.

—— (1993) *Postmodern Ethics*, Oxford: Blackwell Publishers.

—— (1997) 'Education: under, for, and in spite of postmodernity', presented to the *31st Annual Conference of the Philosophy of Education Society of Great Britain*, New College, Oxford: April, 4–6.

Beckett, D. (1992) 'Straining training: The epistemology of workplace learning', *Studies in Continuing Education*, 14(2): 130–42.

—— (1993) 'Professional practice for policy analysts: The getting of wisdom?', paper presented to *The Philosophy of Education Society of Australasian Annual Conference*, Sydney University: October, 1–3.

—— (1996) 'Critical judgement and professional practice', *Educational Theory*, 46(2): 135–50.

Belenky, M. F., McVicker, Clinchy B., Goldberg, N. R. and Tarule, J. M. (1986) *Women's Ways of Knowing: The Development of Self, Voice and Mind*, New York: Bantam Books.

Berger, P. and Luckman, T. (1981) 'The reality of everyday life: A treatise in the sociology of knowledge' in P. Berger and T. Luckman *The Social Construction of Reality*, Harmondsworth: Penguin: 33–42.

Bernstein, R. J. (1991) *The New Constellation*, Oxford: Polity.

Berryman, S. E. (1993) 'Learning from the workplace', *Review of Research in Education*, 19: 343–401.

Berryman, S. E. and Bailey, T. (1992) *The Double Helix of Education and the Economy*, New York: Institute on Education and the Economy, Teachers College, Columbia University.

Billett, S. (1992) 'Towards a theory of workplace learning', *Studies in Continuing Education*, 14(2): 143–55.

Blumer, H. (1962) 'Society as symbolic interaction' in H. Rose (ed.) *Human Behaviour and Social Processes: An Interactionist Approach*, London: Routledge and Kegan Paul.

—— (1969) *Symbolic Interactionism: Perspective and Method*, Englewood Cliffs, NJ: Prentice Hall.

—— (1976) 'The methodological position of symbolic interactionism' in M. Hammersley and P. Woods (eds) *The Process of Schooling*, London: Routledge and Kegan Paul.

Boje, D. M. (1994) 'Organisational storytelling: The struggles of pre-modern, modern and postmodern organisational learning discourses', *Management Learning*, 25(3): 433–62.

—— (1995) 'Stories of the storytelling organisation: A postmodern analysis of Disney as "Tamara-Land"', *Academy of Management Journal*, 38(4): 997–1035.

Boje, D. M. and Winsor, R. (1993) 'The resurrection of Taylorism: Total Quality Management's hidden agenda', *Journal of Organisational Change Management*, 6(4): 57–70.

Bolwijn, P. and Kumpe, T. (1990) 'Manufacturing in the 1990s: Productivity, flexibility and innovation', *Journal of Long Range Planning*, 23(4): 44–57.

Boud, D. (1989) 'Some competing traditions in experiential learning' in S. Warner Weil and I. McGill (eds) *Making Sense of Experiential Learning: Diversity in Theory and Practice*, Buckingham: Open University Press.

Boud, D. and Griffin, C. (eds) (1987) *Appreciating Adult Learning: From the Learners' Perspective*, London: Kogan Page.

Boud, D. and Walker, D. (1992) 'Fostering critical reflection: Opportunities and issues for group learning', *Proceedings of the 3rd International Conference on Experiential Learning*, Pondicherry, India.

Boud, D., Cohen, R. and Walker, D. (eds) (1993) *Using Experience for Learning*, Buckingham: The Society for Research into Higher Education and Open University Press.

Boud, D., Keogh, R. and Walker, D. (eds) (1985) *Reflection: Turning Experience into Learning*, London: Kogan Page.

Brah, A. and Hoy, J. (1990) 'Experiential learning: A new orthodoxy' in S. Warner Weil and I. McGill (eds) *Making Sense of Experiential Learning: Diversity in Theory and Practice*, Buckingham: Open University Press: 70–7.

Braverman, H. (1974) *Labour and Monopoly Capital: The Degradation of Work in the Twentieth Century*, New York: Monthly Review Press.

Bright, B. P. (1989) *Theory and Practice in the Study of Adult Education: The Epistemological Debate*, London: Routledge.

Brookfield, S. D. (1981) 'Independent adult learning', *Studies in Adult Education*, 13(2): 59–71.

—— (1982) 'Independent adult learning', *Adults: Psychological and Educational Perspectives No. 7*, Nottingham: Department of Adult Education, University of Nottingham.

—— (1986) *Understanding and Facilitating Adult Learning: A Comprehensive Analysis of Principles and Effective Practices*, San Francisco: Jossey Bass.

—— (1988) 'Developing critically reflective practitioners: A rationale for training educators of adults' in S. D. Brookfield (ed.) *Training Educators of Adults: The Theory and Practice of Training Educators of Adults*, London: Routledge: 317–38.

—— (1990) *The Skilful Teacher: On Technique, Trust and Responsiveness*, San Francisco: Jossey Bass.

—— (1991) 'On ideology, pillage, language and risk: critical thinking and the tensions of critical practice', *Studies in Continuing Education*, 13(1): 1–14.

—— (1993) *Adult Learners, Adult Education and the Community*, Milton Keynes: Open University Press.

Brooks, A. K. (1994) 'Power and the production of knowledge: Collective team learning in work organisations', *Human Resource Development Quarterly*, 5(3): 213–33.

Burbules, N. C. (1995) 'Postmodern doubt in the philosophy of education', paper presented to the *Philosophy of Education Society Annual Conference*, San Francisco: 29 March–3 April.

Burbules, N. C. and Rice, S. (1991) 'Dialogue across differences: Continuing the conversation', *Harvard Educational Review*, 61: 393–416.

Butler, J. (1993) *Bodies that Matter: On the Discursive Limits of Sex*, New York: Routledge.

Caffarella, R. S. and O'Donnell, J. M. (1990) 'Self directed learning', *Adults: Psychological and Educational Perspectives, No. 1*, Nottingham: Department of Adult Education, University of Nottingham.

Calas, H. B. and Smircich, L. (1993) 'Unbounding organisational analysis: Questioning "globalisation" through third world women's voices', Session T111, *Academy of Management Conference*, Atlanta: 8–11 August.

Candy, P. C. (1988) 'Evolution, revolution or devolution? Increasing learning control in the instructional setting' in D. Boud and V. Griffin (eds) *Appreciating Adults Learning: From the Learners' Perspective*, London: Kogan Page: 159–78.

—— (1989) 'Alternative paradigms in educational research', *Australian Educational Researcher*, 16(3): 1–13.

—— (1991) *Self Direction for Lifelong Learning: A Comprehensive Guide to Theory and Practice*, San Francisco: Jossey Bass.

—— (1993) 'Learning theories in higher education: Reflections on the key note day, HERDSA, 1992', *Higher Education Research and Development*, 12(1): 99–106.

Carnevale, A., Gainer, L. and Villet, J. (1990) *Training in America: The Organisation and Strategic Role of Training*, San Francisco: Jossey Bass.

Casey, C. (1995) *Work, Self and Society after Industrialism*, London and New York: Routledge.

Castoriadis, C. (1992) *Philosophy, Politics, Autonomy: Essays in Political Philosophy*, New York: Oxford University Press.

Cell, E. (1984) *Learning to Learn from Experience*, Albany: State University of New York Press.

Cervero, R. (1992) 'Professional practice, learning and continuing education: An integrated perspective', *International Journal of Lifelong Education*, 11(1): 91–101.

Chalofsky, N. E. (1996) 'A new paradigm for learning in organisations', *Human Resource Development Quarterly*, 7(3): 287–94.

Chang, J. (1991) *Wild Swans: Three Daughters of China*, London: Flamingo Press.

Cherryholmes, C. (1988) *Power and Criticism: Poststructural Investigations in Education*, New York: Teachers College Press.

Chi, A. T. H., Feltovich, P. J. and Glaser, R. (1981) 'Categorisation and representation of physics problems by experts and novices', *Cognition Science*, 5: 121–52.

Cockburn, C. (1985) *Machinery of Dominance: Women, Men and Technical Know-how*, London: Pluto Press.

Commission on the Skills of the American Workforce (1990) *America's Choice: High Skills or Low Wages!*, New York: National Center on Education and the Economy.

Couzens Hoy, D. (1989) *Foucault: A Critical Reader*, Oxford: Basil Blackwell.

Dechant, K., Marsick, V. J. and Kasl, E. (1993) 'Towards a model of team learning', *Studies in Continuing Education*, 15(1): 1–14.

Derrida, J. (1978) *Writing and Difference*, London: Routledge.

—— (1981) *Positions* (trans. by Alan Bass), Chicago: University of Chicago Press.

—— (1982) *Margins of Philosophy* (trans. by Alan Bass), Chicago: University of Chicago Press.

Dewey, J. (1938) *Experience and Education*, New York: Collier Books.

—— (1966) *Democracy and Education: An Introduction to Philosophy*, New York: Macmillan.

Dilthey, W. (1985) *Poetry and Experience. Selected Works, Vol. V*, Princeton, NJ: Princeton University Press.

—— (1987) *Introduction to the Human Sciences*, Toronto: Scholarly Books.

Dodgson, M. (1993) 'Organisational learning: A review of some of the literature' in *Organisation Studies*, 14(3): 375–94.

Drucker, P. (1995) 'The information executives truly need', *Harvard Business Review*, January–February: 35–44.

Du Gay, P. (1996) *Consumption and Identity at Work*, London: Sage Publications.

Durkheim, E. [1933] (1984) *The Division of Labour in Society* (trans. by W. D. Hall), New York: Free Press.

Edwards, R. (1994) 'Really useful knowledge? Flexible accumulation and open and distance learning', *Studies in Continuing Education*, 16(2): 160–71.

Edwards, R. and Usher, R. S. (1993) 'Research: reflecting practice? Modern paradigms, postmodern controversies', *SCUTREA Conference papers*, Manchester: 20–2.

—— (1994) 'Disciplining the subject: The power of competence', *Studies in the Education of Adults*, 26(1): 1–14.

Ellsworth, E. (1989) 'Why doesn't this feel empowering? Working through the repressive myths of critical pedagogy', *Harvard Educational Review*, 59: 297–324.

European Centre for the Development of Vocational Training (1991) *Description of a Framework of Macroprofiles (Archetypes)*, Berlin: CEDEFOP.

Evers, C. W. and Lakomski, G. (1991) *Knowing Educational Administration: Contemporary Methodological Controversies in Educational Administration Research*, Australia: Pergamon Press.

Ewart, G. D. (1991) 'Habermas and education: A comprehensive overview of the influence of Habermas in educational literature', *Review of Educational Research*, 61(3): 345–78.

Fairclough, N. (1992) *Discourse and Social Change*, Cambridge: Polity Press.

Featherstone, M. (1991) *Consumer Culture and Postmodernism*, London: Sage.

—— (1995) *Undoing Culture Globalization, Postmodernism and Identity*, London: Sage.

Field, J. (1991) 'Competency and the pedagogy of labour', *Studies in the Education of Adults*, 23(1): 41–52.

Finger, M. (1990) 'The subject-person of adult education in the crisis of modernity', *Studies in Continuing Education*, 12(1): 24–30.

Foley, G. (ed.) (1995) *Understanding Adult Education and Training*, Sydney: Allen and Unwin.

Ford, B. (1993) 'Customer focussed learning enterprises', paper presented at the *Construction Industry Development Agency National Conference*, Sydney: 3–4 May.

Foucault, M. (1972) *Power/Knowledge* (trans. by C. Gordon), New York: Pantheon Books.

—— (1977) *Discipline and Punish: The Birth of the Prison*, New York: Vintage.

—— (1980a) *Power/Knowledge: Selected Interviews and Other Writings 1972–77* (trans. by C. Gordon), Brighton: Harvester Press.

—— (1980b) 'Truth and power' in M. Foucault *Power/Knowledge: Selected Interviews and Other Writing*, Brighton: Harvester Press: 114–33.

—— (1982) 'The subject and power' in H. L. Dreyfuss and P. Rabinow (eds) *Michel Foucault*, Great Britain: Pathfinder Press: 208–26.

—— (1988a) 'The ethic of care for the self as a practice of freedom' in J. Bernauer and D. Rasmussen (eds) *The Final Foucault*, Cambridge, MA: MIT Press: 1–20.

—— (1988b) 'Technologies of the self' in L. H. Martin, H. Gutman and P. H. Hutton (eds) *Technologies of the Self: A Seminar with Michel Foucault*, London: Tavistock: 16–49.

—— (1988c) 'A dangerous man' in Lawrence D. Kitzman (ed.) *Politics, Philosophy, Culture: Interviews and Other Writings*, New York: Routledge.

—— (1990) *The History of Sexuality Volume 1: An Introduction*, London: Penguin.

—— (1991) *Remarks on Marx* (trans. by R. J. Goldstein and U. J. Cascaito), New York: Columbia University Press.

Francis, G. (1990) 'The experience of being an informal educator' in T. Jeffs and M. Smith (eds) *Using Informal Education: An Alternative to Casework, Teaching and Control?*, Milton Keynes: Open University Press: 49–60.

Freire, P. (1972) *The Pedagogy of the Oppressed* (trans. by Myra Bergman Ramos), London: Penguin.

—— (1985) *The Politics of Education: Culture, Power and Liberation* (trans. by Donald Macedo), London: Macmillan.

Freire, P. and Faundez, A. (1989) *Learning to Question: A Pedagogy of Liberation* (trans. by Tony Coates), New York: Continuum.

Freud, S. (1962) 'Screen memories' in the *Standard Edition of the Complete Psychological Works of Sigmund Freud*, London: Hogarth.

—— [1915] (1966) *Introductory Lectures on Psycho-analysis* (trans. by J. Strachey), New York: W. W. Norton.

Friedman, M. (1962) *Capitalism and Freedom*, Chicago: University Press.

Fuller, G. and Lee, A. (1997) 'Textual collusions', *Discourse: Studies in the Cultural Politics of Education*, 18(3): 409–23.

Gadamer, H. G. (1975) *Truth and Method*, New York: Seabury.

Galbraith, J. (1992) 'Culture of contentment', *New Statesman and Society*, 5(201): 15–25.

Garrick, J. and Solomon, N. (1997) 'Technologies of compliance in training', *Studies in Continuing Education*, 19(1): 71–81.

Garvin, D. A. (1993) 'Building a learning organisation', *Harvard Business Review*, July–August: 78–92.

Gee, J. P. (1994) 'Quality, science and the lifeworld: The alignment of business and education', *Focus*: 4, Stanmore: Adult Literacy and Basic Skills Action Coalition.

Gelder, K. and Salzman, P. (1989) 'Dialogues with history' in K. Gelder and P. Salzman (eds) *The New Diversity*, Melbourne: McPhee Gribble: 140–65.

Gergen, K. J. (1991) *The Saturated Self: Dilemmas of Identity in Contemporary Life*, New York: Basic Books.

Giddens, A. (1986) 'Action, subjectivity, and the constitution of meaning', *Social Research*, 53(3): 529–45.

Giorgi, A. (1985) *Phenomenology and Psychological Research*, Pittsburgh: Duquesne University Press.

Giroux, H. A. (1983) *Theory and Resistance in Education: A Pedagogy for the Opposition*, London: Heinemann.

—— (1992) *Border Crossings: Cultural Workers and the Politics of Education*, London: Routledge.

Glaser, R. (1984) 'Education and thinking: The role of knowledge', *American Psychologist*, 39(2): 93–104.

—— (1989) 'Expertise and learning: How do we think about knowledge structures now that we have discovered knowledge structures?' in D. Klahr and K. Kotosvsky (eds) *Complex Information Processing*, Hillsdale, NJ: Erlbaum and Associates.

Goffman, E. (1959) *The Presentation of Self in Everyday Life*, New York: Doubleday.

Gonczi, A. and Hager, P. (1992) 'The policy context for vocational education and training' in A. Gonczi (ed.) *Developing a Competent Workforce: Adult Learning Statements for Vocational Educators and Trainers*, Adelaide: National Centre for Vocational Education Research: 10–21.

Griffin, C. (1987) *Adult Education as Social Policy*, London: Croom Helm.

—— (1989) 'Critical thinking and critical theory in adult education' in B. Bright (ed.) *Theory and Practice in the Study of Adult Education: The Epistemological Debate*, London: Routledge.

Griffin, V. (1987) 'Naming the processes' in D. Boud and V. Griffin (eds) *Appreciating Adults Learning*, London: Kogan Page: 209–21.

Grosz, E. A. (1989) *Sexual Subversions: Three French Feminists*, Sydney: Allen and Unwin.

Gumpez, J. J. and Berenz, N. (1990) 'Transcribing conversational exchanges', *The Berkeley Cognitive Science Report Series*, University of California, Institute of Cognitive Studies.

Gunnarson, E., Knocke, W. and Westburg, H. (1991) *Research Experience on Learning in Working Life from a Gender Theory Perspective*, Sweden: Swedish Centre for Working Life.

Habermas, J. (1978) *Knowledge and Human Interests* (trans. by Jeremy J. Shapiro), Boston: Beacon Press.

—— (1987) *The Philosophy of Discourse in Modernity*, Cambridge: Polity.

—— (1991) *The Theory of Communicative Action*, Cambridge: Polity.

Hager, P. and Gonczi, A. (1991) 'Competency based standards: A boon for continuing professional education', *Studies in Continuing Education*, 13(1): 24–40.

—— (1993) 'Attributes and competence', *Australia and New Zealand Journal of Vocational Education Research*, 1(1): 36–45.

Hall, S. (1996) 'Who Needs "Identity"?' in S. Hall and P. Du Gay (eds) *Questions of Cultural Identity*, London: Sage: 1–17.

Hart, M. (1993) 'Educative or miseducative work: A critique of the current debate on work and education', *The Canadian Journal for the Study of Adult Education*, 7(1): 19–36.

—— (1995) 'Motherwork: A radical proposal to rethink work and education' in M. R. Welton (ed.) *In Defense of the Lifeworld*, Albany: State University of New York Press: 99–126.

Hayek, F. A. (1960) *The Constitution of Liberty*, London: Routledge and Kegan Paul.

Hayton, G. (1992) 'Workplace reform and vocational education and training' in A. Gonczi (ed.) *Developing a Competent Workforce: Adult Learning Strategies for Vocational Educators and Trainers*, Adelaide: National Centre for Vocational Education Research: 10–25.

Hegel, G. W. F. (1977) *The Phenomenology of Mind*, New York: Humanities Press.

Heidegger, M. (1962) *Being and Time* (trans. by John Macquarie and Edward Robinson), New York: Harper and Row.

—— (1971) *Poetry, Language and Thought*, New York: Harper and Row.

Himmelfarb, G. (1994) *On Looking into the Abyss: Untimely Thoughts on Culture and Society*, New York: Alfred A. Knopf.

Hirschhorn, L. (1984) *Beyond Mechanisation: Work and Technology in a Post-industrial Age*, Cambridge, MA: MIT Press.

hooks, b. (1990) *Yearning: Race, Gender and Cultural Politics*, Boston: South End Press.

Horkheimer, M. and Adorno, T. [1944] (1993) *Dialectic of Enlightenment*, New York: The Continuum Publishing Company.

Husserl, E. (1970) *Logical Investigations, Volume One* (trans. by J.N. Finley), New York: Humanities Press.

Hutton, P. H. (1987) 'The art of memory reconceived: From rhetoric to psychoanalysis', *Journal of the History of Ideas*, 48(3).

—— (1988) 'Foucault, Freud and the technologies of the self' in L. H. Martin, H. Gutman and P. H. Hutton (eds) *Technologies of the Self*, London: Tavistock: 121–44.

Inkster, R. P. (1987) 'How do you know? Polanyi and adult eduction', *Proceedings from the 28th Annual Adult Education Research Conference*, Laramie: University of Wyoming.

Jackson, N. (1991) *Skills Formation and Gender Relations: The Politics of Who Knows What*, Melbourne: Deakin University Press.

—— (1992) 'Training needs: An objective science?' in A. Beckerman, J. Davis and N. Jackson (eds) *Training for What? Labour Perspectives on Job Training*, Toronto: Our Schools/Our Selves Education Foundation, 4(2), 26: 76–83.

—— (1993) 'Reforming vocational learning? Contradictions of competence' in W. Hall (ed.) *What Future for Vocational Education and Training*, Adelaide: National Centre for Vocational Education Research: 105–22.

Jansen, T. and Wildemeersch, D. (1992) 'Bridging gaps between private experiences and public issues' in D. Wildemeersch and T. Jansen (eds) *Adult Education, Experiential Learning and Social Change: The Postmodern Challenge*, 's- Gravenhage: VUGA: 5–18.

Jarvis, P. (1987) *Adult Learning in the Social Context*, London: Croom Helm.

Jeffs, T. and Smith, M. (eds) (1990) *Using Informal Education: An Alternative to Casework, Teaching and Control?*, Milton Keynes: Open University Press.

Jordan, J. V., Kaplan, A. G., Miller, J. B., Stiver, I. P. and Surrey, J. L. (1991) *Women's Growth in Connection: Writings from the Stone Centre*, New York: Guilford Press.

Kahn, R. and Gardell, B. (1989) 'Foreword' in H. Leymann and H. Kornbluh (eds) *Socialisation and Learning at Work: A New Approach to the Learning Process and Society*, Brookfield, VT: Gower: xi–xiii.

Kant, I. (1964) *Critique of Pure Reason*, New York: Everyman's Library.

Kaplan, K. L. (1995) 'Women's voices in organisational development: questions, stories and implications', *Journal of Organisational Change Management*, 8(1): 52–80.

Kasl, E., Dechant, K. and Marsick, V. J. (1993) 'Living the learning: Internalising our model of group learning' in D. Boud, R. Cohen and D. Walker (eds) *Using Experience for Learning*, Buckingham: Open University Press: 143–56.

Kegan, R. (1995) *In Over Our Heads: The Mental Demands of Modern Life*, Cambridge, MA: Harvard University Press.

Kemmis, S. (1985) 'Action research and politics of reflection' in D. Boud, R. Keogh and D. Walker (eds) *Reflection: Turning Experience into Learning*, London: Kogan Page: 139–63.

—— (1991) 'Improving education through action research' in O. Zuber-Skerritt (ed) *Action Research for Change and Development*, Vermont: Gower Publishing: 57–75.

Kierkegaard, S. (1959) *The Journals of Kierkegaard* (trans. by A. Dru), New York: Harper.

Knowles, M. S. (1975) *Self-directed Learning: A Guide for Learners and Teachers*, New York: Association Press.

—— (1980) *The Modern Practice of Adult Education: From Pedagogy to Andragogy*, Chicago: Follet.

Kolb, D. A. (1984) *Experiential Learning: Experience as a Source of Learning*, Englewood Cliffs, NJ: Prentice Hall.

Kornbluh, H. and Greene, R. T. (1989) 'Learning, empowerment and participative work practices' in H. Leymann and H. Kornbluh (eds) *Socialisation and Learning at Work*, Brookfield, VT: Gower: 256–74.

Kosmidou, C. and Usher, R. (1992) 'Experiential learning and the autonomous subject: A critical approach' in D. Wildemeersch and T. Jansen (eds) *Adult Education, Experiential Learning and Social Change: The Postmodern Challenge*, 's-Gravenhage, Den Haag: VUGA: 77–92.

Kuhn, T. S. (1970) *The Structure of Scientific Revolutions*, 2nd edn, Chicago: University of Chicago Press.

La Belle, T. J. (1982) 'Formal, nonformal and informal education: A holistic perspective on life long learning', *International Review of Education*, 28: 159–75.

LaBier, D. (1986) *Modern Madness: The Hidden Link between Work and Emotional Conflict*, New York: Simon and Schuster.

Lacan, J. (1977) *Ecrits: A Selection* (trans. by A. Sheridan), London: Tavistock.

Lasch, C. (1984) *The Minimal Self: Psychic Survival in Troubled Times*, New York: W.W. Norton.

Lash, S. and Urry, J. (1994) *Economies of Signs and Space*, London: Sage.

Lather, P. (1986) 'Issues of validity in openly ideological research: Between a rock and a hard place', *Interchange*, 17(4): 63–84.

—— (1991) *Feminist Research in Education: Within/Against*, Geelong: Deakin University Press.

Latour, B. (1993) *We Have Never Been Modern*, Cambridge, MA: Harvard University Press.

Lave, J. (1990) 'The culture of acquisition and the practice of understanding' in J. W. Stigler, R. A. Sheweder and G. Herdt (eds) *Cultural Psychology: Essays on Comparative Human Development*, Cambridge: Cambridge University Press.

Lave, J. and Wenger, E. (1991) *Situated Learning–Legitimate peripheral participation*, Cambridge: Cambridge University Press.

Lee, A. (1992) 'Poststructuralism and educational research: Some categories and issues', *Issues in Educational Research*, 2(1): 1–12.

Lee, A. and Taylor, E. (1996) 'The dilemma of obedience: A feminist perspective on the making of engineers', *Educational Philosophy and Theory*, 28(1): 57–75.

Lee, C. and Zemke, R. (1993) 'The search for spirit in the workplace', *Training*, June: 21–8.

Lemert, C. (1995) *Sociology After the Crisis*, Boulder, CO: Westview Press.

Letiche, H. (1990) 'Five postmodern aphorisms for trainers', *MEAD*, 21(3): 229–40.

Levinas, E. (1985) *Ethics and Infinity* (trans. by R.A. Cohen), Pittsburgh: Duquesne University Press.

—— (1987) *Time and the Other* (trans. by R. A. Cohen), Pittsburgh: Duquesne University Press.

Lewin, K. (1947) 'Frontiers in group dynamics', *Human Relations* (1): 5–41.

Leymann, H. (1989) 'Towards a new paradigm of learning of organisations' in H. Leymann and M. Kornbluh (eds) *Socialisation and Learning at Work: A New Approach to the Learning Process in the Workplace and Society*, Brookfield, VT: Gower: 281–99.

Littler, C. R. (1991) *Technology and the Organisation of Work*, Geelong: Deakin University Press.

Lukes, S. (1973) *Individualism*, Oxford: Basil Blackwell.

Lyotard, J.-F. (1984) *The Post-modern Condition: A Report on Knowledge*, Manchester: Manchester University Press.

Mac an Ghaill, M. (1991) 'Young, gifted and black: Methodological reflections of a teacher-researcher' in G. Walford (ed.) *Doing Educational Research*, London: Routledge: 101–20.

McHoul, A. and Grace, H. (1993) *A Foucault Primer: Discourse, Power and the Subject*, Melbourne: Melbourne University Press.

Mao Tse Tung (1968) 'On practice' in *Four Essays on Philosophy*, Peking: Foreign Languages Press: 8(7): 20.

Marcuse, H. (1973) *One Dimensional Man: Studies in the Ideology of Advanced Industrial Society*, London: Routledge.

Marginson, S. (1993) *Education and Public Policy in Australia*, Cambridge: Cambridge University Press.

—— (1997) *Markets in Education*, Sydney: Allen and Unwin.

Marsick, V. J. (1987) *Learning in the Workplace*, New York: Croom Helm.

Marsick, V. J. and Watkins, K. E. (1990a) *Informal and Incidental Learning in the Workplace*, London: Routledge.

—— (1990b) 'Towards a theory of informal and incidental learning' in V. J. Marsick and K. E. Watkins *Informal and Incidental Learning in the Workplace*, London: Routledge: 12–40.

Marx, K. (n.d.) 'Critique of political economy', *Selected Works Volume One*, Moscow.

—— (1959) *Economic and Philosophic Manuscripts of 1844*, Moscow: Progress Publishers.

Maurice, M., Sellier, F. and Silvestre, J. J. (1986) *The Social Foundations of Industrial Power: A Comparison of France and Germany* (trans. by A. Goldhammer), London: MIT Press.

Mead, G. H. (1967) *The Philosophy of the Act*, Chicago: University of Chicago Press.

Merleau-Ponty, M. (1962) *Phenomenology of Perception*, London: Routledge and Kegan Paul.

—— (1964) *Signs*, Evanston: Northwestern University Press.

Mestrovic, S. G. (1991) *The Coming Fin de Siècle: An Application of Durkheim's Sociology to Modernity and Postmodernism*, London: Routledge.

Mezirow, J. (1981) 'A critical theory of adult learning and education', *Adult Education*, 32(1): 3–24.

—— (1985) 'A critical theory of adult learning and education' in S. Brookfield (ed.) *Self-Directed Learning: From Theory to Practice. New Directions in Continuing Education*, San Francisco: Jossey Bass.

—— (1990) *Fostering Critical Reflection in Adulthood: A Guide to Transformative and Emancipatory Learning*, San Francisco: Jossey Bass.

—— (1991) *Transformative Dimensions of Adult Learning*, San Francisco: Jossey Bass.

—— (1995) 'Transformation theory of adult education' in M. Welton (ed.) *In Defense of the Lifeworld: Critical Perspectives on Adult Learning*, Albany: State University of New York Press.

Michaelson, E. (1996) 'Taxonomies of sameness: The recognition of prior learning as anthropology', paper presented at the *International Conference on Experience Learning*, 1–6 July, University of Capetown, South Africa.

Millar, C. (1991) 'Critical reflection for education of adults: Getting a grip on the scripts for professional action', *Studies in Continuing Education*, 13(1): 15–23.

Miller, N. E. (1989) *Personal Experience, Adult Learning and Social Research: Developing a Sociological Imagination in and Beyond the T-group*, Adelaide: University of South Australia, Centre for Human Resource Studies.

Mills, C. Wright (1970) *The Sociological Imagination*, Harmondsworth: Penguin.

Mocker, D. W. and Spear, G. E. (1982) 'Life long learning: Formal, nonformal, informal and self directed', *Information Series No. 241, ERIC Clearing House on Adult Career and Vocational Education*, Columbus, Ohio: The National Center for Research in Vocational Eduction, Ohio State University.

Mongardini, C. (1990) 'The decadence of modernity: The delusions of progress and the search for historical consciousness' in J. C. Alexander and Piotr Sztompka (eds) *Rethinking Progress*, Winchester, MA: Unwin Hyman.

Nadler, L. (1992) 'HRD – Where had it been, where is it going?', *Studies in Continuing Education* 14(2): 104–14.

Newman, M. (1993) *The Third Contract: Theory and Practice in Trade Union Training*, Sydney: Stuart Victor.

Norris, C. (1993) *The Truth about Postmodernism*, Oxford: Blackwell.

Noyelle, T. (1987) *Beyond Industrial Dualism: Market and Job Segmentation in the New Economy*, Boulder, CO: Westview Press.

Offe, C. (1985a) *Disorganised Capitalism: Contemporary Transformation of Work and Politics*, Cambridge, MA: MIT Press.

—— (1985b) 'New social movement: Challenging the boundaries of institutional politics', *Social Research*, 52(4): 817–68.

Paracone, P. (et al.) (1991) 'Description of a framework of macro-profiles (archetypes)', *CEDEFOP Document: European Centre for the Development of Vocational Training*, Berlin.

Parker, S. (1997) *Reflective Teaching in the Postmodern World*, Buckingham: Open University Press.

Pateman, C. (1989) *The Disorder of Women: Democracy, Feminism and Political Theory*, Stanford: Stanford University Press.

Payne, M. (1993) *Reading Theory*, Oxford: Blackwell.

Pea, R. D. (1987) 'Socialising the knowledge transfer problem', *International Journal of Educational Research*, 11(6): 639–63.

Pedler, M., Boydell, T. and Burgoyne, J. (1989) 'The learning company', *Studies in Continuing Education*, 11(2): 91–101.

Pennycook, A. (1994) *Applied Linguistics Volume 2*, Oxford: Oxford University Press.

Peters, T. and Waterman, R. H. (1982) *In Search of Excellence: Lessons from America's Best Run Companies*, New York: Harper and Row.

Pfeiffer, J. W. and Jones, J. E. (1983) *Design Considerations in Laboratory Education, Reference Guide to Handbooks and Annuals,* 1983 edn, San Diego, CA: University Associates.

Phillips, A. and Taylor, B. (eds) (1986) *Sex and Skill in Waged Work*, London: Virago.

Piore, M. J. and Sabel, C. F. (1984) *The Second Industrial Divide: Possibilities for Prosperity*, New York: Basic Books.

Polanyi, M. (1967) *The Tacit Dimension*, New York: Doubleday and Company.

Polkinghorne, D. E. (1988) *Narrative Knowing and the Human Sciences*, Albany: State University of New York Press.

—— (1992) 'Postmodern epistemology of practice' in S. Kvale (ed.) *Psychology and Postmodernism*, London: Sage.

Rabinow, P. (1984) *The Foucault Reader*, New York: Pantheon Books.

Rainbird, H. (1988) 'New technology, training and union strategies' in R. Hyman and W. Streeck (eds) *New Technology and Industrial Relations*, Oxford: Basil Blackwell.

—— (1990) *Training Matters: Union Perspectives on Industrial Restructuring and Training*, London: Basil Blackwell.

Raizen, S. (1994) 'Learning and work: The research base' in *Vocational Education and Training for Youth: Towards Coherent Policy and Practice*, Paris: OECD.

Reich, R. (1993) *The Work of Nations: A Blueprint for the Future*, London: Simon and Schuster.

Revans, R. W. (1982) *The Origins and Growth of Action Learning*, London: Chartwell Bratt.

Rogers, C. (1983) *Freedom to Learn in the 80s*, Columbus: Charles E. Merrill.

Rogoff, B. (1990) *Apprenticeship in Thinking: Cognitive Development in Social Context*, New York: Oxford University Press.

Rorty, R. (1989) *Contingency, Irony, and Solidarity*, Cambridge: Cambridge University Press.

Rose, N. (1994) *Governing the Soul: The Shaping of the Private Self*, London: Routledge.

—— (1996) 'Identity, genealogy, history' in S. Hall and P. Du Gay (eds) *Questions of Cultural Identity*, London: Sage Publications.

Sartre, J.-P. (1965) *Nausea* (trans. by Robert Baldick), Harmondsworth: Penguin.

Schön, D. A. (1983) *The Reflective Practitioner: How Professionals Think in Action*, London: Temple Smith.

—— (1987) *Educating the Reflective Practitioner*, San Francisco: Jossey Bass.

Schultz, J. (1985) *Steel City Blues*, Melbourne: Penguin.

Scribner, S. (1984) 'Studying working intelligence' in B. Rogoff and J. Lave (eds) *Everyday Cognition: Its Development in Social Context*, Cambridge, MA: Harvard University Press.

—— (1985) 'Knowledge at work', *Anthropology and Education Quarterly*, 16: 199–206

—— (1986) 'Thinking in action: Some characteristics of practical thought' in R. J. Sternberg and R. K. Wagner (eds) *Practical Intelligence: Nature and Origins of Competence*, Cambridge: Cambridge University Press: 13–30.

Secretary's Commission on Achieving Necessary Skills (SCANS) (1992) *Learning a Living: A Blueprint for High Performance*, A SCAN's report for America 2000, Washington, DC: US Department of Labor.

Senge, P. M. (1990) *The Fifth Discipline: The Art of Practice of the Learning Organisation*, New York: Doubleday Press.

—— (ed.) (1994) *The Fifth Discipline Field Book: Strategies and Tools for Building a Learning Organisation*, Toronto and New York: Currency Doubleday.

Skeggs, B. (1991) 'Challenging masculinity and using sexuality', *British Journal of Sociology of Education*, 12: 127–39.

Skruber, R. (1987) 'Organisations as clarifying learning environments' in V. J. Marsick (ed.) *Learning in the Workplace*, New York: Croom Helm: 55–78.

Soja, E. (1989) *Postmodern Geographies: The Reassertion of Space in Critical Social Theory*, London: Verso.

Sontag, S. (ed.) (1984) 'Writing Itself: On Roland Barthes', *A Barthes Reader*, Toronto: McGraw-Hill Ryerson.

Sorokin, P. (1957) *Social and Cultural Dynamics: A Study of Change in Major Systems of Art, Truth, Ethics, Law and Social Relationships*, Boston: Porter Sargent.

Spear, G. E. and Mocker, D. W. (1984) 'The organising circumstance: Environmental determinants in self-directed learning', *Adult Education Quarterly*, 35(1): 1–10.

Stasz, C., Ramsey, K., Eden, R., Melamid, E. and Kaganoff, T. (1996) *Workplace Skills in Practice: Case Studies of Technical Work*, National Center for Research in Vocational Education, University of California, Berkeley.

Stevenson, J. C. (1994a) 'Current trends in the Australian training reform process', *Australian Vocational Education Review*, 1(1): 32–6.

—— (1994b) *Cognition at Work: The Development of Vocational Expertise*, Adelaide: National Centre for Vocational Education Research.

Sveiby, K.-E. and Lloyd, T. (1987) *Managing Know-how: Add Value by Valuing Creativity*, London: Bloomsbury.

Taylor, C. (1989) *Sources of the Self: The Making of Modern Identity*, Cambridge, MA: Harvard University Press.

Taylor, M. M. (1986) 'Learning for self direction in the classroom: The pattern of a transition process', *Studies in Higher Education*, 11(1): 55–72.

—— (1987) 'Self-directed learning: More than meets the observer's eye' in D. J. Boud and V. Griffin (eds) *Appreciating Adults Learning: From the Learners' Perspective*, London: Kogan Page.

Tennant, M. (1988) *Psychology and Adult Learning*, London: Routledge.

Tough, A. (1982) *Intentional Changes: A Fresh Approach to Helping People Change*, Chicago: Fowlett Publishing Company.

Usher, R. S. (1989) 'Locating adult education in the practical' in B. Bright (ed.) *Theory and Practice in the Study of Adult Education: The Epistemological Debate*, London: Routledge.

—— (1992) 'Experience in adult education: A post-modern critique', *Journal of Philosophy of Education*, 26(2) 201–14.

—— (1993) 'Experiential learning or learning from experience: Does it make a difference?' in D. Boud, R. Cohen and D. Walker (eds) *Using Experience for Learning*, Buckingham: The Society for Research into Higher Education and Open University Press: 169–80.

—— (1996) 'Seductive texts: Competence, power and knowledge in post-modernity' in R. Barnett and A. Griffin (eds) *The End of Knowledge in Higher Education*, Institute of Education Series, University of London.

Usher, R. S. and Bryant, I. (1989) *Adult Education as Theory, Practice and Research: The Captive Triangle*, London: Routledge.

Usher, R. S. and Edwards, R. (1994) *Postmodernism and Education: Different Voices, Different Worlds*, London: Routledge.

—— (1995) 'Confessing all? A postmodern guide to the guidance and counselling of adult learners', *Studies in the Education of Adults*, 27(1): 9–23.

Usher, R. S., Bryant, I. and Johnston, R. A. (1997) *Adult Education and the Postmodern Challenge: Learning Beyond the Limits*, London: Routledge.

Van Manen, M. (1990) *Researching Lived Experience: Human Science for an Action Sensitive Pedagogy*, London, Ont.: The Althouse Press.

Virilio, P. (1997) *Open Sky* (trans. by Julie Rose), London: Verso.

Wain, K. (1987) 'Lifelong education', *Philosophy of Lifelong Education*: 35–60.

—— (1993) 'Lifelong education: Illiberal and repressive?', *Educational Philosophy and Theory*, 25(1): 58–78.

Watkins, K. E. and Marsick, V. J. (1992) 'Building the learning organisation: A new role for human resource developers', *Studies in Continuing Education*, 14(2): 115–29.

—— (1993) *Sculpting the Learning Organisation: Lessons in the Art and Science of Systemic Change*, San Francisco: Jossey Bass.

Watkins, K. E. and Willis, V. J. (1991a) 'Theoretical foundations of models for HRD practice: A critique' in N. M. Dickson and J. Henkelman (eds) *Models for HRD Practice: The Academic Guide*, Alexandria, VA: American Society for Training and Development: 89–105.

—— (1991b) 'Many voices: Defining human resource development from different disciplines', *Adult Education Quarterly*, 41(4): 241–55.

Watkins, P. (1986) *High Tech, Low Tech and Education*, Geelong: Deakin University Press.

—— (1991) *Knowledge and Control in the Flexible Workplace*, Geelong: Deakin University Press.

Weber, M. (1958) *The Protestant Ethic and the Spirit of Capitalism*, New York: Charles Scribner's Sons.

Weil, S. and McGill, I. (1989) *Making Sense of Experiential Learning: Diversity in Theory and Practice*, Milton Keynes: Open University Press.

Welton, M. (1991) *Toward Development Work: The Workplace as a Learning Environment*, Geelong: Deakin University Press.

—— (ed.) (1995) *In Defense of the Lifeworld: Critical Perspectives on Adult Learning*, Albany: State University of New York Press.

Wexler, P. (1987) *Social Analysis of Education: After the New Sociology*, London: Routledge.

—— (1992) *Becoming Somebody: Toward a Social Psychology of School*, London and New York: Falmer Press.

—— (1993) 'Educational corporatism and its counterposes. Keynote address', *After Competence Conference*, Griffith University, Brisbane, 1–3 December.

—— (1995) 'After postmodernism: A new age social theory in education' in R. Smith and P. Wexler (eds) *After Postmodernism: Education, Politics and Identity*, Bristol: Falmer Press.

Whittington, R. (1992) 'Putting Giddens into action: Social systems and managerial agency', *Journal of Management Studies*, 29(6): 693–711.

Wildemeersch, D. (1992) 'Ambiguities of experiential learning and critical pedagogy: The challenge of scepticism and radical responsibility' in D. Wildemeersch and T. Jansen (eds) *Adult Education, Experiential Learning and Social Change: The Postmodern Challenge*, Den Haag: VUGA: 19–34.

Wittgenstein, L. (1982) *Last Writings on the Philosophy of Psychology, Volume One*, Oxford: Blackwell.

Yeatman, A. (1994) 'Research into the costs and benefits of VET: Who costs, who benefits?', paper presented to the *Research Priorities in Vocational Education and Training Conference*, Australian National Training Authority, Sydney: 20–22 April.

Zuboff, S. (1988) *In the Age of the Smart Machine*, New York: Basic Books.

Index